DAYS OF HUMILIATION

# DAYS OF HUMILIATION

## TIMES OF AFFLICTION AND DISASTER

Nine Sermons

For Restoring Favor With

An Angry God

(1696-1727)

BY

## COTTON MATHER

FACSIMILE REPRODUCTIONS

WITH AN INTRODUCTION

BY

## GEORGE HARRISON ORIANS

GAINESVILLE, FLORIDA

SCHOLARS' FACSIMILES & REPRINTS

1970

SCHOLARS' FACSIMILES & REPRINTS

1605 N.W. 14TH AVENUE

GAINESVILLE, FLORIDA, 32601, U.S.A.

HARRY R. WARFEL, GENERAL EDITOR

Grateful acknowledgement is made to the following libraries:

BOSTON PUBLIC LIBRARY: *Things for a Distress'd People to think upon.*

JOHN CARTER BROWN LIBRARY of Brown University: *A Voice from Heaven.*

LIBRARY OF CONGRESS: *Humiliations follow'd with Deliverances.*

TRACY WILLIAM MCGREGOR LIBRARY of The University of Virginia: *Advice from Taberah, Boanerges, The Saviour with his Rainbow,* and *The Terror of the Lord.*

YALE UNIVERSITY LIBRARY: *Advice from the Watchtower* and *The Voice of God in a Tempest.*

L. C. CATALOG CARD NUMBER: 68-24211

SBN 8201-1067-1

Manufactured in the U.S.A.

# CONTENTS

v

# INTRODUCTION

Several interpreters of colonial theological writing have noted the disposition of New England preachers of the seventeenth century to utilize such events of the age as made their sermons not only expositions of piety but of news as well. Every effective preacher had to show adaptability in terms of pulpit opportunities and exigencies. He was called upon when new pastors were inducted, he set the proper tone of seriousness on the eve of elections, he devoted himself to the cause and calling of young people, he witnessed for the Lord in times of peril, he called upon hardened criminals for repentance, he preached funeral sermons for saints in the Lord and innocents, too. He tried, in short, to make his sermons intelligible, interesting, and profitable for listeners and readers. All kinds of temporal occurrences and incidents claimed the preachers' attention: pestilences, public executions, French privateers, Indian raids, wartime expeditions, suicides, great fires, small-pox scares, tempests, seasonal manifestations, explosions, riotous outbursts, captivities, and droughts.

There were two types of days to be found in every year that no preacher eschewed, whether in a fixed calendar or not. These were days of thanksgiving and days of humiliation, days when the beneficences of God were advanced for appreciation and days when congregations were asked to pray and deliberate upon the chastening character of calamities. These last named were labeled as fast-days, and their purpose was to restore harmony between communities and Jehovah.

Early to late in his career Cotton Mather composed and delivered sermons for fast days and for election and commemorative days that showed his grave concern with community piety and his devotion to the doctrine of the covenant. In his exposition of religious concepts Mather gave as full and clear an application of this Old Testament theory as the period afforded. Because he always had one or more printers in his congregation, what he had to say in these matters has been preserved for our examination. The covenantal doctrine was not only universally accepted in New England, but the idea of a contract between a pious community and Jehovah was widely believed and proclaimed throughout Christendom.

For the New England Puritans the covenant did seem to have special relevance, because the Indians were likened unto the pagan dwellers of the plain and because the Christian community was regarded as under the special leadership of Jehovah through whose favor they were guided into the new Canaan, the land flowing with milk and honey. More important, the New Englanders regarded themselves like the Israelites of old as in firm covenant with the Lord, in the fulfilment of which they worshipped him and sought to magnify him, and He on His part afforded the providential aid for them as long as they did not lift their hands in rebellion. Jehovah was their God, and they were His people. As long as they followed in the way of godliness, they prospered; when through pride and vanity they left off true worship, they were warned or punished. This concept, which has come to be known as the doctrine of humiliation or the Deuteronomic formula, had five recognizable stages:

(1) The people worshipped God in sincerity and earnestness and prospered under his divine providence.

(2) They lifted their proud necks in self-assertiveness and put aside the rites of worship. They became wayward.

(3) Jehovah, with concern, warned them of their violation of the contract, and, if they did not heed the warning, sent heavy punishment upon them.

(4) In despair the people appointed occasions for humbling themselves with fasting and lamentations.

(5) The Lord took pity upon their plight and abjection, then restored his favor upon them.

This formula which, found its clearest expression in the D text of the Old Testament, was freely applied to the history of Israel by the D writer in Samuel, Kings, and Chronicles. It can be found illustrated as well in Judges and in the prophets of the eighth century. This formula, undergirding many of the sermons of the period, substantially controlled doctrinal thinking and was responsible for many legislative acts of local or colony councils. When the worshippers were impressed with the majesty of God, His attributes of love, mercy, and watchfulness, they were confirming the first and fifth steps of the Deuteronomic formula, steps concerned with the articulation and summation of the blessings that flowed from divine good-will. In the language of the age these were properly called divine providences. To recite them was to extol divine power

and divine ministrations.  Almost every preacher who
devoted himself to the doctrine of Old Testament covenantal theology divided his thinking into two categories
of praise and punishment, first, the glorification of the
Lord for his maintenance of his children and, second,
the consequences of a broken contract—the sad story of
man's defection from divine worship, his breaking, therefore, of the terms of the celestial covenant, the warning
and punishment which ensued, and the contrition and
humbling that were necessary before the divine beneficence could be restored.

This division of thought is apparent in the writings
of Cotton Mather.  Let us note Mather's devotion to
the doctrine of providences as the first in this two-fold
thought.  Thankfulness involved appreciation for the
largess of the Lord poured out upon a none-too-deserv-
ing generation.  Like Increase Mather with his *Illustrious Providences* and Edward Johnson with his *Wonder-Working Providences* Cotton Mather regarded the
prosperity of New England and the success of the
colonies as evidence of the Lord's beneficence.  Upon
this thought of divine blessing Cotton Mather erected
his famed *Magnalia* and confirmed the doctrine in such
sermons as *The Wonderful Works of God Commemorated* (1690) [reciting the end of the Indian Wars,
the accession of William and Mary, and the wonders of
the universe] and *Christian Thanks-offering* (1696), a
solemn thanksgiving for a bountiful harvest. *Thoughts
for the Day of Rain* (Essay ii, 1712) voiced the hope
that God would remember his covenant with his people
in the "cloudy times that were passing over them," and
*Providence, Asserted and Adored* (1718) again showed
Mather's concern with this concept of celestial blessings.

Mather's thought was summed up in the Biblical text that he several times employed: "Now therefore stand still, that I may reason with you before the Lord of all the righteous acts of the Lord, which he did to you and to your fathers" (I Samuel 12:7).

The second aspect of the covenant doctrine had to do with the days of humiliation or fasting and prayer, in which congregations and communities, contrite and humble for their seeming dereliction in duty or worship, abased themselves before the Lord that the hand of affliction which had been laid upon them might be lifted. This doctrine not only had full Calvinistic warrant in the seventeenth century but was heavily documented in the Old Testament, especially in Deuteronomy XXVIII (a source which led its application to religious life to be known as the Deuteronomic formula). The doctrine back of it we call the covenant theory, for it involves the concept of punishments and rewards for the keeping or breaking of the contract with the Lord. Because men were frail and weak-willed, indulgence was prevalent. Thus the most pronounced feature in the formula was punishment, and the frequent proclamation of fast-days was the standard response to signs of divine displeasure. This application of Deuteronomic thinking was not exclusive with Cotton Mather, for the names of Increase Mather, Samuel Willard, Benjamin Colman, Jonathan Mayhew, Thomas Prince, and others loom as large or larger than that of Cotton Mather. A case can be made out that Mather's notice of fasts, measuring his participation by his printed works alone, was actually much less than one would expect from a preacher who mounted the pulpit for forty years. During the period of his ministry there was in

Massachusetts and Boston alone well over 150 fasts, days of prayer and special thanksgiving, in reaction to which only the really major disasters elicited a sermonized response from Cotton Mather, or at least we are so to judge by his printed utterances. For others, he either spoke from notes or did not regard the results worthy of memorializing in print. In fact, a considerable body of evidence exists to point to his father, Increase Mather, rather than to Cotton as the "preacher of fast days." Judgment would be based on devotion to the subject rather than the literary excellence of the results, which there has been no effort to measure. Increase Mather was especially concerned with what has been called Reformation fasts, an interest evidenced in a half-dozen sermons in the late 1670's; and he shared with his preacher son an interest in tempests and fires. Both, as sincere and devout pastors, were concerned with whatever exhortations might serve to bring about godliness.

In order to understand Cotton Mather's connection with fast-day doctrine we need to glance at representative utterances from his earliest sermon in this field in 1690 to his last in 1727. His first reference to the doctrine on March 20, 1690, was somewhat oblique: *The Present State of New England,* a document of exhortation and stimulus, was evoked by the renewed French and Indian attacks on the scattered settlements. Mather urged decisive action. The proclamation, of Mather's authorship, affixed to the sermon, cited a long series of afflictions and calamities as chargeable "to the anger of the righteous God." The purpose of the document was "a speedy reformation of our *provoking* evils" (ie., debauchery, profaneness, Sabbath breaking, idleness, uncleanness) as well as spiritual sins (heresy, pride, envy, unbelief, etc.). A second notice appeared in *Fair Weather* which recited a catalogue of sins that unleashed the forces of evil upon York and other frontier towns, thus establishing a causal sequence in which frontier troubles were yoked to wickedness. *A Midnight Cry* (1692) sought to arouse a spiritual Reformation. The two sermons of the text were expanded by the *Instrument,* which recited areas for spiritual improvement. But to no avail. In *Magnalia Christi Americana* (V, 98) Mather commented that, since reformation did not come about, God punished the colony for its spiritual failures.

In his *Hortatory and Necessary Address* (delivered May 26, 1692, and included in *Wonders of the Invisible World*) Cotton Mather presented an interesting variation of the Deuteronomic formula. Because of the seducing spirits of unorthodox doctrine, the blight upon the grain, the plagues and pestilences, the charter confiscations, hostile actions by Indians, losses at sea, and finally the witch descent upon New England, it was quite apparent that there was divine displeasure with New England. Mather advanced a variation of the regular formula doctrine, for most of these devastating losses were ascribable to the wrath of the devil in his raging against the godly plantation. Even the devil's wrath was an adjunct of God's punishment; granting divine omnipotence, only with God's permission could this hound of Hell consume with *his* wrath. Were God not angry at the iniquities of his so-called people, He would not permit the devil to lash and rage so violently. At any rate, were the people of the colony to bow themselves in true humbleness before Him, God might withdraw his anger; and if the tribulations were not totally to disappear, at least God might shorten the Devil's chain or leash so that the area he could devastate would be materially reduced.

The next year a day of prayer was kept in the Old Meeting-house at Boston on July 6, 1693, the day following the Commencement at Harvard. The fast had been proclaimed because of a panic over a serious drought at the beginning of the expected growing season. Cotton Mather preached all day. The condensed text of his utterances was printed in *The Day and the Work of the Day*, which expatiated on the function of prayer and the proper spirit of devoutness in which the Lord should be sought. Prayer was interpreted, in short, as the agency for restoring favor with an angry Lord by bringing about divine forgiveness and mercy.

In 1694 Cotton Mather delivered his *Short History of New England* before the General Assembly of the Province of Massachusetts-Bay on June 7. Though Mather underscored the shortcomings of New Englanders in a span of fifty years, shortcomings which caused breaches in their hedges, the sermon, touching upon but unconcerned with spelling out the covenant theory, was mainly devoted to arousing the leaders to higher spiritual efforts.

Two years later Mather made another appearance before the General Assembly; for this occasion he used as a text I Samuel, VII, 6,10, which might well have served for a day of humiliation. His sermon, *Things for a Distressed People to Think Upon*, called for repentance for misdeeds in public and private life. Bewailing God's controversy with New England apparent in sundry deadly tokens of disaster, such as shipwrecks, epidemics, political reverses, and the witch descent, the preacher-watchman sought to bring about a general reformation, to stir men to high endeavor and to the fulfilment of their sworn oaths, to remove open evils and to search out secret provocations to God as well. The obvious way to restore God's favor was for all sensate listeners to weep for the widespread degeneracy, to bewail the horrible sins and the widespread ungodliness, and to pray unceasingly for the rebirth of the rising generation. By their repenting and supplication, by the renovation of the covenant of grace and yielding unto the will of God, the delivering power of the Lord would be felt, and the enemies of the colony would be scattered.

Probably the most characteristic of Mather's sermons was *Humiliations followed with Deliverances*, declaimed in Boston one week before a public fast of May 13, 1697. In its development it followed what might be called steps two, three, four, and five of the formula, the third stage being represented by the recitation of crop failures, losses at sea, widespread sickness, Indian raids, and manifest strokes alleged in Mather's language to have resulted from errors of what he called "our dark time." Mather purposed also to make clear the promise in God's word of renewed favor, proclaiming that if the people would sufficiently humble themselves, the hand of the Lord would no longer be laid upon them in punishment. Deliverances, such as those extensively reviewed, would assuredly come. If only one of Mather's sermons were advanced to show his subscription to Old Testament thinking, this would be the sermon to single out.

During the next decade Mather showed no blindness

to the shortcomings of the age, but he limited his observations in the main to Utopian concepts or to the problems of leadership, or to character development in domestic realms. The second decade of the century furnished catastrophic events to bring his thinking back to covenantal fields.

On July 12, 1711, when a mid-summer storm of destructive force hit Massachusetts Bay, Governor Dudley proclaimed July 26 as a day of humiliation; the sermons of the latter date elicited admonitions that there be more circumspect walking before the Lord. Three months after the storm a great fire broke out in Boston on October 3, 1711, enveloping the meeting-house and the town-house as well as a hundred other structures. This calamity quickly elicited Mather's *Advice from Taberah*. So momentous a fire producing so "calamitous a Desolation" prompted an instructive and moralizing address in which Bostonians were admonished to give heed to God's work and to draw spiritual values from the disaster. The holocaust also led Cotton's father, Increase Mather, to deliver and to print his *Burnings Bewailed*.

Two years afterwards, on April 16, 1713, Cotton Mather turned his eyes upon twenty evil customs of the age, warning that a persistence in them would undoubtedly bring the wrath of the Lord upon the community. *Advice from the Watch Tower* described by its title the hortatory vein Mather indulged in and confirmed his purpose of preventing evil. To evil customs, the usual accompaniment of ungodliness, people had become accustomed and reconciled. Their consciences had become deaf; they became emboldened, turned away from the Lord, and He in turn withdrew his grace from them. Recognizing that it was not easy to penetrate the stoniness with which evil customs were surrounded, for evil was now second nature, Mather admonished parental guidance, self-scrutiny, and a series of special resolutions to bring about a speedy Reformation. Six years later in 1719 the vile customs of the age were still his concern; he joined with Benjamin Wadsworth and Benjamin Colman in a renewed testimony against them. Their comment is almost a rationale of the social analyses of the age.

In fine, let it be remembered, That our Glorious Lord is an Holy God, and Requires and Expects His People to be Holy in all manner of Conversation; his Jealous and Flaming Eyes are upon us. And Evil Customs, whereof he says unto us from Heaven, *Such Things I hate them*, will be more offensive to the Eyes of His Glory, if they be found among us then if they be seen among many other People. They will provoke him To *Depart* from us; And, *Wo to them when I Depart from them, saith the Lord*. It will not be long before he makes Our *Plagues Wonderful*. We would *persuade* our People, to be *full of Goodness*, and shun the *Works of them, who turn aside*: We do it, *Knowing the Terror of the Lord*.

It is a Day of dreadful *Degeneracy* among the Reformed Churches; and the Dread of our having a Share in it, has produced from us, this Testimony against such Things as may contribute unto it. For the Efficacy whereof

we now look up to the God of all Grace, in
Obedience to whom it is that we have Offered
it.

                          Cotton Mather
                          Benjamin Wadsworth
                          Benjamin Colman
Boston, 1719

*The Voice of God in a Tempest* advanced lessons of
piety seasonably prompted by a destructive hurricane
on February 24, 1723. The sermon emphasized the
way of God in all storms, human as well as physical,
and spelled out what the individual worshipper should
do, especially in understanding God's gracious designs
and acknowledging His sovereignty. The tempest was
a summons to duty and a reminder that regularly we
shall meet with storms of emotions and passions. The
sermon was related to covenantal thinking by stress
upon God's providences and the citation of the means
to prevent worshippers from departing from the Way.

The last of the events to stir Mather to expression
on humiliation was a succession of earthquakes in the
autumn of 1727. The first of these fell on October
28-30, the tremors of which were felt all the way to the
West Indies. The sheer power of the cataclysm dic-
tated Mather's title, *The Glorious God has Roared out
of Zion.* Before this destructiveness all of New England
cowered and immediate days of fasting and supplication
were designated and observed. The running title affixed
to Mather's sermon—*The Terror of the Lord*— appro-
priately defined the fourth phase of the Deuteronomic
formula, for there was slight doubt of the sincerity with
which the congregations of New England humiliated

themselves before the Lord. Mather's sermon was delivered the next morning when the congregations out-
paced the preachers to the churches. At least four
of the sermons delivered on that day by New England
preachers were subsequently printed.

*The Terror of the Lord* was almost an impromptu
performance. More leisurely brooding on the subjects
of earthquakes as indexes of God's wrath led Mather
to deliver a Thursday lecture on December 14, 1727, a
sermon printed with the title of *Boanerges.* The title
seems to have implied not so much the later meaning
of vociferous preacher or orator as the denotative one
of speaking in thunder. Mather's concern was with the
fleeting character of morality that was prompted by
fear. He hoped that the reformation which ensued
from such violent events would prove enduring. Thus
the statement of purpose in the running title: "to preserve and strengthen the good impressions produced by
earthquakes on the minds of people that have been
awakened with them."

Minor references to fast-day thinking occur in many
other sermons of Cotton Mather, but the works cited
are sufficient to illustrate his exposition of the doctrine
and to indicate how thoroughly it entered into his own
meditation and the background thinking of almost every
serious New Englander. It was their way of explaining
supernatural happenings which their science could not
account for. It constituted also their application of
Old Testament doctrine to daily living, and represented
the general force of community morality. The frequent
characterization of New England as a theocracy is in
no way more apparent than in this interpretation and
application of God's government of the world.

The covenant doctrine was one which the Israelite descent upon Canaan easily engendered, and which New Englanders applied to their conquest under God of a new country. One must be on guard, however, against assuming that Cotton Mather's concern was solely with Old Testament theology and involved an exclusive devotion to Jehovah. Since any selection of Mather's sermons on any topic of interest (considering the 444 potentialities) tends inevitably to be arbitrary, one needs to maintain always an awareness of what lies on the periphery of one's observation. Mather's thinking was Christian as well as Hebraic; in scores of sermons he examined fully and adequately the nature of true Christian righteousness. He was concerned for New Testament virtues, for Pauline thinking and for Trinitarian doctrines. Like Jeremy Taylor he pointed to individual responsibility in holy living and in holy dying. Not primarily from the mercy of Yahweh but from the intercession of Christ was providential and redeeming salvation extended unto man. Thus in many sermons Mather advanced the divine perfections of Christ, the achievements possible unto man when he grows strong in the Savior's grace, and the supreme ascendency that he arrives at when his life is patterned after a glorious Christ.

In such sermons as *Manly Christianity* (1711), *Faith at Work* (1697), *El Shaddai* (1725), and *Thaumato-graphia Christiana* (1701) Mather, so far from expounding the power of a God of supreme natural forces, was feelingly engaged in recapitulating the wonderful mysteries of the Lord Jesus Christ. Doctrines such as humility, charitable speaking, sympathy, godly conversation, consecration, social virtues—all are attributes of individual attainment which he commends to Christian congregations.

While New Englanders, in their attempt to conquer a wilderness, saw marked parallelism between their state and that of the Israelites moving in on Palestine, the doctrine of the covenant which they believed and acted upon was not peculiar to New England. It was a solid doctrine in the Christian world of their day. This is nowhere more apparent than in the reaction of English divines to the earthquake of 1580 and their response to the great fires of 1666 and 1725 and to other catastrophic events early in the eighteenth century. It was clearly apparent in the theological writings of all northern Europe. Witness the ready interpretation of this theory in the writings of William Price, Johann Alsted, William Perkins, William Ames, Wollebius and Hornecke, works known to many pious readers in New England as well as in Protestant Europe.

The doctrine was not a shallow one limited to a narrow seventeenth-century outlook. It persisted as a doctrine in America as late as the Civil War. "A day of solemn humiliation, fasting and prayer, was proclaimed by President John Adams on May 8, 1798. There were fast-days proclaimed on April 25, 1799, on June 18, 1812, and on November 16, 1814. We hear of fast-day proclamations in 1850, 1860, August 5, 1861, and July 2, 1864. In the case of the later dates, however, the action was not universally approved and led to some partisan dissent. Still, the fast-day thinking was not purely a conservative, out-dated seventeenth-century concept.

One other consideration needs to be noted in closing.

Cotton Mather was concerned as a preacher with improving on the moral implications of events, and utilizing the immediate for the divine instruction of the soul. But this was not his whole concern. He also regarded himself as scientist and natural philosopher. His *Christian Philosopher* was an attempt to reconcile science and theology. Starting out with the premise that the universe is the handiwork of God, Mather proceeded to the view that the unfolding of the wonders and mysteries of the universe, which was the function of science, clearly led to a fuller appreciation of the majesty and power of the ruler of the universe. Thus the more we know of mountains and rainfall and plants and mammals, for instance, the greater is the appreciation of the wonder-working powers of a supreme being.

Under such an interpretation, the glory of God could as clearly be perceived in the sustaining of the world and in the complexities of created things as in the sudden and mighty forces unleashed upon the works of man. Many operations of scientific laws, therefore, were means by which the might of the Divine could be studied. God was glorified by the entire range and depth of forces in the world, and this view of divine function represented a considerable expansion in concepts of power over the primitive literalness of an Old Testament mountain people. In his sermons Mather restricted his observation of divine agency to the more colossal events that interrupted the normal operations of the universe. Mather did not believe that all the manifestations of the natural law should be heralded as exhibitions of divine agency. If Cotton Mather did not assume the position of the extreme Deists that God made the world like a giant clock which he set running

and departed thereform, neither did he believe that all
events, instances, incidents, occurrences were the consequence of divine intervention and impulse. God was
not a mere control center of multifarious electrical
impulses. Not every manifestation was in direct response to divine decrees. The normal operations of the
physical world could go along without the continuous,
jealous, and persistent supervision of a celestial monitor.
Thus to Mather not all that occurred in the world was
entrapped in a moral scheme, nor were all discoverable
laws to be confined in the narrow channel of divine
theodicy. Less judicial were numerous contemporaries.
Many people in Cotton Mather's day were addicted to
an unthinking belief in signs and wonders, and looked
for meaning and guidance in every heavenly manifestation. Against such superstition Cotton Mather had
inveighed as early as 1690 in his *Way to Prosperity*;
he warned against regarding oddities, malformations,
strange accidents and events out of the ordinary as
omens or portents,—or in terms of moral instruction—
against confounding warnings and mere phenomena.
Thirty years later he resumed the text in his *Aurora
Borealis* (1719). Addressing himself to the question as
to whether or not sporadic celestial phenomena could
be regarded as warnings of divine anger or vengeance,
he concluded that such prognostication was not only
unreliable but usually conceited: "It is a weakness to be
too apprehensive of prodigies in all *Uncommon Occurrences.*" As for the belief so rife in his day that
every unusual sign was an index of God's will, Mather
pronounced such gullibility as a cause for high-minded
compassion. Take the following as a vigorous statement
of his meaning: "Were so many *Comets* (four hundred

and fifteen comets . . . appearing since the beginning of the world) all seen Blazing at once, I must freely say, That tho' such *Worlds in a state of Punishment,* would be an awful Spectacle, yet I should not be apprehensive of such *horrid Presages* in them, unto a *Baptized Nation.*" Not prodigies nor signs in the sky but lax living and theological sin brought on the wrath of God.

Only when the forces were so great as to represent what we even today call the "Acts of God" and only when the signs of adversity everywhere evoked fear and wonderment did Cotton Mather regard them as worthy of notice. Always he was concerned with catastrophic events. Earthquakes destructive of countless human lives, fires that wiped out cities, hurricanes that swept everything before them in their devastations —these to the preacher in him seemed to rise above and beyond the ordinary operations of cosmic forces and might be interpreted, theologically, as the wrath of God. No minor manifestations on the scientific scene nor normal functioning of earthly forces need be examined with reference to divine pleasure or displeasure. Of course the homiletic spirit sought always to capitalize on the immediate for the divine instruction of the soul. Even with his scientific spirit Mather would have been prone to improve on the moral implications of events. But he was not led into easy temptation. And he did insist that the sins of the people were "surer and blacker signs of Judgment than any Signs in Heaven that we think of."

GEORGE HARRISON ORIANS

*University of Toledo*
*March 20, 1966.*

𝕿𝖍𝖎𝖓𝖌𝖘 for a 𝕯𝖎𝖘𝖙𝖗𝖊𝖘𝖘'𝖉 𝕻𝖊𝖔𝖕𝖑𝖊 to think upon.

Offered in the

# SERMON

To the *General Assembly* of the Province, of the *Massachusetts Bay*, at the Anniversary ELECTION.
*May,* 27. 1696.
*Wherein,*

I. The Condition of the *Future,* as well as the *Former* TIMES, in which we are concerned, is Considered.

II. A Narrative of the late Wonderful Deliverance, of the KING, and the three KINGDOMS,& all the English DOMINIONS, is Endeavoured.

III. A Relation, of no less than SEVEN MIRACLES, within this little while wrought by the Almighty Lord 𝕵𝖊𝖘𝖚𝖘 𝕮𝖍𝖗𝖎𝖘𝖙, for the Confirmation of our Hopes, that some *Glorious Works,* for the welfare of His Church, are quickly to be done, is annexed.

By *COTTON MATHER.*

*Boston* in *N E.* Printed by *B Green,* and *J. Allen,* for *Duncan Campbel* at his Shop over-against the Old-Meeting House. 1696.

Uttered unto the Great and General Affembly, of the *Maſſachuſetts Bay, New-
England* : Convened, *May* 27. 1696.

IN a General *Aſſembly* there is this Day
Convened, a whole *Province,* that hath
Eminently profeſſed the *Religion* of the Lord
JESUS CHRIST ; and ſome Advice from
the *Lively Oracles* of the Lord JESUS CHRIST,
unto ſuch a *Province,* now Labouring under the
*Deadly Tokens* of *His* Diſpleaſure, is this Day
called for. The *Text* now to be Recommended unto you, from theſe *Oracles* of Heaven,
ſhall be one, wherein you ſhall ſee deſcribed,
the Behaviour of the only People that the
God of Heaven then had in the World, meeting together in a General *Aſſembly,* upon the
Advice of his being Diſpleaſed with them.
The moſt Reaſonable, and the moſt Seaſona-
ble Things, that I can Recommend unto you,
in this critical Time, are thoſe Three Things
which were done by the General *Aſſembly* of
*Iſrael,* in the *Text* whereto I now deſire your
ſerious Attention.

A 2                     1 Sam.

---

### 1 Samuel VII. 6, 10.

*And they gathered together to* Mizpeh, *and they drew water, and poured it out before the Lord ; and they Fasted on that Day ; and they said there, We have Sinned against the Lord.* [ Unto which, if we duely Attend, we shall be ready for the following passages ; ] *And* Samuel *Judged the Children of* Israel ; *But the Lord Thundered with a great Thunder upon the* Philistines, *and discomfited them.*

I Confess, that I now Entertain you with a *Text* very proper, for a *Day of Humiliation :* but it is for this very cause that I pitch upon this *Text,* as a very Agreeable Entertainment for us : inasmuch as we are generally agreed, That we are in most *Humbling* Circumstances.

'Tis possible, that it was an *Anniversary* Solemnity of a *Sacred* Importance with the People of *Israel,* when the memorable Actions here mentioned were performed. Jewish and Ancient Records have told us, that at the *Feast of Tabernacles,* they did every Day fetch a silver Flagon of *Water,* and pour it out at the *Altar,* with the *Wine,* for the *Drink Offering ;* to signify

nify the pouring out of the *Holy Spirit*, after the Coming of the *Messiah*, who indeed, was afterwards Born at the very Time of that *September Festival.* For this Custome, we find no Institution; but the countenance which our Lord Jesus Christ gave unto it, when He thence formed a Reflection upon the *Living Waters* of the *Holy Spirit* which He has to give, would make one think, whether it were not first Instituted by the Inspired *Samuel*, in that History which is now before us. But we have a further Assurance, that five dayes before the *Feast of Tabernacles*, namely, on the *Tenth* Day of the *Seventh Month*, a *Fast* was kept for a *Day of Expiation*: Even on the same Day that *Moses* having *Thrice Fasted* forty dayes together, came down to his people, with the News of the Lords being Reconciled unto them. I know not, whether the Prophet *Samuel*, might not, a little divert some Actions of that Great Solemnity, unto the Designs of *Repentance*, which the extraordinary Calamities upon his people did now require. But still, our *Anniversary* Solemnity of a *Civil* Importance, this Day recurring, will be the better accommodated, by our proposing those Actions to our present Imitation.

The People of *Israel*, were, by their Sins, like us, the poor People of *New England*, brought into very dismal circumstances. Those Taw-

ny

ny Pagans the *Philistines*, had made cruel and bloody Depredations, upon several of their Villages: and besides their Loss of men, by the Hand of the *Philistines*, they lost a great number of their *Principal men*, by the more Immediate Hand of Heaven upon them. The *least computation* of that mischief, is that of them, who thus read the Story: When they were together met from all Quarters at *Bethshemesh*, about *Fifty Thousand People*, the Lord smote *Threescore and ten men* : and it may be those *Threescore & ten men* were equivalent unto *Fifty Thousand People*, of the more common sort. Under these awful Judgments of God, they continued Impenitent, for as many years, as have ran out, since the Children of those *Philistines* were first let Loose upon our selves; even for *Twenty* years together. But it was well for them, that they had a *Samuel* among them ; a faithful Minister of God, who had no little part of their *Civil*, as well as of their *Sacred* Affairs, falling under his Direction. Upon the Exhortations of that Blessed *Samuel*, they began to *Lament after the Lord*, that is, to cry unto the Lord for His Help, with grievous *Lamentations* ; and they joyned many *private Reformations* of their Families, all the Land over, to their *Lamentations*. But *Samuel* must have something more publickly done in this matter: the whole Body of that People must
Assemble

Assemble at *Mizpeh,* a Town of some Note
in the Confines of *Judah* and *Benjamin,* near
the center of the Countrey, where we suppose
there might be an *Altar* Erected for the Worship of God ; and at *Mizpeh* they do *Three
Things,* whereto, may the Body of this People,
to Day, endeavour some Conformity.

We have *Three Things* here done, by a *General Assembly* of *Israel.*

First, *They Drew Water, and poured it out before the Lord.* This passage puts *Interpreters,* as
the Dead Body of *Asahel* did the Travellers,
and Spectators, unto a *Stand* ; they almost content themselves with saying, *Mirabilis hic locus,
ac Difficilis* ; 'Tis too hard for us to *Interpret*
it. But, if the Exposition, which we have already *guess'd,* will not *hitt,* there are several o-
ther Conjectures to be made upon the *Literal
Sense* of this passage, which we will at present
wave ; that we may in the room thereof sub-
stitute that *Figurative Sense,* which has no less
Authority, than that of the *Chaldee Paraphrase*
to support it ; *Hauserunt Aquas e puteo cordis sui,
et abunde Lacrymati sunt coram Domino.* And
indeed, Expositors do mostly go this way ;
Expounding it of the plentiful *Tears* which
they shed in such abundance, as if, to use the
the words of the *Weeping* Prophet elsewhere,
*Their Heads had been Waters, and their Eyes a
Fountain of Tears.* However, Let us take what

*Sense*

*Sense* we will, of all that the Commentators have ordinarily offered us, the words will still have some Sense of *Humiliation* in them. The other two passages, are more Intelligible.

Secondly, *They Fasted on that Day* :

Thirdly, *They said there, we have Sinned against the Lord.* Behold, the *Supplication,* and, Behold, the *Reformation,* which this *Humiliation* was attended withal. The circumstances of it, here specified, that it was, *On that Day,* and that it was, *There,* intimate that they were not willing to *Delay,* the Work of *Repentance* any longer : they counted it *High Time* for them to make thorough work of it, and they would not rise from the *place* until they had accomplished the work.

There are *Three Things,* which the Text thus laid before us, would Awaken us all unto : *Three Things* which if duely attended, *Thrice* and *Four Times* Happy from this Day, will be our Land, which is at this Day *Trembling* and *Shaking,* by the *Breaches* that God makes upon it. I will not leave my Text, though I do now call in another Text, for the *Application* of it, and make, *The present State of* NEW-ENGLAND, the Text which we shall now insist upon.

I. May the Tears of a profound HUMI-LIATION, be this Day shed among us, upon the

the Sorrowful Occasions of those *Tears*.

The *Tears* of an *Humbled*, a *Melted*, a Broken Heart, O let us *Draw that Water*, and *pour it out before the Lord*.

When the General Assembly of *Israel, poured out Water before the Lord*, it is the Opinion of some, that they designed with an *Hieroglyphick* of much *Humiliation*, to express their own Calamitous Condition. A State Irretrievably calamitous, is thus described, in 2 *Sam.* 14. 14. *We are as water spilt upon the ground, which cannot be gathered up again.* Thus the Intention of the General Assembly here, might be, most significantly to say, *Lord, see whether we are not a People so utterly Lost, and Spoilt, and Gone, that it is as impossible to Retrieve our doleful Circumstance's, as to gather up the Water which is poured out upon the Ground.* Now, thy Condition, O poor *New England*, is indeed so very like that of *Water poured out*, that it pathetically obligeth us all, to *pour out the Water* of our *Tears* before the Lord. *Weeping*, is one of those Exercises, whereto the God of *Heaven* calls His people, to *Humble* themselves before Him. And in the Bible we have many Instances of a *Practice*, according to that *Precept*, in Joel 2. 12. *Turn ye to God, with all your Heart, with weeping, and with mourning.* Indeed the *Tears* of the *Eye*, are to be expected of men, more or less, according to their *Natural Constitutions*.

It

It is defirable, that the *Eye*, which has been
the Grand *Broker for Sin*, fhould by its *Tears*
bear its part in difcovering the paffions of our
minds thereupon. But where the *Eye*, does
not Naturally afford fo free a Channel to that
Brine, which the compreffion and conftriction
of the *Brain* upon *Grief* produceth, we have
ftill our *Sighs*, which *Auftin*, well calls, our *In-
teriour Tears*. And now, O our *Tears*, where
are you!

We read concerning a General Affembly,
in *Judg.* 2. 1. *An Angel of the Lord came unto
them, and faid, I brought you unto the Land, which
I fware unto your Fathers ; but ye have not obeyed
my voice ; wherefore there fhall yet be Thorns in
your fides : And it came to pafs, when the Angel of
the Lord fpake thefe words, the people lift up their
voice and wept ; And they called the Name of the
place Bochim* ; 1. e. Weepers. Oh! why fhould
not *Bofton* this Day, be thus called *Bochim*. So
*Autocratorically* fpoke that *Angel*, that it feems
to have been the *Meffiah* himfelf, appearing in
an Humane Shape ; even, the fame *Angel of
the Covenant*, that had formerly appeared unto
*Jofhua* at *Gilgal* ; and therefore 'tis here faid,
*He came up from Gilgal*. Permit a poor Servant
of that Bleffed *Meffiah*, thus to Expoftulate
with you ; *The Lord of Heaven from whom I
come unto you, brought our Fathers into this Good
Land, which He provided for us* ; *But we have*
*not*

*not obey'd His voice ; and this our Disobedience He has chastised with continual Thorns in our sides.* Why should we not *Lift up our voice & weep,* at such doleful Tidings!

I am sure there are such Things as these to bespeak our *Tears.*

First, The Horrid *Sins* committed in the Land , yea, commonly committed, loudly call for our *Tears.* Alas, it may be said of us, That *we have been Drinking in Iniquity like water.* How much ought we then to, *Drop it away in Tears,* as I may say,, when we *pour out Water before the Lord !* *Bloody* Crimes, like those, the Imputation whereof, made our Lord Jesus Christ, *Sweat* out His very *Blood,* have abounded among us ; and will they not cause us to *weep?* Truly, *Tears of Blood,* were little enough to bewayl our *Bloody, Scarlet, Crimson* Abominations. There is not one of all the *Ten Commandments,* in the Law, which our God has given us, but people are notoriously violating of it, from one end of the Land unto the other. While our Land is full of Unconverted, Unrenewed, Unsanctifyed *Sinners,* how should it be any other than full of all *Ungodliness !* And yet such is the vast multitude of *Dead Souls* among us, or of Souls which do not *Live* unto God, by vertue of *Union* with the Lord Jesus Christ, that we may with Horror say, *There is hardly an House, in which there is not one Dead :*

*Dead* : Nor may we wonder at it, if the Holy God in His Difpenfations, treat our *Land,* as *Unclean,* when the *Dead* in all Societies are fo very many. Truly, If we had a real kind-nefs for the *Holy and Juft and Good Law of our God,* or for our Neighbours, that Ruine them-felves by finning againft that *Law,* we fhall in fome fort fay with him, in *Pfal.* 119. 136. *Rivers of waters run down my Eyes, becaufe they keep not thy Law.* Oh! fhall we not *mourn,* when we fee, That the *World* is become the *Idol,* of almoft all our little World, but the Lord Jefus Chrift, and His *Great Salvation* very *little* con-fidered ? That the *Inftitutions* of the Lord Je-fus Chrift are fhamefully neglected, and the *Superftitions* of a *vain Converfation* practifed ? That the *Names, Words, Works* and *Ordinances,* and *Providences,* of the Lord Jefus Chrift, are moft Irreverently & Unprofitably look'd upon ? And, That we have a *Profane* Indifpofition to the *Sabbaths* of the Lord ? Shall we not *Mourn* when we fee the *Diforder* which confounds all Societies, and the *Selfifhnefs* which depraves the moft in all Societies ? Our *Hating* & *Vexing* of one another ? Our *Unchaftity* in all forts of *Pollution* ? Our *Injuftice* in our Dealings ? Our ma-nifold *Falfhood* in our Affayrs ? Our *Difcontent* in every Station ? We could, in a *Synod* of our Churches, near Seventeen years ago, charge our felves with Epidemical Breaches of all the Rules of

of *Love,* to God, and man. And verily, t'would be a brave Sponge to Dry up our *Tears,* if we could say, that we are mended since the Admonitions of that faithful *Synod.* But besides the more common Violations of the Divine Law among us, there are more Special out-breakings of Sin, in the midst of us, for which, no *Tears* are enough. We may say, but Oh! not without our *Tears,* as in Jer 5.30. *A wonderful & Horrible Thing is committed in the Land.* The Land was fearfully Defiled, by the Impieties of the *Indians,* which were the first Inhabitants. Now, is it not *A Wonderful & an Horrible Thing,* for so many *English* that have Succeeded them, to *Indianize,* and by the *Indian* Vices of *Lying,* and *Idleness,* and *Sorcery,* and a notorious want of all *Family Discipline,* to become obnoxious unto the old Score, and Store of wrath due unto the Land? Is it not *a Wonderful & an Horrible thing,* that the Sins of *Sodom,* should so much prevail in a Land, which was once a *Land of Uprightness?* For, *this was the Iniquity of our Sister Sodom, Pride, Fulness of Bread, and Abundance of Idleness; neither did she strengthen the Hand of the Poor & Needy:* The whole *Spirit* of all their *Dealings,* was, it seems, a General contrivance to *Oppress,* one another. Is it not a *Wonderful & an Horrible Thing,* that in such a Land as this, there should be the Sins that made the *Old Land of Canaan, Vomit out*
her

*her Inhabitants?* For so did those Infandous, &
Confounded, Mixtures, that have openly shown
their Heads among our selves.    There was a
Time, when one Returning from hence to
*England,* could in a Sermon to a very Honourable Auditory, give this Report concerning us,
*I have been Seven years in a Country, where I ne-*
*ver beheld one common Beggar, I never saw one*
*man Drunk ; I never heard one Profane Oath, for*
*all the Time of my being there.*    But is it not a
*Wonderful & an Horrible Thing,* that the Vices of
*Drinking & Swearing,* are now every Day, the
objects of our Observation ;  I pray,  let it be
a *Sorrowful* Observation ?  And is it not a *Won-*
*derful & an Horrible Thing,* that  it should  be a
Complaint made about *New England, Righteous-*
*ness once Lodged in it, but now Murderers ?*    I do
speak it, with a Great concern of Soul ;  The
*Tears* of a bitter Detestation, are necessary to
cleanse this Land, from the Guilt & Shame, of
the *Murderous* Things, that have been with too
much credibility Reported, as done  by some
*New-Englanders* !  God forbid, That  I should
Reproach my Country.   As the Apostle could
say, *I do not make my Appeal, as having any thing*
*to Accuse my Nation of :* So I would say, *I do not*
*Accuse my Country, of any Thing,  but what any o-*
*ther Nation may as much be charged withal.*    But,
when *Cæsar* saw one that  was nearly Related
unto himself, among the Wretches that were
Stabbing

Stabbing of him, he cryed out, with a Singular Agony, *What ? You my Son ! Have I a Son among you !* Thus, there is *this* Aggravation upon all of our Miscarriages : Our Lord JesusChrist from Heaven may thus Argue with us ; *If other People do Wound me by their Sins, 'tis not such a Wonderful and horrible Thing : But for you, O my People, of* New-England, *a People that for the Liberties of my Gospel, I have known above the other Families of the Earth ; a People that are obliged unto me, above the rest of mankind : For these Vile Things to be done among you, my Children !* Oh! This is a *Lamentation, & it should be for a Lamentation?*

Secondly, No *Tears* are enough to Bewayl the visible *Degeneracy*, which is to be Instanced, let me *plainly*, and *humbly* say so! in all Orders of men throughout the Land. When there was a Second Edition of the *Temple*, among the People of God, it is noted, in Neh. 3. 12. *The Ancient men, who had seen the first House, when the Foundation of this House was laid before their Eyes, they wept with a loud voice.* Truly, the few *Ancient men* that are left among us, do *weep with a loud voice,* when they see how miserably *Temple work* is now circumstanced, in the *Second* and *Third* Generation of the Countrey. Tho' we may *Shout aloud for joy,* when we see *so much* of Christ, and of *Truth,* and of *Grace,* among us ; for indeed, *so much* there is, that if they who talk of *Deserting* this Country,

try, would please to stay, as methinks they should, until they hear of a Country that has proportionably more of CHRIST in it, there would for the present, be little said of a Removal! Yet let not this Hinder our joyning with such as *weep with a loud voice* for our Degeneracy. It is affirmed, That many sorts of Inferiour Creatures, when Transplanted from *Europe* into *America*, do Degenerate by the Transplantation ; But if this Remark must be made upon the *People* too, what can we do, but spend our *Tears* upon such a sad Remark? Our Lord Jesus Christ from Heaven seems to bestow that Rebuke upon us, in Jer. 2. 21. *I planted thee a Noble Vine; How then art thou Turned into the Degenerate Plant of a strange vine unto me!* New England once had a famous Governour, namely, *Hopkins* of *Connecticut*, whose words were, *I fear, I fear, the Sins of* New England *will e're long be read in its punishments. Blessed hast thou been, O Land, in thy Rulers; but alas, for the generality, they have not considered, how they were to Honour the Rules of God, in Honouring of those whom God made Rulers over them; and I fear they will come to smart by having them set over them, that it will be an hard work to Honour, and that will hardly be capable to manage their Affairs.* Now can we without many *Tears*, look upon the Tendencies, with the words of that Excellent man have towards an Accomplishment!

It

It muſt be acknowledged unto the praiſe of God, that *New England* is yet Bleſſed with very Worthy men in all Orders; but alas, we have not ſuch a *Choice* of them, as once we had. I ſuppoſe, 'twere eaſy to ſingle out, it may be, *leſs* than *Twenty men*, upon whoſe Removal from us, all our Affairs would be *Palſey-Struck*, with an Irrecoverable Feebleneſs, and the Countrey would almoſt fall, for want of *Pillars* to ſupport it. Indeed, the beſt ſymptom that *New England* has to boaſt of, is an *Hopeful Iſſue*, of Learned and Pious *Young men*, from a well-governed *Colledge*; a *Colledge*, which the Sons of Barbarity among us perhaps care not, if it might be *Raſed unto the ground*. But thoſe thy Sons, O *New-England*, will be no ſooner Hatch'd and Fledg'd, but it may be, they will fly away from thee, as faſt as they can. Among the Firſt Planters of *New-England*, there was a vaſt variety of Generous, Notable, *Brave Spirited* men; yea, ſome of thoſe very men, that were afterwards found able to conquer and manage mighty Kingdoms, would have been but *New-England* Farmers, if their ſilly Perſecutors had not hindred them: *Choice Grain from three ſifted Nations* filled this Wilderneſs. But, the Poſterity do for the moſt part ſtrangely Looſe that *Brave Spirit*, which Inſpired their Anceſtors. I Remember, That the Writer of the *Iſraelitiſh* Chronicles,

B in

in 1 *Chron.* 4. 22. reports, That among the Children of *Judah,* there were Degenerate Creatures, who were *Potters,* and Wretches *Dwelling among Plants, and Hedges; there they dwelt with the King, for his work;* a slavish Generation they were: But what were their Ancestors? Why, they were Brave *Hero's,* who had the Dominion in *Moab:* and it is added, *These are Ancient Things.* *New-England* once abounded with *Hero's* worthy to have their Lives written, as Copies for future Ages to write after; But, *These are Ancient Things!* A *Publick Spirit* in all that sustained any *Publick Office,* and a fervent *Inclination* to Do Good, joyn'd with an Incomparable *Ability* to do it, once ran through *New England;* But, *These are Ancient Things!* A *New England-man,* once was as much as to say, A man that scorns to do an Ill Thing, and *One whose word is as good as his Bond;* But, *These are Ancient Things!* There seems to be a shameful *Shrink,* in all sorts of men among us, from that *Greatness,* and *Goodness,* which adorned our Ancestors: We grow *Little* every way; *Little* in our Civil Matters, *Little* in our Military Matters, *Little* in our Ecclesiastical Matters; we dwindle away, to *Nothing:* I do not mean, for our *Numbers,* but for our *Actions.* Those things, which have been our *Glory,* they are gradually Removing from us. Oh! with *Tears,* do our Ancient

ent men cry out, *Where is the Glory of the Ancient Things!* And shall I say it? As the Grand-child of *Moses*, 'tis judged, became an *Idolater*: So, There are very many Families, of Everlasting Renown throughout *New-England*, wherein some or other of the Grand-children, are become either foolish, or wicked, and it may be notorious *Children of the Devil*: the first and great *Apostate.* Those Things, which their *Grand-fathers* would sooner have dy'd, than have Done, these Degenerous Creatures, do them every Day.------*At non ille Satum, quo te mentiris.* Wretch, If thy Grandfather had imagined, that ever thou wouldest have become, such a pittiful Thing, he would have swum in his own *Tears*, unto his Grave upon it. Yea, our people, have for many years been going on in a course of long *Apostasy.* I will not Enquire, Whether the Principles of *Church-Reformation*, upon which we were at first Established, begin to be Deserted among us? I won't so much as Enquire, Whether we are Loosing that Principle, *That no party of men whatsoever, have any just Authority to appoint any parts or means of Divine Worship, which the Lord Jesus Christ has not in the Scriptures Instituted?* I won't so much as Enquire, Whether we are Loosing that, Principle, *That a probable, and a credible, and a try'd Profession of a Saving Faith is to be expected from all that we Admit unto the*

B 2　　　　　　　　　　　*Table*

*Table of the Lord?* For us to Loose those Principles, *already,* would be too quick a *Degeneracy,* to be imagined. I know very well, that *Apostasy* has been sometimes unreasonably charged among us: Those things that were Incontestably, *The First Principles of New-England,* when asserted and practised, have been called, an *Apostasy.* The *Principles* of *Morellianism,* and *Separation,* were none of our *First Principles*: Nevertheless, the *Principles* of a *Scriptural Purity* in our Whole Worship, were so much our *First Principles,* that the Lord Jesus Christ, I am verily perswaded, will abhor us, and forsake us, upon our Abandoning thereof. But, I will Enquire, Whether our *First Love* to the Lord Jesus Christ, and his Evangelical Appointments be not almost Lost ? And, whether we have not almost Lost the old *Power of Godliness,* in our Conversations? And, whether, A Christian full of *Piety,* and *Charity,* and *Self-Denial,* and universal *Holiness* and *Fruitfulness,* do not grow a rare sight among us? Christians, our Lord Jesus Christ is this Day Holding His *Bottel,* to take the *Tears,* which we are to drop for our *Apostasies !*

Thirdly ; The prodigious and astonishing *Scandals,* given by the extraordinary Miscarriages of some that have made a more than ordinary *Profession* of Religion ; These call for our *Tears,* and our Bleeding Lamentations.

When

When some Church-members, yea, some Tea-
chers and Rulers in *Israel*, were fallen into
*Scandal*, says that good man, in *Ezra* 9. 3.
*When I heard this Thing, then I rent my Garment,
and my Mantle, and I sat down Astonied; and I
said, O my God, I am Ashamed.* Alas, It would
*Astonish* any good man, into *Tears*, to be informed of the Detestable Things done by some
that have highly Profess'd *Better Things.* Indeed, Let a man do never so well, yet a great
many Ill Things may be spoken of him; yea,
a man shall Hear Ill, for Doing Well. One
of the most faithful men among the whole
People of God, could say, *I heard the Defaming
of many.* But if those *Defamed* Servants of the
Lord Jesus Christ, will be a little patient, *He*
will at last give an Honourable *Resurrection* unto the *Names*, that had so much *Dirt* cast upon them, when the *Names* of their Envious
Accusers, will either lie Buried in *Oblivion*, or
be mentioned no otherwise, than as *Judas* in
the Gospel, and *Pilate* in the Creed. It is a-
nother matter, and oh! a very *Tearful*, and
*Fearful* matter it is! When such as have made
an high profession of *Godliness*, are left of
God, unto the Doing of those *Ungodly* Things,
upon which it may be said unto them, *The
Name of God is through your means Blasphemed.*
Syrs, It were infinitely better, for one to *Dye
immediately!* There are some, who do with

pleasure, Entertain the Stories of Base Things done by the strict Professors of Religion; and with Triumph exclame thereupon, *Ay, These are the Members of such an one! who would be a Professor? They are all so!* Unto every such person I must without hæsitation say, Man, Thou hast an infallible mark of an Unregenerate Soul upon thee. If thou hadst the Heart of a *Christian* in thee, thou wouldst never speak at such a rate: such Language would rather proceed from the Heart of a *Devil!* But the Lord Jesus Christ has an *Holy People*, who do themselves *Hate every false way*, and are in exquisite Agonies of Soul, when they see any others to step aside into such a *Way*. The Wise man says, in Prov. 25. 26. *A Righteous man falling before the Wicked, is as a Troubled Fountain, and a corrupt Spring.* Some have made such a profession of *Righteousness*, that much Notice has been taken of them; others have been ready to think, *Well, Christianity, is just such a Thing, as the Lives of these men do Represent it.* Now the *Falls* of these men, before the *Wicked*, are just as if one should throw *poison* into the *Well* that all the Town is to fetch Water at. So were the Heathen of old *Poisoned*, when they said, *Christiani sanctè vixissent, si Christus sancta docuisset!* Oh! *Lamentable* Thing! *Satan*, who is often the Executioner of the Wrath of God upon a sinful World, hath

hath *Defired*, leave to fingle out fome high Profeffors of Religion,& pufh them on to fome fcandalous Iniquities : he would fain do the part of a Devil, it may be, on fome one man, that he might *poifon* all the Town, by the *Falls* of that man. The Dreadful Juftice of God, who *gives none account of His matters*, hath faid, *Go, Satan, go make an Experiment upon them* ? And lo, upon the *Experiment*, fome ftrict, and it may be, fome old Profeffor, that had been formerly Troublefome to all the Sinners that were about him, *He* not only proves a *Coveteous Worldling*, but he acts as driven by an *Unclean Devil*, or by a *Cheating Devil*, or by a *Lying Devil* : and he plays the Devil horribly. Such Doleful Inftances there have been among us, as would *poifon* a whole Neighbourhood, yea, a whole Colony, with *Atheifm*, if the Lord Jefus Chrift, had not an Almighty Arm, to fecure His own Religion. *Wo, wo, wo*, to Hundreds of Souls, in the midft of thee, O *New England*, for the *Offences* that are given by fome of thy *Church-members* ; Let *Them* think of the reft. But, Oh! how fhould we all come to fuch Lamentations, *My Eyes do fail with Tears, my Bowels are Troubled*. The fcandalous Fall of *David*, is by as tranfcendent a Myftery of Divine Soveraignty *Recorded*, as it was *Ordered*. Some of the *Pagans* in the Primitive Times, would not be *Chriftians*, becaufe

*David*, forsooth, was one of our greatest *Saints*
tho' he did such Damnable Things; and, many of the *Christians* would then Sin Damnably, pleading, *Si David, cur non et ego* ? Why,
mayn't I, as well as *David*? I believe, There
are a million of men in *Hell*, whose Damnation was occasioned by the Fall of *David*, tho'
*David* himself be gone to *Heaven* after all. Ay,
but this *David* therefore comes to cry out, *I
water my couch with my Tears, mine Eye is consumed!* Have any of our Eminent Persons, ever
miscarried like *David*? We should with an Impartial Fidelity, do what we can, that they
may Repent like *David* : No doubt, the most
Holy Lord Jesus Christ, who has *Eyes like a
Flame of Fire*, makes his Jealousy burn *like fire*,
against the Churches, which do not bear due
*Testimonies* against such Offendors: It may be,
He'l set them on fire, for their Unfaithfulness.
But still, we must even *Consume our Eyes with
Tears*, when we bear our *Testimonies*.   Oh! the
Irreparable Wrongs that we have seen done to
the dear and sweet Name of our precious Je-
sus ! Methinks, we should broach our *Tears*, on
this Lamentable Provocation ; and be like the
Church of *Corinth*, when an Unclean Fellow
was found among them ; [ 2 *Cor.* 7. 11. ] for
*Godly Sorrow*, for *Carefulness*, for *Clearing of our
selves, for Indignation, Fear, Desire, Zeal, and
Revenge.*

Fourthly,

Fourthly ; The Evident *Blowes* from the
Hand of an Angry God, in a long Train of *Difafters* upon all our Affayres,How much do they
Sollicit our *Tears* before the Lord ?  A Recapi-
tulation of the fad things, which have befallen
us, while our *Dayes have paffed away under the
wrath of God,*in this *Wilderness,*and we have feen
one *Deftruction* after another, almoft without a-
ny *Intermiffion,* might juftly bring us to that Lamentation,in Lam.3.48,49.*Mine eye runneth down
with Rivers of Water, for the Deftruction of the
Daughter of my People ; Mine eye trickleth down,
& ceafeth not, without any Intermiffion.* The *Vials*
of the wrath of God, have been long *Pouring
out* upon us, in Continued, & Horrendous Defolations ; it becomes us therefore to *Draw Water,* and pour our *Tears* into the *Vials* of the
Lord.  God began to fmite us, with an Annual
*Blaft* upon feveral forts of our *Grain,* juft Forty
years ago : and although, if our *Husbandman
were taught Difcretion by his God,* no doubt,many
Natural Remedies for much of that *blaft,*might
be lit upon, a kind of Dead fleep upon men ftill
detains them under *Blafting* Difadvantages : &
behold, by an Alteration come upon the very
*Courfe of Nature* among us, our *Indian Grain* it
felf, the very *Native Grain* in the Country, is
the laft year fo *Blafted,* that we hear fuch an
hideous Cry, for, *Bread! Bread!* this year, as
was never heard in this Land before. And how
very

very much have our *Estates* been Diminished, by *Losses* that have been *Multiplied*, upon us? On *Shore*, once and again such *Fires* have laid wast the Treasures of our *Metropolis*, that we have had cause to Cry, *Oh ! What means the heat of this Anger !* And at *Sea*, besides our Frequent *Ship-wracks*, I suppose, no part of the English Dominions, have proportionably had near so many *Ships*, taken by the common Adversary, as *New-England*; poor *Boston* & *Salem*, I am sure, has *Felt* what I *Speak* : Yea, it is the Discourse among the Vertuous Merchants upon the Exchange at *London*, *That surely, Almighty God is much offended at* New-England, *for they miscarry from no Quarter so much as they do from thence* : But what Havock, ha's been all this while, ever now and then making upon the *Lives* of our People, by the *Angels of Death*, in *Epidemical Sicknesses* ? We have ever now and then, been visited with *Mortal Contagions* ; the *Arrowes of Death* have been flying thick among us; A *Thousand Persons*, if I have not misreckon'd have been from one Town, in one year, carried unto their Eternal Home ; And, *Oh ! The slain of the Lord have been many* !

Shall I proceed ? We have seen our selves Deprived, not only of *Charter*-Liberties, but all of *English*-Liberties, with such Things done to us, as the High Court of *Parliament*, by the Vote numbred among the *Grievances* of the Nation

tion. Any confiderate man, that compares the
Prodigious *Invafiors* then made upon all our Interefts, with Two Things that have fince come
to light ; the *Irifh* propofals, *For the Irifh to be
fettled near* New-England, *to check the growing*
Independants *of that Country* ; and the Letter to
the *Pope,* engaging to *fet up the Roman Catholick
Religion in the Plantations of* America : cannot
but fay, That *all Things* were then under a
Dreadful Profpect with us. An Happy RE-
VOLUTION hath Saved us, out of thofe
Diftreffes ; But we have immediately been Diftreffed with New Difafters, wherein a Righteous God, ha's been *Punifhing us yet Seven Times
more for our Iniquities.* The Salvages fill'd this
Land from one end unto the other, with direful
outrages, with which they cut off many Hundreds of our Inhabitants, in a *Former War* ; and
now a *Later War,* wherein the *Revolution* found
us Entangled, ha's been confuming us for more
than Seven years together. Herein, God ha's
been *Pouring* out the *Blood* of our *Friends* ; Yea,
Horrid Stories might be told, of the Barbarous
Cruelties, wherewith fome of them have been
butchered, by the Hands of the *Barbarians* :
And fhall not we, *Pour* out our *Tears* upon their
*Graves* ?

*---Quis talia fando,*
*Temperet a Lacrymis ?---*
The moft Compendious & Effectual way to
come

come at a lasting *Peace*, was well contrived, in an Expedition formed, for the cutting down of a *Tree*, that was the Roost of the *Rooks*, which Troubled us; but a marvellous Frown from Heaven, so defeated this contrivance, that although it was at first next unto a *Miracle* that so Important a Thing, as the Conquest of *Canada*, was not accomplished, yet Now our Armies not being All cut off, by the whole Force of *Canada* now arriv'd into *Quebeck*, was a Deliverance next unto a *Miracle*. Our compassionate Lord, Marvellously answered the *Faith*, which we then Expressed in our *Prayer* before Him, *That the English Army should not fall by the Hands of the French Enemy* : And therefore, about fourteen Hundred Raw men, tired with a long Voyage, were not made a Prey to more than twice as many Expert Souldiers, then *Crowing on their own Dunghil*. Nevertheless, the heavy *Debts*, and the many *Deaths*, which ensued upon the failure of that *Great Action*, the *Greatest* that ever we attempted, have so confounded us, that it becomes us to Ly *Low*, before that Just God, who *Show'd us Great and Sore Troubles,& brought us down to the Depths of the Earth*. And, as if all this had not been enough to lay us *Low*, the *Spirit* of God against whom we had *Rebelled*, permitted the *Devils*, from the *Depths of Hell*, to assault us, with as Prodigious Vexations, as ever befel any People under the whole *Cope of Heaven*.

*ven.* The *Devils,* thofe *Powers* of *Darknefs,* had been horribly plaid withal, by *Magical Tricks,* ufed among many People in this *Land of Light,* and thefe *Devils* now broke in upon the Country, with fuch *Præternatural Poffeffions* as may be the perpetual Aftonifhment of the World. In the *Storm* now Raifed, upon a Land, which by the *Wrath of the Lord of Hofts was Darkned:* a *Storm* Raifed by *Wicked* Spirits in *High Places,* that had the *Upper hand* of us : a *Storm* that would have made the beft of *Pilots,* to want the beft *Advice* that could be given : It was, and it will be, paft all *Humane Skill,* Exactly to *Underftand* what *Inextricable Things* we have met withal. But yet it may need fome Difquifition with us, *What matter of Humiliation in them?* O *New England* fuch as thefe, have been thy *Difafters* : And indeed, there is hardly a *Family* among us, wherein there ha's not fome Terrible Thing or other, fallen out, which will caufe particular Perfons, to go Drooping, with *Sorrow* to their *Graves.* T'will be Endlefs to Enumerate the *Temptations,* that we have all had in this *Wildernefs* : But as it was faid of *Miriam,* that feems to have been a Figure of the Church then with her in the *Wildernefs* ; Numb.12.14. *If her Father had Spit in her Face, fhould fhe not be afhamed ?* Thus, O *New England* ; Thy *Father* has been *Spitting* in thy *Face;* but, Oh! Let thy *Tears* now run down that fhamed *Face,* let thy *Tears* wafh waſh that ſhame of thy *Face* away for ever.    If we did thus *Pour out Water before the Lord,* we might at laſt, as the Scripture ſpeaks, come to *Forget our Miſery, and Remember it as Waters that paſs away.*

*II.* May the Prayers of a fervent SUP-PLICATION, be from this Day, raiſed among us, upon the manifold Occaſions for ſuch *Prayers.*    I do not ask you to *Faſt on this Day,* as the General Aſſembly of *Iſrael* did, on the day when they were all together.    But thoſe things may be Uttered *on this Day,* and Reſolved *on this Day,* that many a Day of *Prayer,* with *Faſting,* may be the effect of *this Day:* And it may be, a *General Aſſembly,* will before they break up, ſome time or other ſet apart a Day, for *Prayer* with *Faſting,* together, before the Lord that ſo a whole *Province* together at once, may *Hear what God the Lord will ſpeak unto them.* Some think, that when the General Aſſembly of *Iſrael,* did *pour out water before the Lord,* they did it, as a ſymbol, expreſſive of the Devotion with which they made their *Prayers* before Him; as the devout perſon could ſay, in 1 Sam. 1. 15. *I have poured out my Soul before the Lord* And indeed, they ſeem to me ſo intent on *pouring out their Prayers,* that they would *pour nothing,* not ſo much as a little *water,* in.    For ſuch *Prayers* unto the God and Father of our

Lord

Lord Jefus Chrift, I do *this Day* make my moft zealous Addreffes unto you, O Inhabitants of *New England* : I Addrefs you, That you would *Pray always with all Prayer and Supplication;* and that with a publick Recommendation of pub- lick *Supplication,* to be maintained by our Chur- ches, in a fucceffive and a repeated pra- ctice thereof, *Houfhold Prayer,* and *Secret Pray- er,* may be confcientioufly practifed by all forts of men.

It is with a Threefold *Advertifment* that I would urge this Defire of my Soul.

Firft ; All the *Bleffings,* that we can want, or wifh ; yea, the very Beft of *Bleffings,* are to be obtained by *Supplication* to the *Bleffed God* for them. Why fhould I lanch forth into the vaft Ocean of *Affurances* and *Experiences,* which our God has given unto His People, *That they fhall not feek his Face in vain?* All *New-England,* has been filled with Demonftrations from its firft Settlement unto this Day, That *Prayer* is as it has been fometimes called, *A Golden Key to Un- lock all the Treafures of Heaven.* Many, and many, and many a time, it might be faid, *This poor Land cried unto the Lord, and the Lord has heard and faved.* And what is the ufe that we fhould make of all the Salvations, wherein we have fo wonderfully feen, *The prevalency of Prayer* demonftrated ? What but this, That we will with our *Prayer,* again & always come unto
Thee,

Thee, O *Thou Hearer of Prayer!* We would have a Supply of Provifion ffom the Bounties of Heaven fent unto us in our Scarcity. Why, *Supplications,* like thofe of *Elijah,* will manage the very Corks on the *Bottles* of *Heaven.* We would have the *Lions* that are threatning to Devour us, Reftrain'd from doing fo. Why, *Supplications,* like thofe of *Daniel,* will muzzle the moft Ravenous *Lions.* All our *Undertakings,* would they not profper the more, if by more *Prayer* over them, like the Servant of *Abraham,* we *acknowledged the Lord in all our ways?* Would any of our *Churches,* have *Paftors after the Lords own Heart* beftowed upon them? I pray, mark what I fay; I wonder exceedingly, How any Church dare proceed fo far as to vote, and call a Minifter, for their fixed Service, until they have by a *Day of Prayer,* firft made their *Supplications* unto the Lord Jefus Chrift, for His Direction: The jealous Lord Jefus Chrift, may juftly fhow them, that they *make more Hafte than good fpeed,* when the *chief Shepherd,* is thus forgotten with them, Whereas, if you will go to the Lord Jefus Chrift, O ye *Flocks* of the Lord, He will give you thofe *Paftors,* that fhall be *Good men, and Full of the Holy Ghoft,* & men, by whom *there fhall be much people added unto the Lord:* Men, in whom you fhall be, on a thoufand accounts unfpeakably Happy, as long as they live among you.

Briefly,

Briefly, The *Beſt Thing* that *New-England* can poſſibly be Bleſſed withal, would be, the *Regeneration* of the *Riſing Generation*; the general Converſion of our Young People, to know, and prize, and ſerve our Lord Jeſus Chriſt. We are Trembling, at the *Controverſy*, which we ſee the Great God managing againſt you, O our Young Folks, in Fiery, Deadly Rebukes. *You* do not *Keep the Covenant of God*; and now, the Almighty God ſeems to ſay over *New-England, I will take no pleaſure in your young men.* Some of our *Young men* are given up to the furtheſt ſallies of Extravagant and Exorbitant Impiety: And others of our *Young men* periſh either by the *Wars* at Home, or by the *Seas* abroad, until we almoſt become, as *Bede* reports once *England* was, *Omni milite, et floridæ Juventutis Alacritate Spoliata.* Miſerable *Young men*; your *Converſion* to the Lord Jeſus Chriſt, would certainly prevent all of this miſery. Now, to procure ſuch a *Converſion*, it would be a courſe of admirable Efficacy, for our *Churches* to keep now and then, whole *Dayes of Prayer* unto the Lord, on the behalf of their poor Poſterity. *Awake then, what mean you, O ye ſleeping Churches? Ariſe, and call upon your Lord!* The Holy *Spirit* of the Lord Jeſus Chriſt, Oh! could we *Pray* that *Holy Spirit* into the Hearts of our Children, they would fall to Glorifying of the Lord Jeſus Chriſt immediately!

C

mediately! How much might our *Counsils*
work upon them, if they saw our most ardent
*Prayers* accompany those *Counsils*? If *Grace*
were more own'd, and sought, who can say,
What the *Spirit of Grace*, would then do for
our *Offspring*?

Secondly; The *Times* which we are fallen into, do Loudly call for our *Supplication* to that
God, in whose *Hand* are *all our Times*. All the
whole Tribe of Thinking men, that have any
*Understanding in the Times*, do *know* this, that of
all the Things, which we *ought now to do*, there
is nothing more Seasonable, than *Unfained Prayer* unto the Lord. There are those Things now
come unto the *Birth*, which require us to *Lift
up our* Lively *Prayer*, unto the *Living God*;
There are those *Calamities* impending, that
strongly require us to *Cry unto the God that per-
formeth all things for us*. When *Daniel*, did *understand by Books*, that the *Number of the years*, for
the Captivitie of the Church of God, was very
near accomplished, *Then*, sayes he, in Dan.9.3.
*I set my Face unto the Lord God, to seek by Prayer
and Supplications, with Fasting & Sackclothe and
Ashes*. Truly, We may *Understand by Books*,
That the *Number of years*, for the Church of
our Lord Jesus Christ to Ly under its
Desolations, is very near to its Accomplishment : and therefore, *Hæc sunt Orandi Tem-
pora* : I may say, *Pray, Pray, Pray, never more
Need than Now*. When the *Seventy years*, for

the Churches confinement in *Babylon*, were almoſt out, Good men might have *Known* that
they were ſo : Holy *Daniel* did *Know* it. When
the *Four Hundred & Thirty* years for the Churches Expecting the Promiſed Reſcue from *E-
gypt*, were almoſt out, Good men might have
*Known* that they were ſo : The Lord made the
Doubting *Moſes* to *Know* it. When the *Four Hundred & Ninety years* for the coming of the *Meſſiah*,
after the Rebuilding of *Jeruſalem*, were almoſt
Expired, Good men might have *Known* it ; &
many Good men *did* then *Know* it, *Waiting for
the Conſolation of Iſrael* : Yea, the *Phariſees* themſelves, the High Church-men of thoſe Dayes,
*They* alſo did *Know* it ; and our Lord call'd them
*Hypocrites*, for their not conforming themſelves
accordingly. Well, When the *Twelve Hundred &
Sixty years* aſſigned unto the Reign of the *Anti-
chriſtian Apoſtaſy*, draw towards their *Period*, this
*Period* alſo may be *Known*, as well as any of the
former.   The *Miſtakes* that have been in the
*Gueſſes* of ſome Learned men, about this *Happy
Period*, are far from Inferring a Neceſſity of
*Wrong Reckonings* to the Worlds end ; No, they
rather make it more eaſy now to *Reckon Right.*
Now I do this Day appear among you, O People of God, with ſuch a Meſſage from Heaven
unto you, as This ; *Behold, I bring unto you Good
Tidings of Great Joy, that ſhall be to all the faith-
ful People of God* : The *Tidings* which I bring

unto you, are, *That there is a* REVOLUTION *and a* REFORMATION *at the very Door, which will be vaſtly more Wonderful, than any of the Deliverances, yet ſeen by the Church of God, from the Beginning of the World.* I do not ſay, That the *Next year* will bring on this *Happy Period* ; but this I do ſay, That the bigger part of this Aſſembly, may in the courſe of Nature, Live to ſee it.: There ſtand thoſe within theſe Walls this Day, That ſhall ſee, *Glorious Things done for Thee, O thou City of God ! The Day is at Hand,* when Thunder & Lightning and Earth quake, ſhall Prodigiouſly Swallow up that *Abominable City,* which now indeed her ſelf begins with *Proceſſions,* to deprecate ſuch an Exterpation. *The Day is at Hand,* when the *Turkiſh Empire,* inſtead of being any longer a *Wo* to *Chriſtendome,* ſhall it ſelf become a *Part* of *Chriſtendome. The Day is at Hand,* when the *Vail* that ha's been upon the Hearts of the *Jewiſh Nation,* ſhall be taken off, and that Nation ſhall *Fear the Lord, and His Good Thing,* the *Meſſiah.* Concerning the *Day of the Lord,* wherein theſe Things will be done, I do with all Freedome ſay unto you, *That Great Day of the Lord, it is Near, it is Near, and it haſteth greatly!* Yea, If I could ſpeak with a Voice as loud, as that of the *Seventh Trumpet,* which we are certain will *Sound Quickly,* I would Sound this Alarm to all mankind, *The Kingdom of God is at Hand ! The Kingdom of*
*God*

*God is at Hand!* This is not meer *Conjecture,*
or *Opinion* ; but there is *Demonstration,* I assert
nothing short of *Demonstration* for it.   For, I
pray, when the Kingdom of *Satan,* managed by
his *Vicar* at *Rome,* is Expired, whose *Kingdom*
shall next Succeed upon it?   Now, Tis very
certain, That there will be no more than
*Twelve Hundred & Sixty* years allow'd unto that
Papal Kingdom : Tis very certain, That when
*Ten* Soveraign Kings arise, in the broken Roman Empire, the *Twelve Hundred & Sixty* years
of the Papal Kingdom, are Commenced : And
It is very certain, That by the middle of the
*Fifth* century, *Ten* several Distinct Kingdomes,
took advantage from the Distractions then upon
the Roman Empire, to set up for themselves.
By this Calculation, we have nothing less than
a Demonstration, that the *Papal Kingdom,* ha's
the last Sands, of its last *Hour-glass,* now running for it.   Nor is it *Unlikely,* no, but all
Things conspire, even to *Demonstration* it self,
That the last *Half Time,* or, Hundred and Four-
score years, of the Papal Kingdom, Entred at
the *Reformation* in the *Former* Century.   All the
*Schæmes,* that put off this most *Happy Period,*
unto further and future Ages, are easily con-
victed of manifest *Inconsistences :* And therefore,
I question, whether there be so much as one
Judicious and Considerate Student, in those
Prophecies, which, *Blessed are they that Study,* but
C 3

what

what concurs to this Expectation, *That the Kingdom of God is at Hand. Lift up your Heads* then, O you that *Love the Appearing of the Lord Jesus Christ* : For there seems as if there were an *Age of Miracles* now *Dawning* upon us. Proper *Miracles* were continued in the Church of God, for Two or Three Hundred years together, even until the Antichristian *Apostasy* was come on to some Extremity. And when that *Apostasy* is over, tis possible, there may be a Return of proper *Miracles* ; those, *Powers of the World to come.* Such *Miracles* have been lately Wrought, more than two or three of them, in the City of *London*, that, what if they should be a Few Drops of the *Spirit* of the *Messiah*, falling before a Mighty Shower of that *Spirit* ? Persons who have had their *Limbs* miserably disjointed, Persons that have had Inveterate *Palseyes*, Incurable *Fistula's*, Desperate *Leprosies* ; These Persons, as they have been Reading the Ancient *Miracles* of our Lord Jesus Christ, the *Spirit* of Christ hath wonderfully given them, the *Faith* of His doing the like for them ; and Behold, they have, to the Astonishment of mankind, been by the like *Miracles*, perfectly and presently recovered out of all their Maladies. What shall we make of these things ? Do not Sinfully Expect *Miracles* ; and yet say I, *That the Lords Name is Near, His Wondrous Works declare* ! However, They may be *Symbolical* Representations, and Exhibitions, of the *Miraculous* Things, which the Lord is going to Do for His People : For, I do again affure you, The *Trumpet* is going to Sound, that fhall make the *Kingdomes of this World, become the Kingdoms of the Lord, and of His Chrift.*

But I am fure, we had need be much upon our knees, in *Supplications* before the Lord, if it be a Day of fuch *Expectations.* For you muft expect, That thefe Things will come on with fuch Horrible Commotions, and Concuffions, and Confufions, that *Mens Hearts every where fhall fail them for Fear, and for looking after thofe Things which are coming on the Earth.* The mighty *Angels* of the Lord Jefus Chrift, will make their Defcent, and fet the World a Trembling at the Approaches of their Almighty Lord : They will *Shake* Nations, and *Shake* Churches, and *Shake* mighty Kingdoms, and *Shake once more, not Earth only, but Heaven alfo.* The very next Thing, I freely tell you, that I look for, is, That there will thofe Horrible *Shakes* be given unto certain Kingdoms in *Europe,* that fhall bring the pure Worfhippers of the Lord Jefus Chrift into fuch *Employments &* *Advancements,* as they never had before. But fuch Things will be done, that it may be queftioned, *Who fhall Live, when God doth thefe things?* and it muft be Anfwered, *Your Hearts fhall Live, that feek the Lord?*

Thirdly ; No men are under fo much obli-

C 4                                        gati-

gation to be *Men of Prayer*, as the *Ministers* of the Gospel, who should be as much by their *Study*, as they are by their *Office*, the *Men of God*.

My Fathers, and Brethren ; You that are the *Samuels* of this *New-English Israel*, you are concerned more than any men Living, to be among them that *Call upon the Name of God* ; *Call you upon the Lord, & He will Answer you.* The First Ministers of the *New-Testament*, expressed a Resolution, well worthy to be follow'd, by all that shall come after them, in Acts 6. 4. *We will give our selves continually to Prayer, and the Ministry of the Word.*

Our Lord Jesus Christ, gave unto His *Disciples* a *Directory*, for their *Supplications :* And in this *Directory*, methinks, I see the condition of His *Ministers* most particularly Accommodated. Our *Prayer* should be, as it were our *Breath* ; and oh! how should we *Live*, if we were *Breathing* of *Prayer*, on all Occasions every day continually! The Success of our Ministry, in those three Things, *The Sanctifying of Gods Name*, and, *The Coming of His Kingdome*, and, *The Doing of His Will*, these are the first and main Things, for which we are to be concerned in our daily *Supplications*. But if we will be Faithful in our Ministry, we must run the hazard of loosing all the Comforts of this Life ; 'twill be well, if even they that
                                                          are

are bound by *Compact*, as well as otherwife by
*Juftice*, to fupport us, do not *Sacrilegioufly* cheat
us of our *Daily Bread*. We muft therefore Go
to God as unto our *Heavenly Father*, for our
*Bread* with our daily *Supplications*. But in our
Miniftry we fhall commit many Errors, being
*Flefh* and *Blood*, and having a *Fountain of Sin*
in us, as well as other men. We muft therefore cry for the *Forgivenefs of our Sins*, with
our Daily *Supplications*. And the many *Inju-*
*ries*, which an Ungodly World will treat us
withal, will furnifh us with opportunities e-
nough, to Infert in our Daily *Supplications*, that
claufe, *Lord, we forgive them who Trefpafs a-*
*gainft our felves!* But our Miniftry, will be attended with various *Temptations* from the *Wick-*
*ed One* : Oh! how glad will the *Devils* be, if
*We*, whofe Bufinefs 'tis to thwart and crofs *his*
Defigns, may be Trepan'd by him into any
thing that fhall promote them! For this caufe,
our Daily *Supplications* muft cry to Heaven,
That we *may not be Led into Temptation, but*
*Sav'd from the Evil.*

Thus are we to *Pray without ceafing*, and we
are to interweave *Prayer*, into all the *Affairs* of
our Miniftry. Our *Sermons* efpecially, oh! if
we did but *Pray* much over them, how much
would the *Spirit* of Chrift adjoyn Himfelf unto them! 'Tis very fure, *Bene Oraffe, eft bene*
*Studuiffe.* But fhall we not *Faft*, as well as
                                        *Pray?*

*Pray?* Our Excellent *Hooker* would fay, *That Prayer was a principal part of a Minifters work*; *'twas by this, that he was to carry on all the reft* : He would alfo fay, *That fuch an Extraordinary Favour as the Life of Religion, and the Power of Godlinefs, muft be preferved by the frequent ufe of fuch extraordinary means, as Fafting with Prayer* : and accordingly, he did himfelf ftill Devote one Day in a *Month* unto a fecret *Faft* before the Lord. Thus, our Excellent *Mitchel*, would once in two months, keep fuch a *Faft*, wherein he would make a Catalogue of all the Afflictive Things that he faw, not only in himfelf, but in all our *Three Colonies,* and in the Nations of *Europe* alfo, and he would fpread them all before the Lord, with the matters of *his own* Everlafting Welfare. Yea, I fuppofe, there hath been hardly one very famous man, in the Churches of *New England,* but what has familiarized himfelf to fuch Exercifes ; and thefe were the Exercifes that Ripened, & Enlarged their Souls, and refcued them from Enchantments, and fitted them to become fo famous : And they that have hereto Exercifed themfelves, have left this *Obfervation* to us, *I foon Loofe that ferious, that gracious, that generous, and that watchful and ufeful Difpofition of mind, that I gain by thefe Devotions, if I do for many dayes together intermit them.* I remember, There are three perfons Renowned in the Scripture,

for

for their *Fasting*; and every one of those persons, was Honoured, with the Doing of Miraculous Things, in *Feeding* the People of God.
And I Remember a *Golden* Passage of *Chry-*
*sostom, That the very Angels themselves cannot but*
*Honour the man, whom they see familiarly and*
*frequently, admitted unto the Audience, and as it*
*were Discourse, with the Divine Majesty.*

*III.* May the **Cares** of a Thorough RE-
FORMATION, be from this Day used among
us, upon the multiplied Occasions for such
*Cares.* When the General Assembly of *Israel,*
were all together, *They said, we have Sinned a-*
*gainst the Lord* ; but when they so said, it is
implied, that they *did* something, in pursuance
of this Confession ; that is to *say,* They set
themselves to Redress the *Provoking Evils,*
wherein they had *Sinned.* Certainly, there is
not one man, in our *General Assembly,* but what
will readily confess, *We have Sinned against the*
*Lord* : Yea, the Lord, has by *Scourging* made
this whole People, many a Time, over, to confess thus much before Heaven and Earth. But
now, Just, and Quick, and Warm *Cares* to *Re-*
*form* what we *Confess,* are needful to show the
Sincerity of our *Confession,* or, to prove, that we
had a *Spirit without Guile,* in our *Confession.* 'Tis
thought by some, That when the General Assembly of *Israel* did *Pour out Water before the*
Lord,

*Lord*, they did thereby, as it were, Sacramentally Profess, that they thoroughly *Cleansed* themselves from all their *filthy Idolatries*, and utterly *cast forth* all their *Filthiness & Wickedness*, with a full purpose, to *Take up* nothing of it, any more. Truly, The Command of our God, now unto us, is that, in Isa.1.16. *Wash yee, make you clean, put away the Evil of your Doings, from before mine Eyes.* I must say unto you, That whatever man, shall in any Thing Obstruct, the *Reformation* of *New England*, he is *therein*, and *so far*, a *Publick Enemy* of the Land. There is much Talk, oftentimes Impertinently Enough carried on, whether such a man, or such a man, be *True to the Interest of the Country.* But you shall give *Me*, that am never present at any of your *Elections*, leave to Suggest unto you, who those men are, that are *True to the Interest of the Country.* Syrs, Those men, that will do all they can, for the *Reformation* of the Country, from *Ignorance*, from *Idleness*, from *Dishonesty*, from *Uncleanness*, from all *Profaneness*, and *Paganism*, and from *Drunkenness*, and all the Execrable Incentives thereunto ; THAT, That is the man ! Those men are *True to the Interest of the Country* ; for indeed, our Peace with God, is our *True Interest.* Nor do I, by saying this, go to set by, an *English* Tenderness of our *Liberties*, from the Reputation, of a Commendable, yea, and a Necessary Quality, in all that we call to Serve the Publick.

Publick. If there should be any Sons of *Esau,* that will not be Tender, and Tenacious of such precious *Liberties,* as the Country is, by a Royal Grant, at this Day, priviledg'd withal, those persons also cannot be *True to the Interest of the Country.* But, still it must be asserted, That our *Best Friends,* are those, that most Vigorously Endeavour to Restrain, and Redress, and *Reform,* that *Liberty of Sinning,* which men are too ready to give unto themselves. Now, to Invigorate our Endeavours after this *Reformation,* Let us give *Earnest Heed* unto a Five-fold *Admonition.*

First, What tho' we shan't *Agree* about *Every Thing?* Is there *Nothing* therefore to be done, for the *Reformation* of a Land *Pining away in its Iniquities?* Possibly, We are yet somewhat in the *Dark,* about that Quæstion, *What is the Controversy that the Lord Jesus Christ hath with* New-England? And it might occasion some *Controversy* our selves with one another, to pull that Quæstion, under too close and hard, and arbitrary Disquisitions. However, There are several Provocations to God, so *Evident,* and so *Notorious,* among us, that methinks, we cannot be to seek, for many *Causes* of the judgments that are daily breaking of us; and where we see those uncontestable *Causes* of Wrath, Oh! Why may we not *Unite,* as *one man,* for the Removal of them? 'Tis true,

true, We don't *Know all Things* ; But shall we
therefore *Do Nothing* ? Let us Examine, How
far we can go, hand in hand, for the *Reformation* of what we do plainly *see* to be amiss ; &
what we *see* not, the *Lord will Teach us*, that
*wherein we have done Iniquity, we may do so no
more.* A Lady of a very suspected Chastity,
Apostatising to Popery, complained unto a
Protestant Minister, that the Reason of her
Apostasy was, *Because the Scriptures were not
plain enough, to have their Sense determined by
private Christians, and therefore she must Embrace
a Religion, where an Infallible Judge could be had
for all* : but the Protestant Minister, gave her
that sharp Reply, *Good Madam, say not so* ; *For
what can be more plain, than one Instance, that I
can give you instead of many* ; 'Tis that, Thou
shalt not commit Adultery. Thus, when, *Reformation* ; *Reformation !* is urgently called for,
perhaps, 'twill be objected ; *It is not plain to us,
what are the Things most Needful to be Reformed,
nor what are the wayes most likely to Reform
them ?* Now, suppose a man should make this
Reply ; *Syrs, Can any thing be more plain than
this ? That except the Drinking Houses throughout
the Countrey come under more of Regulation, and
except the Town-Dwellers in many places be allow'd
less to Ly Tipling at such Houses, all the Evil Consequences of slothful Drunkenness, are like to Drown
us in Confusion.* Or, suppose, a man should
make

make this Reply ; *Syrs, can any thing be more plain than this? That except we leave off Oppreſſing one another, in our Dealings, and leave off our Abuſing and Injuring of them that ſerve the Publick, above the reſt of our Neighbours, the Great God will ſtill Interpoſe His Revenges upon us.* Or, ſuppoſe a man ſhould make this Relpy ; *Syrs, Can any thing be more plain than this? That if men would every where ſet themſelves to the well-ordering of their own Families, and Revive generally, ſuch Family Prayer, and ſuch Family Inſtruction, and ſuch Family-Goverimnent, as our firſt Planters Exemplified unto us, the whole Countrey would preſently be mended thereupon.* All that I ſhall ſay is ; There are *plain matters,* wherein we all *Know the will* of our Heavenly Lord ; and oh ! to what *Stripes* do we Expoſe our ſelves, if we cannot Agree plainly and fully to promote thoſe matters ! The Laſt Queen, that adorned the *Britiſh* Throne, even the Late Queen *Mary,* of Glorious Memory, was in this thing a Pattern moſt worthy of our Imitation; She would ſay, *She feared there might be ſome ſecret Sins, that might Lye at the Root, and Blaſt all the* Engliſh *Affairs ;* but then ſhe would come off and ſay, *There is ſo much Sin viſible, that there is little Need of Divination concerning what may be ſecret.* And yet I will venture to go on and ſay,

Secondly. Are we ſure that we have no *Se-cret*

*cret Sins* to be Repented of ? Let us, with all *Humility of Soul,* Enquire after *them,* that so, nothing may be wanting to the *Reformation* of the Land.   There was once a People in a Wilderness, who being harassed by sore Desolations, could thereupon say, in Psal.90.8. *Thou hast set our Secret Sins, in the Light of thy Countenance.* There is at all Times, a Room for that Exclamation, *How Unsearchable are the Judgments of God !* And at some Times, tis peculiarly difficult for us, vain Mortals, to *Search* out the causes of those *Judgments.*   There were such Diabolical practices among the *Israelites* of old, that it is said, *Therefore the Lord was very Angry with them, and Removed them out of His Sight :* and yet it is also said, of those things, in 2 King.17.9. *They did Secretly those things, which were not Right, against the Lord their God.*   Yea, There was a Time, when the *Judgments* of God, made all the Armies of *Israel* to fly and fall before them, so that *the Hearts of the People melted, and became as Water :* No doubt, the Sins usual in other Armies, and an abundance of *Debaucheries* and of other Disorders, and Distempers were among them : Nevertheless, These were not the *Accursed Thing,* that procured 'em all their Trouble ; nor did any one man among all their Leaders understand what was that *Accursed Thing,* until God Wonderfully helped them to discover it.   Yea, There was a Time, when the *Judgments* of God
pursued

purfued a whole Company of Sea-faring people; a Storm came upon them, that had like
to have Sunk them all : No doubt, they were
as faulty and as vicious, as any other Sea-faring
Folks ufe to be : Neverthelefs, the Storm came
for the Sins, of that perfon, that one would
have leaft fufpected among them all; that man
was the *Jonas,* whofe Error had Expos'd them
all. So *Uunfearchable are the Judgments of God !*
And that which renders them yet more *Unfearchable* is, The wondrous *Diftance of Time,*
which the Lord may take, to punifh a people,
for *Former Iniquities,* and even ( as that paffage
of Scripture which I am now quoting, may be
Tranflated ) for the *Iniquities of thofe that have
gone before them.* The Children of *Jacob* were
once brought into aftonifhing Diftreffes ; and
in thofe Diftreffes, Then *Jofephs Bloody Coat* is
laid before their Eyes ; The Hard *Things* done
by them to a *Brother* of theirs, Things done
*Twenty years ago,* fo came unto Remembrance,
as to make them cry out with Horror, *We are
verily Guilty !* If none of all thefe Inftances are
enough to perplex our Thoughts, about the
*Unfearchable Judgments of God,* I'le give you
one more. I take Notice, That when *David*
Numbred the *People,* there was a *Great Sin*
cleaving to that matter ; and it was not Holy
*David* alone, but it was the *People,* whom the
Lord was in that matter chiefly offended at.

D God

God had Required, That when the People
were Numbred, *Every man should give a Ran-
some for his Soul unto the Lord, That there be no
Plague among them* ( says he ) *when thou Num-
brest them.* Now, because the Lord had a
Controversy with that People, for their *Former Iniquities,* he leaves *David,* the Best man in
the Nation, to act in this weighty matter,
without the Advice of the *Priests of the Lord*;
Hence, tho' it was not a Sin simply to *Number
the People,* yet the *People* not being put upon
their part, that they might be *Ransomed* from
a *Plague* among them, it became a Sin and a
Snare unto them : Now, as an effect hereof
I take Notice of a strange Threatning, in 2
Sam. 24. 13. *Shall seven years of Famine come
unto thee, in thy Land?* Whereas, the Threatning runs no more than so, in 1 Chron. 21.
12. *Three years of Famine.* I pray, How shall
these two passages be Reconciled ? Attend,
and you shall see a very Remarkable Thing,
in the Reconciliation.    There had been *Three
Years* of a Famine upon the People, for an old
Sin, of slaying the *Gibeonites*; God thus chastised the people, for a Sin that had been Committed more than Forty years before: and
while the *Fourth Year* was Running, there was
that *New Provocation,* about the *Numbring* of
the People, added unto the former : and that
*Fourth year* being well nigh Expired, *Three years*
more

more of a Famine denounced, make up the *Seven* : The firſt of which *ſeven years* Famine, was the year that next followed after the Rebellion of *Abſalom* : as *That* was Forty Years, after the Anointing of *David* at *Bethlehem.* Oh ! What a world of *Intricacies,* were there, in theſe Diſpenſations of Providence! The only Thing, that I deſign here to Recommend, from the mention of theſe Intricate & Myſterious Matters is, A moſt Self-jealous and Self-loathing, *Humility of Soul,* in our Enquiries, after thoſe Things, that are to be acknowledged as *Provoking Evils,* eʻre peace will be Reſtored unto our Land. This is very ſure, that this Land has often had its *D ayes of Temptation* ; and when the People of God come with *Second Thoughts* to Reflect upon thoſe Dayes, they often ſee cauſe to cry out, *Peccavimus omnes* : we have one and all been out of the way. On the whole, The *Temper* which I would propound is This ; Let us not be without ſome *Suſpicion,* that our God may be Angry with us, for ſome *Evil* or other, which is not yet univerſally Acknowledged : But yet let us manage that *Suſpicion* ſo Humbly, ſo Modeſtly, ſo Seriouſly, that we may not thereby add a *New Evil* unto the old ſcore. ʻTis very certain, That when a *Secret Cauſe* of a Divine Controverſy, is Enquired after, there *is* nothing more uſual, than for

men

very

men *To Enquire not wisely concerning that matter.*
An Assembly of *Lutherans* coming together to
Enquire, after the *Cause* of the *Judgments* which
God had brought upon their Churches, most
unhappily determined, *That their not paying Re-
spect enough unto Images, in their Churches, was
one cause of the Lords Controversy with them.*
Unhappy Enquirers ; Instead of your Dream
that you had not Sinn'd enough against the
*Second Commandment,* you should have thought
whether you had not Sinn'd too much against
the *Fourth.*  But we hear not a word, concerning their universal prophanations of the
*Lords-Day* to this Day.   That which I therefore say, is This ;  In a just Apprehension of
our own *Darkness,* and *Weakness,* Let us make
that Prayer to our Lord, *Lord, show us wherefore thou contendest with us.*  Let us then have
our *Debates,* with one another hereupon ;  but
let us come to those *Debates,* alwayes with a
*Disposition* to judge our selves rather than any
one else, and a *Resolution* to take any shame to
our selves, that Scripture and Reason, shall cast
upon us.   Wherefore,

Thirdly.  In pursuing the Designs of *Reformation,* why should not *Every man,* even *E-
very one* concern himself, according to the *Ca-
pacities* of the Station, wherein God has placed
them ?  That a General *Reformation* may be
effected, *Every man* should begin with *Himself* ;
and

and if *Every man* would *mend one*, the *Emenda-
tion of Manners* among us, would indeed be
very general. Men fhould be as defirous in
point of *Repentance*, as they ufe to be in point
of *Charity*, to *Begin at Home!* *Self-Reformation*
every where confcientioufly endeavoured, would
prevent a double *Evil*, very *common under the
Sun*. Sometimes, men make a *Noife* about
*Reformation*, when they do but follow the Di-
ctates of their own *Malice* and *Revenge*, in all
the Noife. There was once a *Shimei*, who,
feeing the Judgments of God come upon the
Land, he prefently fell to Railing at the chief
Rulers in the Land: he falls upon *David*, with
fuch out-cries, as thofe, in 2 *Sam.* 16. 8. *Thou
Bloody man, the Lord has now Returned all the
Blood of the Houfe of Saul, in whofe ftead thou haft
Reigned.* This poor man, was himfelf of *the
Houfe of Saul*, and becaufe he thought his *own
Houfe* had met with fome hard meafure from
the *Government*, he falls to Reviling as if the
Land had no Sins, but thofe of the *Government*
men to anfwer for. But I can tell you, That
we was egregioufly miftaken! And men had.
deed beware, left by giving way to their own
exafperated Spirits and Paffions, they become
*Shimei's*, in exclaming for a *Reformation.* Sometimes again, there is a cry made about *Reformation*, by men that only cover their own vile
*Hypocrifie*, by the Diverfion of fuch a cry. 'Tis

very clear, that there are *Vanities* of Apparell to be Rebuked and Retrenched among us; those little Female, foolish *Vanities,* are *utterly a Fault among us :* the Holy *Angels* of the Lord Jesus Christ, are doubtless grieved, when they see the *Flags,* and *Signs* of a vain mind, hung out by the children of men ; else the Lord would never have said, as in Isa. 3. 16. *Because the Daughters of Zion are Haughty, and walk with stretched forth Necks, therefore the Lord will take away the Bravery of their Tinkling Ornaments,* as *thy men shall fall by the Sword.* But now there are persons, who are themselves *Drones,* or *Thieves,* or *Cheats,* or *Lyars,* or *Drunkards,* or *Fornicators,* or some other way horribly *Depraved Creatures :* And these, to quiet their own guilty Consciences, will Declame very bitterly against certain *Vanities* in other people, and perhaps will with more *pride* than *Scripture* croud in many lawful and needful Things among those *Vanities :* These are the Things that want *Reformation,* they say ; But thou wouldest say it, with a better Grace, O may it some of the zeal were spent upon thy own Enormities. However, Thus they'l fall into a fiery rage about those Things, *As if nothing else brought the Judgments of God upon the Land.* But that which we are first of all to do, is This : It becomes *every one* of us, first of all, to *Judge* themselves, and throw the *First Stone,* at

our *own Iniquity.* It was greatly Refented, in
Jer. 8. 6. *I hearkened, and heard, but they fpake
not aright ; No man repented him of his Wickednefs, faying, What have I done ?* Then, Oh !
Then, fhall we *fpeak aright* about the *Reformation* incumbent on us, when *Every man* fhall
fay, *What have I to do, towards the Reforming of
my felf, and of my own Family ?* Let *Every one*
fet before himfelf, a *Catalogue* of Things *Forbidden,* and of Things *Required,* in the *Ten Commandments ;* our ordinary *Catechifms* will advan-
tageoufly fet before us, the *Glafs* of the Law,
wherein we are to take a view of our felves ;
Thereat, Let us with a fecret *Self Examination*
find out our own Delinquencies, and fo Requeft for, and Rely on, the Aids of *Grace,* for
a *Self Reformation.* Having done thus *much,*
we are then bravely qualified for the Doing of
*more :* Let us now, as far as ever we are capable, *Extend* our Influences. *Houfholders,* They
are firft of all to Rectify all that is amifs, where
they reckon themfelves a fort of *Kings,* that is to
fay, in *their own Houfes.* Oh ! Ask your felves,
whether you have no *Bad Orders* to be Rectified there? Whether your *Devotions* there might
not be more Edifyingly carried on ? Whether
your *Children* and *Servants* may not have a
better Education beftow'd upon them ? Upon
which, let all the World befides take what
courfe they will, do you Refolve, *As for me,*
*and*

*and my House, we will serve the Lord.* But is this all? No; 'Twould be a very Laudable Thing, for the Worshipful *Justices* in the several Counties, now and then to hold a *Consultation,* upon that Question, *What may we do, to Reform any Spreading Evils?* Gentlemen, I take Leave humbly to Represent it unto *You,* That you have singular *Opportunities,* to *Reform* almost all the *Growing Evils* in the midst of us; and such is your *Wisdom,* that without any further Advice from us, You need but a little Discourse now and then with one another, to be informed of Your own *Opportunities:* But, Let me say unto You, That these *Opportunities* are precious *Talents,* for which You are Accountable to the Eternal Son of God. The same that was done by *Jehoshaphat* for his Land, has in You, been done by the Lord Jesus Christ, for *this* Land. He hath set *Judges* throughout the Land; & now His words from His *Excellent Glory,* unto every one of you, are like those, in 2 Chron. 19. 6. *Take heed what you do; For ye Judge not for man, but for the Lord: Let the Fear of the Lord be upon you; Act in the Fear of the Lord, faithfully, and with a perfect Heart; ye shall warn men, that they Trespass not against the Lord, and so Wrath come upon you, and upon your Brethren: The Levites also shall be Officers before you, Deal courageously, and the Lord shall be with the Good.* But those *Consultations* for a *Reformation* of

pernici-

*pernicious Things* among us, which have been Recommended unto thefe *Worfhipful* Perfons, may likewife be moft profitably practifed, by the *Grand-Jury-men,* the *Conftables,* the *Tithing-men,* in their feveral Precincts. Syrs, If you alfo would have your Stated, or Frequent Meetings, to confider, *What may be done by us, to Reform any Common Evils?* You might be wonderfully Serviceable.

But above all, O ye *Watchmen* in our *Churches* ; 'Tis from *You,* that the Lord Jefus Chrift expects the moft critical *watchfulnefs,* in Advifing your feveral *Churches* and *Charges,* of the feveral *Evils,* that are to be Reformed among them. That which you have lately been doing towards *Gofpellizing* thofe Out-lying parts of the Countrey, has been very *worthily done:* And, I do humbly pray the *Recompencing Benediction* of Heaven, upon thofe Worthy Merchants and others in this place, who by their pious Expences have affifted the Undertaking. I wifh thofe parts of the Countrey might now be effectually put in mind, of the concernment that lies upon them to make a due Improvement of the *Price put into their Hand.*If any that belong, or travel to thofe parts, are now in this Affembly, I pray, carry them this Advice, That if they flight the *Gofpel* now fent unto them, there is Danger, the Lord Jefus Chrift will never grant them another Offer of it ; no, there

there is Danger that they will *never be Healed*, but *be given to Salt for ever* : there is Danger, that *a Wrath unto the uttermost will overtake them.* And now, there are further Inftances of our *Watchfulnefs*, over our own Flocks, to be maintained. It may be, 'twould be one very fignificant piece of our *Watchfulnefs*, over the Churches, if fome fafe methods might be taken that all thofe who go forth unto the Work of the Miniftry, might carry with them fome Teftimonial of their Qualifications, from fit Judges of thofe Qualifications ; and that Raw, Rude, Lewd Young Men, and profane Sons of *Eli*, may not go forth, to make a *Living* of their *Preaching*, and Ruine Chriftianity among us,by not *Living* according to their *Preaching.* Yea, I do earneftly Befeech the Congregations of *New England*, That, if they have any Regard unto the *Things of their Peace*, they would none of them, Invite, or Accept, any man, to conftant Preaching among them, unlefs that fome Holy, and Faithful, and Able Paftors of other Churches, do, upon a thorough Trial, Teftify, *That fuch a man is Worthy to Labour, and be very Highly Efteemed for his Labour, among them.* Nor is this All that we have to do. Can we not, in *Vifiting* our *Flocks*, inform our felves about the *Morals* of our People, in every Quarter, and thereupon both Publickly and Privately fet our felves to cure all that fhall
be

be found amiß ! May we *Lift up our voice like a Trumpet*, againſt every thing that we ſee offenſive unto our Lord Jeſus Chriſt ; and let us therefore, by the Anticipations of our Faith, have in our Ears continually, the Sound of the *LaſtTrumpet*, which will fetch us before the Tribunal of our Lord. Much,very,very much will be done towards a Glorious *Reformation*, by our Diſcharging the work of our Miniſtry, as under the Awe of that moſt awful Conſideration, in Heb.13.17. *They watch for Souls, as they that muſt give an Account.* I Remember, 'Tis Related concerning the Holy Mr. *Herbert Palmer*, That obſerving of Sundry Evils to have been become common in his Town of *Canterbury*,he took ſuch Pains to convince the People of thoſe Evils, that at laſt, they generally Signed an Inſtrument, wherein they Declared their *Diſlike* of thoſe Evils, and their *Purpoſe* to take heed of them forever ; and a wondrous *Reformation* enſued upon it. Syrs, who can tell,how far the concern of *Reformation* may poſſeſs the Hearts of our People, in almoſt every Town, if we took due pains to convince them, and perſwade them ; yea, if our Perſonal, Prudent, Loving Admonitions, might but operate, upon that one part of Neighbours, the *Inn-keepers*,who can tell how far the Deſired *Reformation* might be Befriended and Attained ! But this leads me into another Article of our Diſcourſe.

Fourthly.

Fourthly. To Assist the Designs of *Reforma-tion* among us, Why should we not Review, & Renew, and Apply, the *Obligation*, which is by *Covenant* Lying upon us thereunto ? If one would say at once, what it is, that hath procur-ed the Indignation of Heaven against us, to be written in such Dismal and Bloody Characters, methinks, I could find a passage in our Psalter, that should Expressively enough describe it. While the Time was not yet come, that the *Israelites* in *Egypt* should be delivered out of their Difficulties, the Active Colony of *Ephrai-mites* formed a Lively *Expedition*, against the *Philistines* to the *North-ward*, from whom they had Received many Injuries ; they reckon'd themselves Numerous and Powerful enough, to attack the *Canaanites* in their own Country ; but they came off unhappy loosers in it ; and the Psalmist ha's told us, what was the reason of the loss that befel them : T'was, as in Psal. 78. 10. Because, *They kept not the Covenant of God.* This I venture to say, whatever else may be said ; *Covenant Breaking*, I say, *Covenant-Break-ing*, or, the Neglect, and Contempt of that *Cove-nant*, even, the *New-Covenant*, wherein the Lord Jesus Christ, ha's been tendring Himself unto us ; *This*, is the most comprehensive Cause of all our *Disasters.* I will say so, as long as I can Read that horrid Picture of our own condition, in Isa. 24. 4. --- *The Lord makes the Land Empty,*
*and*

*and makes it waſt, and turns it upſide down, and*
*Scatters abroad the Inhabitants thereof;* *The Land*
*mourns and fades.* And why is all this? *Becauſe*
*they have broken the everlaſting Covenant; there-*
*fore the Inhabitants of the Land are Burned, & few*
*men are left.* Wherefore, if we would be Recovered out of our Condition, 'tis the *Covenant*
of our God, that muſt Recover us,& *Reform* us.
'Tis imagined by ſome,That when the General
Aſſembly of *Iſrael* here, *Poured out Water before*
*the Lord,* they uſed a Rite of making of a *Cove-*
*nant;* q. d. If we Return to our Sins, let our
*Blood* be thus *Poured out.* This we all know;
A Renovation of *Covenant,* ha's been always
preſſed, as a very ſpecial and Important Expedient of *Reformation.* The *Covenant of Grace,*
which is *Brought* unto us all, is very particularly
*Seal'd* and *Own'd,* with ſuch as have been Admitted unto any *Eccleſiaſtical Priviledges* among
us. Let all Perſons, by the Help of *Grace,* give
the conſent of their Souls unto this *Covenant;*
Conſent, O Immortal Souls, That God ſhould
be your *God,* and be unto you, better than all
your Idols; that the Lord Jeſus Chriſt ſhould be
your *Prophet, Prieſt,* and *King;* that the Holy
Spirit ſhould Poſſeſs you, and incline you to
Glorify Him according to the Gracious Terms
of this *Covenant* for ever. But then, Let them
that have Enjoy'd the *Seals* of this *Covenant,* a-
gain, and again, with all poſſible Solemnity
Repeat

Repeat the Confent of their Souls thereunto.
Syrs, A moft wondrous *Reformation* would follow hereupon Immediately ! Now, In the doing of this Thing, Why fhould not our Churches, moft Explicitly *Apply*, the *Covenant of
Grace*, unto all the Defigns of *Reformation*, as
well as they *Apply* it unto the particular Defigns,
of a *Particular Church-ftate* before the Lord ?
Our *Covenant* will to the moft Edification, and
the moft Satisfaction,be *Renewed*,when we moft
of all Exprefs the *Spirit of the New Covenant* in
all that we do.   Now, 'Tis the *Spirit of the New
Covenant*, for us to Acknowledge, That our
*Juftification* only by *Faith* in the *Righteoufnefs*
of our *Saviour* and our *Surety*, does powerfully
oblige us to *Depart from all Iniquity* : And,Then,
to Acknowledge,That this and that Evil Thing,
whereof we are advifed, is an *Iniquity*, from
which we do, with our very Hearts within us,
Defire to *Depart* for ever : But with fuch Acknowledgments,we are to *Proteft* in all Sincerity
of Soul, That we ask the *Grace* of Heaven,
to *Watch* againft every fuch *Abominable Thing*,
both in our felves, and in one another.  What
one *Chriftian* upon Earth would fcruple to
confent unto fuch *Acknowledgments* and *Proteftations* ?  Now, if our *Churches*, yea, and other
*Societies* too, would thus ufe the *Covenant of
Grace*, with pertinent Applications thereof, to
every *New Iniquity*, that they Difcern arifing
among

among them, how glorioufly might the *Spirit
of Grace*, then *Lift up a Standard* againft every
*Flood* of Iniquity ! As faft as we fee any Sin
gaining of ground upon us, Let us make our
*Evangelical Acknowledgments* and our *Evangelical Proteftations*, againft that Sin ; Thefe are
the *Sanctified Wayes* in which the Almighty
Spirit of Chrift, will make us *Conquerors, and
more than Conquerors*, over that Sin for ever.
And fhall I add this one thing more ? There
are many forts of *Officers* among us, that are
under very fpecial *Oaths*, unto God, for *Well-
Doing* ; and thefe would furely *Do well*, to
have Copies of their *Oaths*, well Explained
unto them, often before their Eyes. Our Honourable *Counfellers* are under the *Oath* of God,
*That they will to the beft of their Judgment at all
Times freely give their Advice*. Our Worfhipful *Juftices* are under the *Oath* of God, *That
they will Difpenfe Juftice equally and impartially
in all cafes, and for no caufe forbear truly to do
their Office*. Our *Grand Jury-men* are Sworn
by the Ever living God, *That they will diligent-
ly Enquire, and true Prefentment make, of all
things given them in Charge ; and prefent no man
for Envy, Hatred, or Malice, nor leave any man
unprefented, for Love, Fear, Favour and Affection,
or Hope of Reward*. Our *Conftables* are Sworn
by the Ever-living God, *That in all that the
Law has made part of their Office, they will deal*

*ferioufly*

*seriously and faithfully, whilst they are in Office, without any sinister Respects of Favour or Displeasure.* And are not our *Tithing-men*, under an Oath of the like Importance : Yea, I suppose, there is hardly a *Clerk* of a Company, but he is under the Bonds of a Dreadful *Oath*, to Discharge his Duty faithfully. Now, This one thing would exceedingly contribute unto the *Reformation* of the Land, That men often *Read* and *Think*, what they are *Sworn* to *Do* : For this would put the Good men, upon more usual *Thoughts* in themselves, *What Good they may do in their several Places for other men ?* It is mentioned, as a Commendable property, in a Citizen of *Zion*, Psal. 15. 4. *He sweareth to his own Hurt, and Changeth not.* It may be rendred, *He Sweareth to an Ill man, and Changeth not.* If he have made a *Lawful Promise*, though it be to a Wicked man, a Pagan, an Enemy, he will not reckon that the Wicked unworthiness of the man, will Release him from his Promise. But, Syrs, You that are Sworn to a *Good God*, and Sworn to a *Good King*, & Sworn to a *Good Work*, & Sworn, for the Service of a *Good People* ; how much ought you to Study, that you may be the Genuine *Citizens of Zion*, for your Fidelity ! The *Land will mourn, because of Swearing*, if men ordinarily, Lift up their Hands to the Eternal God, in *Oaths* to Deal faithfully and honestly, but Swear indeed *Hand over Head*, without any
                                                    *After-*

*After-care* to obferve their *Oathes* : As on the other Hand, For men to *Fear an Oath*, is one way to keep clear of many *Fearful* Sins & Evils. Behold the *Reformation*, that is to be laboured for.

But then, Laftly, to put an *Edge* upon thefe Things ; That we may be in Earneft about the Neceffary *Reformation*, Let us confider the loud calls of Heaven, that moft earneftly befpeak it of us. *The Neceffity of Reformation*, is a Thing that ha's been long and oft Preach'd unto us, ever fince that the *Judgments* of God, began to make us more generally miferable ; but the *Judgments* of God, are going on ftill to further and further Degrees of mifery upon us, while the *Cares* of a *Neceffary Reformation*, continue faft afleep in our Souls. We do one year after a-nother feel the formidable Executions, of thofe Threatnings, in Lev.26.23. *If ye will not be Re-formed by me, through thefe things, but will walk contrary unto me, Then will I alfo walk contrary unto you, and I will Punifh you yet Seven Times for your Sins.* Our moft Intolerable Indifpofition, to do any Significant Thing, towards our *Ne-ceffary Reformation*, ha's been already Revenged, with *Sore Plagues, and of long Continuance* ; Yea, The Lord ha's made our *Plagues Wonderful*, for this our Obdurate & Obftinate Impænitency. Wherefore, As they cryed unto *Pharaoh, Let the men go ; know/eft thou not yet that Egypt is deftroyed ?*

E                    Even

Even such a cry muſt I this Day awaken you
withal ; *Know you not, that* New England, *is very
near deſtroy'd, by the Sins that have been Harboured
among us ?* Oh ! Let them *Go !* Let them *Go!*
Leſt we periſh in them. Chriſtians, Let us take
Warning.   There have been many *Thouſands,* I
ſay, many *Thouſands,* of Churches in *Europe,* not
much leſs famous  for the Proteſtant Religion,
than that little Handful & Hundred of Churches,
whereof this Country is compoſed ; Every one
of which, have been made an utter Deſolation,
within theſe few years ;  even ſince the Time
that ſo Young a Man as I am, came into the
World.   And, is not the Fate of thoſe Churches, a Solemn Warning to us, in theſe  *Ends of
the World ?* I ſay again, Let us  take the Warning, and, *Repent, Leſt we likewiſe Periſh.*   Don't
you ſee,the Tokens of the Divine Wrath againſt
us, ariſe apace towards an horrible Extremity ?
O *Lord, They who dwell in theſe uttermoſt parts,
are afraid at thy Tokens !* I'l ſay only theſe Two
Things.   One thing is this ; If there be not an
Extraordinary Appearance of *God, from Heaven,*
to give a check unto a Great *Leviathan,* who is
at this Day Troubling all the *European* Waters,
*New England* will be ſoon overwhelmed in Deſolation.   Another thing is this ; If we ſhould
have ſuch a *Summer* this year,  as we had the
laſt, for the *Unſeaſonable Weather,* which,  alas,
hitherto does hold,upon the Fruits of the Earth,
the

the Defolation of *New-England* will be more
horrid, than any Tongue, ha's hitherto Expreffed, or Heart Conceived.   On every fide of us
then, we have that  cry Roaring  in our Ears,
*Reformation, or Defolation ! Reformation, or Defo-*
*lation !* Oh! Tis *High Time to Awake out of our*
*Sleep,* and to do fome Signal Thing for the *Re-*
*formation* of our Land.   Confider, O our *Zerub-*
*babels,* O our *Jofhua's,* and O all ye People of
the Land :  *Neceffity is laid upon us, and Wo unto*
*us if we Do it not.*
And now, if thefe calls of Heaven, are, by
your *Tears,* and by your *Prayers,*  and by your
*Cares,* duely complied withal, there is a twofold
*Benediction,* from  our Lord Jefus Chrift, our
*High Prieft,* who went  away  from  hence  to
Heaven, *Bleffing* of us, that I do from the Word
of His, now before us, Conclude withal.

I. You fhall have *Samuels* to be *Judges* over
you.  How vaft  was  the  Felicity of *Ifrael,*
when a *Samuel,* who formerly had been a
moft faithful *Preacher,* by whom they were alwayes advifed of their *True Intereft,* now became a *Ruler,* who fo acquitted himfelf in his
Government over them, that when he came
to put off his Government, he could make
that Appeal to all the World, *Behold, Here I*
*am ; Witnefs againft me before the Lord ; whom*
*have I defrauded ! whom have I oppreffed ?* or of

*whose Hand have I Received any Bribe, to blind mine Eyes withal?* Many fuch a *Samuel* will thy God give unto thee, O *New England,* if thou thus Turn unto Him. It was a Sentiment, for which we have the Authority, of the greateft perfons, both among the *Ancients* and among the *Moderns,* who count that they have alfo for it, the greateft Authority of the Sacred *Scriptures* themfelves *That every Province is under the fpecial care of fome Angel, by a fingular Deputation of Heaven affigned thereunto.* But befides that *Invifible Guardian,* our God, upon our Turn to Him, will give us a GOVERNOUR, that fhall be like a *Guardian Angel* unto us, Employing his whole Strength to *Guard* us from all Difafters. Although we are Invefted with a *Royal Charter,* which leaves not any *Governour* capable to Enact one *Law,* or Levy one *Tax,* or Conftitute one *Counfeller,* or one *Judge,* or one *Juftice,* or one *Sheriff,* without fuch a *Negative* of the *People* upon him, as the *People* are not in the other *American Plantations,* no, nor in *Ireland,* no, nor in *England* it felf, priviledged withal ; Neverthelefs, we fhall have caufe to Receive a *Governour* that like a *Nehemiah,* fhall *Seek our Welfare,* with all Thankfulnefs to God, and the King, as a very Rich *Bleffing* from Heaven unto us. We have *Already,* and *Hitherto,* Enjoy'd that *Bleffing,* above any people at this Day under

the

the whole Expanſe of Heaven ; and, if our God be not Angry with us, we ſhall with ſuch a *Bleſſing* ſtill be, *A People Saved of the Lord.* Our God will ſend us a *Governour,* who will caſt a *Favourable,* and a *Fatherly* Aſpe, upon all that is valuable to us ; a *Governour,* who ſhall have the brave Motto of the Emperour *Hadrian* Engraved upon his Heart, *Not for my ſelf, but for my People.* And with ſuch a *Governour,* He will give us, *Our Judges as at the Firſt, and our Counſellers as at the Beginning.*

II. God will *Thunder with a great Thunder* upon your *Philiſtian* Adverſaries, and gloriouſly *Diſcomfit* them. The Lord had promis'd unto His People, that if they would *Go up* duly to *Worſhip* Him, at His Tabernacle, He would keep off the Invaſion of their Adverſaries ; and now when they were together at *Mizpeh,* He fulfilled that Promiſe, by a ſtrange Diſcomfiture of the Invading *Philiſtines.* *New England* never was without its Adverſaries ; but at this Day, we are more Eminently under that Alarum, *The Philiſtines are upon thee, O Land much Maligned !* Now, by our Conforming our ſelves unto the Will of God, we ſhall get Him on our ſide ; The Almighty would then ſoon ſcatter our Enemies with His Hot Thunderbolts, and *Thunder* them into Ruine for ever ; and that Sentence which the Emperour *Max-*

E 3 *imili-*

*imilian* wrote upon his Table, we shall see written on all our Houses, and all our Vessels, and all our Fields, *If God be for us, who can be against us ?* By comparing of certain passages in the Bible, not commonly observed or understood it appears; that there was a *General Circumcision* of the *Israelites* in *Goshen*; & at that very Time God sent the *Three Dayes* Darkness upon the *Egyptians*; God sent Three Dayes of Darkness and Horror upon the *Egyptian* Adversaries, that they might then be Able to *Do Nothing* against His People, who *Rebelled not against His Word.* Oh ! might there be a *General Obedience* of *New England* unto the Lord Jesus Christ, that Lord of Heaven would soon *Darken* our Adversaries, with His Plagues upon them. Hear O *New-England,* Hear thy Lord, saying over thee, *O that my people would Hearken to me; I would then soon Turn my Hand upon their Adversaries ; but their own Time should Remain for ever and ever.*

---

### THE CLOSE.

*Containing a Relation, of the Wonderful Deliverance newly received, by the* KING, *the Three Kingdomes, & all the English Dominions.*

BUT, Behold, O my dear People of *New England,* while I am telling you, of

Thun-

*Thunder* to fall upon our *Philiftean* Adverfaries, there do this very Week arrive unto us the Joyful and the Wondrous Tidings, which give us a Stupendous Inftance of this very matter; *The Philiftines drew near to Battel againft Ifrael, but the Lord Thundred with a Great Thunder on that Day, upon the Philiftines, and difcomfited them, and they were Smitten before Ifrael.* It is but juft now that we have Advice from the other fide of the *Atlantick* Ocean, That Great *Britain* is Miraculoufly delivered, from the utmoft Perils, of becoming an *Enflaved,* and perhaps a *Dragooned,* Province of the *French Empire,* or, at leaft from a *Bloody War,* that muft have coft many Thoufands of the Beft Lives in the Nations, to have fhaken off the *Chains,* which a French Force would have laid upon them : And then, I am fure, that thou, O little *New England,* haft, above all the *American* Plantations, a fhare in this Deliverance; for if the *Great Houfe,* whereof thou art but a poor *Leanto,* had fallen, how horribly hadft thou been crufh'd in the *Ruines* of it ! *O come, and Behold the Works of the Lord, the Defolations which He is bringing* upon the *French Philiftines,* by the Hand of His Omnipotency ! There hath been all along, a large party of *Bigotted* and *Befotted* People, the Sons of *Nimrod,* in the Englifh Nation, who have long been feeking to overthrow thofe things, wherein the Real Welfare of the Nation lies ; and, *Many a*

*Time*

*Time have they afflicted me, from my Youth, may* England *now say*; *Many a Time have they afflicted me, from my Youth*; *Yet have they not Prevailed against me.* It may be those Adversaries, were never more confident of their prevailing, than in their late Execrable *Plot*, for the Murdering of our Illustrious King WILLIAM, in that horrid Juncture, when a French Army, with an *Abdicated Prince* in the Head of it, was coming over to join his Friends in *England*, and have made that Land such a stage of Blood, Fire, & Horror, as it never was before.   But we have now appointed, by the Authority of this Province, a Day of Publick and Solemn THANKSGIVING unto the God of Heaven, for the [ It was Observed, *June* 16.] Miraculous Defeat of that *Plot*; and upon the Invitation thereof, give me leave now to Entertain you, with a brief Relation of that Wonderful Providence, which ha's now been after an astonishing manner display'd, for the Preservation of us all.

The miserable *Male-contents* had for a long while been fomenting and augmenting, *Discontents* throughout the Kingdom, in hopes, by the means of those Confusions, to Recover all that they had lost, in the late 𝕳𝖆𝖕𝖕𝖞 𝕽𝖊𝖛𝖔𝖑𝖚𝖙𝖎𝖔𝖓. The Kingdom had been long Disastered with many *Losses*; besides the Heavy *Taxes* that lay upon it : & the Prodigious Depravation, brought,

as

as it were at Once, upon the *Coin* current throughout the Kingdom, coming upon all the reſt, had thrown the Nation into ſuch a Ferment, that the Exquiſite Wiſdom & Succeſs of the Parliament, in ſince getting through it, is to be annumerated perhaps among the *Greateſt Appearances* of God, for His Poor People there : Moreover, There had been particular methods uſed, through the Artifice of theſe Incendiaries, to Diſtreſs, yea, to Deſtroy, the *Sea-faring* part of the Kingdom, that ſo a *French Invaſion* might be facilitated : Nor were they unwilling to Encourage themſelves from a Bone of contention caſt between the Two Kingdoms of *England*, and *Scotland*, about their Trade : And the Servants of the late King, had in Great Numbers pretendedly Deſerted him ; Returning Home, that they might *Live Quietly under a Mild Government*, though not intending, it ſeems, To, *Study to be Quiet*. It was at this Critical Time, That Great *Britain*, with all the Dominions pertaining thereunto, was upon the point of being overwhelmed in, *A Conſpiracy for the Aſſaſſinating of His Majeſties Perſon to encourage an Invaſion from* France, *at the ſame Time intended, for the utter Subverſion of the Proteſtant Religion, and the Liberties of the Kingdom.*

It being underſtood in *France*, that many Hundred Ships of *Merchant-men*, were ſetting out from *England*, for divers parts of the World, and

and that a great *Convoy* was also going to the
*Streights*, whereby the Kingdom would have
been left extreamly Naked, immediately in *Fe-*
*bruary* laft, near Thirty Thoufand *French* were
drawn down to *Dunkirk*, and *Calice*, and other
Ports, Headed by the Late King *James*, with
an huge Fleet, wherein were between Three
and Four Hundred *Tranfport Ships*, to bring
them over, unto the *Thames* Mouth, *Suffex*, or
*Kent* ; and fome unto the *North*, to ftrengthen
thofe that fhould make an Infurrection there.
They Embarked, before it was known in *En-*
*gland* ; but the Lord Jefus Chrift, who Com-
mands the *Winds*, did by *Crofs winds*, conftrain
them to ftand in again.   In the mean time, the
Duke of *Wittenberg*, having obtained fome
knowledge of the *French Invafion*, prefently fent
over to King *WILLIAM*, the Notice of it, by
a Meffenger, in a *Fifher boat*, where, by lying
hid among the *Nets*, he fo efcaped the *French*
*Infpection*, that he was able to inform the King,
of the *Nets*, which the common Enemy had
laid for Him, and for more than Three Kingdoms.   At this Inftant, Admiral *Ruffel* being
difpatch'd, on this vaft occafion to re-inforce
the *Englifh Fleet*, found, that by a furprizing
Hand of Heaven, our *Merchant-men*, with this
*Convoy*, had been out at Sea, but were by contrary Weather driven back into their Harbours
and by this moft feafonable Accident, the *Fleet*
which

which elfe might have been a prey to the *French*, was within a few hours, all *Manned*, and *Fitted* out; and immediately they Block'd up the *French Fleet* in their Harbours, with no little damage to them at the prefent, befides the future Devaftations, which may attend, the total Difappointment of the Defcent by them Defigned.

But this was not all. The Almighty Lord JESUS CHRIST, hath Employ'd the mighty WILLIAM, as an *Hook* in the *Noftrils* of that *French Leviathan*, who has been fo long *Troubling the Waters of Europe*; and the Confpirators thought it impoffible for them to do a more fignificant Thing, than to get Him out of the way. It was therefore concerted and refolved, among a Defperate Crew of Ruffians in *England*, that in *February* laft, they would make an Attempt upon that *Royal Life*, upon which the Fate of all *Europe* does at this Day depend, it may be more than upon that of any one man Living in the World. After feveral Confults held among thofe Wretches, about this wretched Enterprife, it was at length Agreed, That upon the Kings Return from *Richmond*, they would, at the end of a Lane, by *Turnam Green*, a place which they not only *marked*, but *fitted* for that Hellifh purpofe, with Forty five perfons on Horfe-back, fall upon the *Kings* Perfon, and in fpite of His *Guards*, whereof fome, 'tis said,

said, were in the Conspiracy, Assassinate Him; upon the Accomplishment whereof, the Printed Accounts report, that a Signal, was to have been given to the *French* Coast, by a *Fire* on *Dover Cliff*; And indeed, there had been seen *Fire* enough, if this Barbarous and Villanous Thing had been Accomplished! The *Tenth* of *February*, was the Day first Appointed, for the perpetration of this *Comprehensive Murder*: But upon the failing of some circumstances, it was put off unto the *Fifteenth*. In the mean while our Lord JESUS CHRIST, who *Giveth Salvation unto Kings*, thus wonderfully *Delivered His Servant* our King, *from the Hurtful Sword!* There were Two or Three of the Conspirators, who, as it seems, unknown to each other, discovered the Treason; what it was that put them, upon the making of the Discovery, I can at present, say no further, than that the Papers Printed thereupon inform us, That their Threatning one of their Company, *To kill him for his being Absent from some of their Cabals*, did contribute not a little thereunto: though a Generous Abhorrence of so barbarous an Action, as the Murder of the King, inspiring the Heart of one, to whom the Design had been communicated, seems to have been the true original of the Discovery. The King being satisfied in the Truth of the matter, took effectual care, to have the rest seized, in the most con-

convictive circumstances; for upon finding
Things, the *Fifteenth* of *February* look suspici-
oufly upon them, they began to fly from the
Storm, which they fear'd thus breaking upon
them : and upon their Trial fince, the Fact has
been fo convictively proved upon them, that
fundry of them, have been with the general
fatisfaction of the Nation, Executed.

In this *Plot*, things were fo laid, that the
Adverfaries, were very fecure, of carrying all
before them. It cannot but create an *Horror*
mix'd with *Pleafure*, to reflect on the Affurance,
which the Adverfaries, both at home & abroad,
had, that their machinations could not mifcar-
ry. It is affirmed, That on the Day when
the *Plot* was judg'd ripe for Execution, One
of the *Nonjurant Parfons*, Preached on thofe
words, in Jer. 46. 10. *This is the Day of the Lord
God of Hofts, a Day of Vengeance, that He may
Avenge Himfelf of His Adverfaries; and the
Sword fhall Devour, and it fhall be Satiate, and
made Drunk with their Blood.* But, behold, by
the aftonifhing Providence of our Lord JESUS
CHRIST, it is come to pafs, that it may be
there never did fo great a *Rout* befall thofe
Adverfaries of God, and of the Nation, as the
mifcarriage of this *Plot* has given them. A Remarkable *Zeal* infpires, one of the beft *Parlia-
ments* that ever the Nation faw, to *Affociate*
for the Safety of the King, and *Meditate* fuch
Things

Things as cause the whole Kingdom to Rejoyce. A prodigious Consternation falls upon
the Adverſaries; and they daily feel the fulfilment of the Label, which the Dutch Sculptures
on this occaſion, put into the mouth of the
Abdicated Prince, *Fruſtra Tentare, nocebit*. Many years are now paſt, ſince that from the
*Preſs*, as well as from the *Pulpit*, we have ſaid
unto you; ' If any man, be he High or Low,
' Rich or Poor, ſhall go to introduce Popery,
' in a Kingdome, wherein it has been Abo-
' liſhed, the Curſe of *Joſhua*, never fell ſo hard
' on the Rebuilder of Demoliſhed *Jericho*, as
' the Curſe of *Jeſus* will fall upon the Authors
' of this Accurſed Enterprize; neither ſhall
' they proſper in it, any better than the Jews,
' who at the Invitation of the Apoſtate *Julian*,
' going to Re-Edifie their Temple, God ſent
' the Terrible *Earthquake*, that Overthrew all
' they had already done, and by *Fire* from
' Heaven, burnt up the Tools, and ſome of
' thoſe that uſed them. And this year, has
now ſtrangely added, unto the many Confuſi-
ons, that we have ſeen every year of late be
falling the Enemies of the *Reformation*. Prepare now, your *Praiſes* to the Glorious Lord
Jeſus Chriſt, O ye People of God, for the
*Great Things* which He has done. But *Believ-
eſt Thou? Thou ſhalt ſee yet GREATER THINGS
than theſe!* For I do once more aſſure you
The Kingdom of God is at Hand.

## A POSTCRIPT.

*Giving an Account of some late* MIRACLES, *wrought by the* Power *of our Lord* *JESUS CHRIST.*

HAving in the preceding Sermon, mention'd the late MIRACLES, with Hopes that they may be *Symbolical* Representations & Exhibitions of the *Miraculous* Things, which the Lord is going to Do for His People, I am willing to Entertain the *Faith* of the Christians in this Remote Wilderness of *America*, with a brief Relation of those *Miracles* ; for all which, we have Incontestable Evidences, that they are not like the *Lying Wonders,* by *Popery* sometimes imposed upon the World, but the *Wondrous Works* of the God, which declare that His *Name is Near.*

### The First Example.

In the Preface of a French Treatise, Entituled, *Harmonie des Propheties Anciennes avec les Modernes,* which was Printed at *Cologne,* in the year 1687. I find this very Wonderful Passage, which I choose to mention in this place, as contributing to the Explication of them that are to follow.

Madam *Mingot,* the Widow of a Cheirurgeon, of the City of *Caen* in *Normandy,* had several unaccountable Revelations made unto her, that she kept wholly Secret ; but there was one, which by a *Miracle* that accompanied it, was put beyond the possibility of Secrecy. She was afflicted with a *Palsey,* Eight or Ten years together

gether in her Limbs, which rendred her altogether Impotent ; and her Impotency was not the
lefs, for her being Fourfcore years of Age.  But
one Day, when fhe was at *Prayer* before the God
of Heaven, for the Deliverance of His Church,
from the Confufions then upon it,  in the  heat
and heighth of the French Perfecution,  it was
audibly faid unto her, *Thy Prayers are heard* ;
*The afflicted Church fhall  be fpeedily and glorioufly
delivered* ; *But it ha's yet fomewhat more to fuffer.*
She was Commanded herewithal, to make this
Revelation known unto her *Brethren* ; and that
they might give credit unto her words, it was
added, *The Lord has Reftored thy Health and
Strength unto thee.*   She was Immediately,  and
Miraculoufly, Healed of her Malady,  and fhe
Walked her felf, and  carried unto her *Paftors,*
the Account of this Revelation.   They wondered at the *Miracle,* and would  fain have
concealed th  *Prophecy* ; but the *Prophecy* could
not poffibly be hid, becaufe of the famous *Miracle* that attended it.   All the Paftors of *Caen*
and a good Number of other Proteftant Refugees, belonging to the  Town,  being in the
Low Countryes, *Anno* 1687. offered their U-
nanimous and  Uniform  Teftimony,  to the
Truth of this marvellous matter.

*The Second Example.*

*Mary Maillard,* a *French* Damfel, (the Daughter of Proteftant Refugees, ) about  Thirteen
Years

Years of Age, Living in *Weftminfter*, was thro'
a Diflocation of her Left Thigh, very *Lame*
from her Birth, and her *Lamenefs* increafed
with her Age, into much Deformity and Infirmity, infomuch that fhe became Ridiculous
to the Children in the Streets, who would
Throw *Dirt* upon her, with other Abufes & Injuries, as they faw her pafs along. Her *Leg* was
become fhorter by four Inches than the other,
her *Knee* was turned Inwards, and her *Foot* was
diftorted fo, that the Inward Ancle bone almoft fupplied the place of the Sole of that
Foot , and much pain attended this Malady,
which the Chirurgeons and Phyficians pronounced *Incurable.* The Ill treatment of the
Children in the Streets, one *Lords-Day, Nov.*
26. 1693. befpattering her with Dirt, as fhe
returned from the Publick Worfhip of God,
much afflicted her : She wept extreamly, with
Complaints to her Miftrefs, of the Affronts that
had been offered her ; but her Miftrefs Exhorted her to be patient, and put her Truft in
God. In the Evening fhe took the Bible ; and
Reading the Second Chapter of *Mark,* wherein is related our Lords Miraculous Cure of one
Sick of a *Palfey,* fhe feemed much affected therewithal. She told her Miftrefs, that fhe could
not but wonder at the Unbelief of the Jews ;
adding, That if fuch a Thing fhould now happen, fhe would run to the Lord *Jefus Chrift* for

F

a

a *Cure* also. She had no sooner spoke this, but her pain began to Return with violence upon her; and suddenly stretching out her *Leg*, the Bone audibly snapt into its place, and her *Knee* and *Foot* were instantly restored unto their Natural Posture. Her pain immediately went off; and she supposed that she heard a voice declaring to her, *Thou art Healed :* whereupon she presently found her self to be fully Cured of all her Lameness, and she *Walk'd* up & down her Chamber ; still continuing well, and affirming to the great multitudes that came to visit her, *That without any Humane Help she was healed, in Reading the Gospel of the Lord Jesus Christ.*

*The Third Example.*

Mrs. *Elizabeth Savage*, the Wife of Mr. *John Savage*, a Minister and School master, Living in *Middle Moor Fields*, was afflicted with a *Palsey* on her Right-side; and her Mother knows nothing to the contrary, but that she brought it into the World with her. Her Distemper was judged Remediless, and her Right Thumb was distorted, & three other fingers, were bowed round, almost close to the palm of her Hand; nor could she, by that Hand ( which also was alwayes cold ) bring any Sustenance unto her mouth. She was now upwards of Twenty-eight years old ; and her Husband agreed with her, to set apart the Twenty second of *December,* 1693. for *Prayer* with *Fasting,* in secret before
the

the Lord; not upon any Temporal Account, but purely to obtain Spiritual & Eternal Blessings. About eleven of the Clock, when he was upon his knees, the late *Miracle* wrought for the *French* Damsel came into his mind, with such Impression, that he gave solemn Thanks unto the Lord Jesus Christ, for Displaying of His Power, in such a work, at a Time of prevailing Infidelity. He then asked his Wife, whether she believed that our Lord Jesus Christ, was able to Cure her Weakness also; whereto she answered with Tears, That she question'd not His *Power*, but she knew not whether it might be good for her to have such a *Comfort*, inasmuch as her Weakness was useful many ways to Humble her. He began to Read the Eighth Chapter of *Matthew*; and when he read those words, *Lord, if thou wilt, thou canst*, he said, That he had as much *Faith* in the *Power* of the Lord Jesus Christ, for the Cure of her Infirmity. Proceeding then to the third verse, *I will, be thou clean*, she presently felt a great pain in the middle Joynts of her crooked Fingers; which before the Chapter was ended, were stretched out, and she was able to move them nimbly, like those on her other Hand. A new warmth also came into that Hand, and though it were poor and lean, as well as weak before, it began to Recover *Flesh*, with *Strength*, and its natural colour came into it. When her Husband had finished the Chapter, she show'd unto him, in her warm Hand, now opened and expanded, what the Lord Jesus Christ had newly done for her; whereupon they sat some while drown'd in Tears of Admiration, from which when they Recovered themselves, they solemnly praised the Lord Jesus Christ, on their Knees, for His Mercy to them: And the day following, her whole *Paralytic* Side also, had a New Life return'd into it, so that she was able to Walk four or five miles, without any weariness.

*The Fourth Example.*

*David Wright*, who was Twenty Seven or Eight Years of Age, had been grievously mortified with the *Kings Evil* for divers years; but there was a *Worse Evil* than this upon him, for he was also a very vicious and profane sort of a Fellow. Following the Employments of a *Shepherd*, because his Distemper had Enfeebled him, for any harder Labour, he desired a Religious Gentlewoman, in the year 1693. to take him into her Service. But she was afraid of Employing him, until he promised a *Reformation* of his Lewd courses, and particularly, a due care to Hear the Word of God; which promises nevertheless he sadly violated. However, on the Twenty Ninth of *November*, understanding that there was to be a Sermon Preached at *Hitchin*, by one Mr. *Edward Coles*, his mind became unaccountably so Resolved for the Hearing of him, that though his Brother came for him, with an Horse, to go another way, he could by no means be prevailed withal, to bear him company. While he was Hearing the Sermon, he found his *Blind Mind* strangely Enlightened, and his *Hard Heart* strangely mollified: He had new Visions of his own Sinfulness and Wretchedness, and of the Remedy provided for him in the Lord Jesus Christ; and before the Sermon was ended, he did with a conquered Soul and with inexpressible Agony and Reflection, give himself up unto the Lord Redemer. And whereas, he had been fifteen or sixteen years, horribly Tormented with *Scrophulous* Tumors and Ulcers, and
now

now came unto the Meeting under great pain with them, while he was hearing the Sermon, his ugly Sores all infensibly funk upon him, and he was well on a fudden. So that, as they Returned home from the Meeting, he went in the Head of the Affembly, Admiring and Adoring the Wonderful Glories of the Lord Jefus Chrift, in thus dealing with him; and it made an Heaven upon Earth among them, to joyn with him, in the Heavenly Praifes rendred unto the Lord Jefus Chrift, on the occafion of this *Double Miracle.*

### The Fifth Example.

There is likewife, an undoubted Relation, of a poor, but a good Woman, belonging to the Congregation of the Reverend Mr. *Daniel Burgefs* in *London.* She had for many years, laboured under a *Fiftula* in her Hip, which had proceeded fo far, that the very Bone was tainted, and fhe was turned out of the Hofpital as Incurable. This perfon, Reading, with Prayer over it, that paffage, in *Mat.* 15. 28. *Jefus faid unto her, O Woman, Great is thy Faith ; be it unto thee as thou wilt*; and feeling her Soul, by the Spirit of the Lord Jefus Chrift, carried forth unto a Great Faith in Him, fhe found her felf immediately and miraculoufly, Cured of all her Malady. I have not now the Relation of this matter at hand ; but this is as far as I can Remember, the fubftance of what I received concerning it. It was about the beginning of *December,* 1694.

### The Sixth Example.

In a Letter from the Reverend, Mr. *John How,* I find the Enfuing paffages, which I take the leave to Expofe unto the Publick.

'It gives among us ( Writes that Worthy Man )

fome

'some Reviving to the Languishing Interest of Christi-
' anity, and some check to the *Infidel Spirit*, that ( un-
' der the falsly assumed Name of *Deism* ) would turn
' all *Revealed Religion*, and indeed all *Religion* into *Ri-*
' *dicule* ; that God is pleased to own it, by some late
' *Miraculous Cures*, wrought upon the Acting of *Faith*
' in CHRIST.

That Excellent Person, proceeding then, to recite
some of the Instances, which we have already mentioned, he adds ;

' A Fourth, I have late certain knowledge of ( but
' the Thing was done Six years ago ) of a *Blackamoor*
' *Youth*, Servant unto a Religious *Baronet*. He lately
' dining at my House, assured me, That his Servant
' having a Great Aversion to Christianity, & refusing
' Instruction, was struck with Universal Pains in all his
' Limbs, which continued upon him a year & half,
' like *Rheumatical*, but Releived by none of the apt
' usual means, that are wont to give Relief in such
' Cases. At length, in his Torments, which were
' Great, he grew Serious, Instructible, Penitent ; and
' by the frequent Endeavours of the Parochial Minis-
' ster ( a Good man, known to me ) brought to an
' understanding Acknowledgment of Christ ; upon,
' which, *Baptism* being promised to him, he consented ;
' but pressed to be carried unto the Assembly, that he
' might own Christ Publickly ; Upon the doing
' whereof, he was *Immediately Cured*, and hath conti-
' nued well, ever since. These are Great Things
' *Hallelujah* ! Preparatives, I hope, to the Revival of
' Christianity ; and, I fear, to terrible Acts of Ven-
' geance, upon Obstinate Persevering Infidels.

*The Seventh Example.*

*Susanna Arch*, was a Miserable Widow, for diverse

years, overwhelmed with an horrid *Leprofy*, which the Phyficians that faw it, pronounced, *Incurable*; but from that very Time that they told her fo, a ftrange per-swafion came into her mind, *That the Lord* JESUS CHRIST *would Cure her.* That Scripture came frequently into her mind, Math. 8.2. *Lord, if thou wilt, Thou canft make me clean*; and fhe found her felf En-abled to plead this before Him, with fome Degree of confidence, *That at laft fhe fhould prevail.* She Re-folved, That fhe would Rely on the Lord JESUS CHRIST, who, in the Dayes of His Flefh, when on Earth, cured all Difeafes and Sickneffes among the People, and who had ftill as much *Power,* now that he is Glorified in Heaven. She felt many *Tempta-tions,* to weaken her Confidence; but ftill, there came in Seafonable, and Agreeable Scriptures, with a mighty Force upon her to Strengthen it; As, at one time, that in Mark 11.22. *Have Faith in God*; At another Time, that in Joh. 11.40. *Said I not unto thee, that if thou wouldeft Believe, thou fhouldeft fee the glory of God?* At another Time, that in Heb. 10.35. *caft not away your Confidence, which hath Great Re-compence of Reward.* Her *Leprofy* had been Compli-cated with a *Phtifick,* which for many years afflicted her; but in the Month of *November,* 1694. fhe found her *Phtifick* Removed without any Humane means, and fhe took that as a *Token for Good,* that fhe fhould alfo be cured of her *Leprofy*; and the late *Miracles* upon others, Enlivened this her Hope Ex-ceedingly. In *December,* the Diftemper of this Godly Woman grew worfe and worfe upon her; and when her Mind was uneafy, thofe paffages came to Mind, *I know, O Lord, that thou canft do every Thing,* and, *Our God, whom we Serve, is able to deliver us.* On

December,

*December* 26. at Night, ſhe was buffeted with ſore Temptations, That her *Faith* for her *Cure*, having proved but a *Fancy*, her *Faith* for her *Soul* muſt be ſo too : but ſhe cryed out unto the Lord Lord, *I have caſt my Soul upon thee, and my Body up to thee, and I am Reſolved now to caſt all my Diſeaſe upon thee.* Her Mind was hereupon Compoſed and the Next Night, putting up her Hand unto her Head, firſt on the one ſide, and then on the other, ſhe felt a *New Skin*, on both ſides, which very much amazed her ; whereupon ſhe cryed out *Lord Jeſus, Haſt thou begun ? Thou wilt carry it on.* She then taking off her Head Clothes, found the Scurff gone off her Head, and a firm Skin appearing there ; and her Diſtemper, which had Extended itſelf all over her Body, from Head to Foot, with *Putrifying Sores*, was in like manner, ſuddenly taken away, to the Admiration of all Beholders.

*Reader,* Do not now Encourage thy ſelf in a Vain Expectation of *Miracles,* to Relieve thy particular Afflictions, but Improve theſe *Miracles,* as Intimations of what the Lord Jeſus Chriſt can and will quickly do, for His Afflicted Church in the World.

# F I N I S.

# Humiliations follow'd with Deliverances.

A Brief Difcourfe
On the MATTER and METHOD,
Of that

# HUMILIATION

which would be
an Hopeful Symptom of our Deliverance
from Calamity.

Accompanied and Accommodated
## WITH
# A NARRATIVE,

Of a Notable Deliverance lately
Received by fome

## English Captives,

From the Hands of Cruel Indians.

And fome *Improvement* of that *Narrative.*

Whereto is added
A Narrative of *Hannah Swarton,* containing
a great many wonderful paffages, relating to
her Captivity and Deliverance.

*Bofton* in *N. E* Printed by *B Green,* & *J. Allen,*
for *Samuel Phillips* at the Brick Shop. 1697.

# Humiliations, follow'd with Deliverances.

At *Boston Lecture* ; 6 d. 3. m. 1697. The Week before a General FAST.

2 Chron XII. 7.

*When the Lord saw, that they* Humbled *themselves, the Word of the Lord came unto* Shemajah, *saying, They have* Humbled *themselves, I will not Destroy them, but I will grant them some Deliverance.*

WHen the Punishment of *Scourging* was used upon a Criminal in *Israel,* it was the Order and Usage, that while the Executioner was Laying on his *Thirteen* ( and therein *Forty save one* ) Blowes, with an Instrument, every stroke whereof gave *Three* Lashes to the Delinquent, there were still present

A 2      sent

4     𝕳𝖚𝖒𝖎𝖑𝖎𝖆𝖙𝖎𝖔𝖓𝖘 𝖋𝖔𝖑𝖑𝖔𝖜'𝖉

fent *Three* Judges, whereof, while one
did *Number* the Blowes, and another kept
crying out, *Smite him!* a Third Read
*Three* Scriptures, during the Time of the
*Scourging:* and the *Scourging* Ended with
the *Reading* of them: The firſt Scripture
was That in Deut. 28. 58. *If thou wilt not
obſerve to do all the words of this Law, that
be written in this Book that thou mayſt Fear
this Glorious and Fearful Name, THE LORD
THY GOD; then the Lord will make thy
Plagues wonderful.* The ſecond Scripture
was That in Deut. 29 9. *Keep therefore
the words of this Covenant, and do them,
that you may proſper in all that ye do.* The
laſt Scripture was That in Pſal. 78 38.
*But He, being full of Compaſſion, forgave
their Iniquity, and deſtroy'd them not.* This
was done, partly for the *Admonition*, partly for the *Conſolation* of the Chaſtiſed
Criminal.

    *Chriſtians,* We are all ſenſible, That
the *Scourges* of Heaven, have long been
Employ'd upon us, for our Crimes againſt
the *Holy and Juſt and Good Laws* of the
Lord our God: Alas, our *Plagues* have
been *wonderful!* We have been ſorely
Laſhed, with one Blow after another,
                        for

for our Delinquencies. Who is there to *Number* the Blowes ? Yea, *The Anger of God, is not for all this Turned away, but His Hand stretched out still !* It is but proper, while we are thus under our Punishment, for us, to have a *Text* of the Sacred Oracles, agreeable unto our present State, Read unto us. Behold, an *Agreeable Text*, now singled out, for our Entertainment ; & I do the rather single it out becaufe the next Week, a General HUMILIATION is to be attended among us ; for which, I cannot eafily do a more *Ufeful* Thing, than to give you a *Preparative*; while I am speaking unto the Chriftians of many Churches, here come together, in One Great Affembly.

In our Context, we find the People of God, beginning to *Forsake the Law of the Lord* : They many wayes *Transgreffed* againft Him. Sad *Calamity* overtook them, for this their *Iniquity*, and *Apoftafy* ; But God bleffed the Preaching of His Prophet *Shemajah* unto them, under this *Calamity* to produce a Notable Dumiliation in them. The Claufes now before us, reprefent a bleffed Effect of that *Humiliation*; a gracious Promife of fome *Delive-*

A 3 *rance*

6    𝕳umiliations follow'd

*rance* from *Destruction*, was, by that Prophet of the Lord, when they *Humbled*
themselves, brought from the Lord unto
them.

The Truth which Lies plainly before
us, is, *That when a Sinful People Humble
themselves before the Almighty God, it is an
Hopeful and an Happy Symptom, that He
will not utterly Destroy such a People.*

Now, The CASE, which this Encou-
raging Truth, does at this Time Encourage us, to speak unto, is,

*After what manner is the* 𝕾elf-𝕳umilia-
tion *of a People that would Escape a*
𝕾ore 𝕯estruction, *to be Expressed and
Excited?*

Which to speak yet more pertinently
and profitably, is to say.

*After what manner are we our selves,* O
*our Dear People, to Humble our selves
before the Lord?*

Give your Attention.

*I.* When we *Pœnitently* Confess our
Sins,

*Sins*, and much more, when we vigorously Reform *our Sins*, we *Then* do to
good purpose *Humble* our selves, before
the God, against whom we have Sinned.
More distinctly ;

Firſt, A *Pœnitent Confeſſion of Sin*, is
that *Self Humiliation* which our God expects from ſuch a people as our ſelves.
Thus, in Luk. 18. 13, 14. He that ſaid,
*God be merciful to me a Sinner*, is, *He that
Humbleth himſelf.* Thus, Lev. 26. 40, 41.
They that *Confeſs their iniquity, and the I-
niquity of their Fathers*, have their *Uncir-
cumciſed Hearts Humbled* in their doing
ſo.

Accordingly, Firſt, In our *Humiliations*,
we ought ſeriouſly to *Confeſs* our *Provocations* to the Moſt Holy God, and the *Iniquities* that we have done, before Him
who is *of purer Eyes than to behold Iniquities.* But, what a ſad *Catalogue* of *Provocations*, have we to bring forth before
the Lord.

When we *Humble* our ſelves,

I. Let us Humbly Confeſs, That the
People of this Land, in a growing *Apoſtaſy* from that Religious Diſpoſition that
Signalized the firſt Planting of theſe Colonies,

lonies, have with multiplied Rebellions against the Almighty, Sinned exceedingly.

II. Let us Humbly Confess, That the *Spirit of this World*, hath brought an Epidemical Death, upon the Spirit, and *Power of Godliness*.

III. Let us Humbly Confess, That the Glorious *Gospel* of the Lord Jesus Christ, here Enjoy'd, with much *Plenty* as well as *Purity*, hath not been *Thankfully* and *Fruitfully* Entertained by those that have been *Blessed* with the *Joyful Sound*.

IV. Let us Humbly Confess, That the *Covenant of Grace* Recognized in our Churches, hath been by multitudes not submitted unto ; and of them that have submitted unto it, multitudes have not walked according to the Sacred *Obligations* thereof.

V. Let us Humbly Confess, That the Unreasonable Vices of Rash and Vain *Swearing*, with Hellish *Cursing* in the Mouths of many, have rendred them *Guilty Sinners.*

VI. Let us Humbly Confess, That a *Flood* of *Excessive Drinking*, hath begun to *Drown* much of *Christianity*, yea, and of

Civility

*Civility* it felt, in many places among us.

*VII.* Let us Humbly Confefs, That fome *Englifh,* by Selling of *Strong Drink* unto the *Indians,* have not only prejudiced among them, the Succeffes of the *Word of Life,* but alfo been the Faulty & Bloody Occafions of *Death* unto them.

*VIII.* Let us Humbly Confefs, That a *Vanity of Apparrel,* hath been affected by many perfons, who have been fo *vain,* as to *Glory in their Shame.*

*IX.* Let us Humbly Confefs, That wicked *Sorceries* have been practifed in the Land ; and yet in the Troubles from the *Devils,* thereby brought in among us, thofe *Errors* on both Hands were committed, which, *Who can underftand ?*

*X.* Let us Humbly Confefs, That the Dayes of *Sacred Reft* among us, have been difturbed with fo many Profanation, that we may not wonder if we *See no Reft.*

*XI.* Let us Humbly Confefs, That the woful Decay of good *Family Difcipline,* hath opened the Flood Gates, for Innumerable, and almoft Irremediable *Woes,* to break in upon us.

*XII.* Let us Humbly Confefs, That *Magiftrates*

*giftrates, Ministers,* and others that have ferved the *Publick,* have been but great *Sufferers* by their *Services,* and met with Unrighteous Difcouragements.

*XIII.* Let us Humbly Confefs, That the *Pyracies,* which, 'tis to be feared, fome who belong to thefe, have perpetrated in other parts of the World, are *Scandals,* that call for much Lamentation.

*XIV.* Let us Humbly Confefs, That we have in former years ufed *Unjustifiable Hardships,* upon fome that have Confcientioufly Diffented from our perfwafions in Religion.

*XV.* Let us Humbly Confefs, That we have treated one another, very Ill, in the Various *Temptations, Contentions,* and *Revolutions,* which have been upon us.

*XVI.* Let us Humbly Confefs, That the Sins of the moft *Filthy Uncleannefs,* have horribly *Defiled the Land.*

*XVII.* Let us Humbly Confefs, That the *Joy of Harvest,* hath been filled with Folly, and Lewdnefs, and Forgotten the *Glad Service* of God, whom we fhould have Served *in the Abundance of all things.*

*XVIII.* Let us Humbly Confefs, That much *Fraud* hath been ufed in the Deal
ings

ings of many, and the *Spirit of Oppreffion*
hath made a *Cry.*

*XIX.* Let us Humbly Confefs, That
*Falfehood* and *Slander* hath been commonly carrying of *Darts* through the Land
and the *Wounded* have been many!

*XX.* And, Let us Humbly Confefs,
That the Succeffive and Amazing Judgments of God upon us, for our thus Tref-
paffing, have not Reclamed us, but we
have prodigioufly *Gone on ftill in our Trefpaffes.*

In our *Humiliations,* Let thefe things be
Reflected on ; and with our moft Hum-
ble Reflections, Let us do like them, in
1 Sam. 7. 6. *Gather together, and Draw
water, and pour it out,* [ in a Showre of
Tears ] *before the Lord, and Faft on that
Day, and fay, we have Sinned againft the
Lord.*

But that this our *Confeffion* of our *Provocations,* may be *Penitent,* we muft, Secondly,
Incorporate thereinto, a *Confeffion* of what
we have *Deferved* by thefe *Provoking Evils.*
Particularly.

We have feen many *Troubles :* but on
our Day of *Humiliation,* concerning all
our *Troubles,* Let us Humbly make that
*Confeffion,*

*Confeſſion*, in Ezra 9. 13. *Thou, our God, haſt puniſhed us, leſs than our Iniquities Deſerve.*

Have we loſt many Thouſands of Pounds, by the *Diſaſters* of the *Sea* ? Let us Humbly Confeſs, our Sins have *Deſerved*, that inſtead of making one Good Voyage, we ſhould have been ſtript of all the Little that is left unto us.

Hath one *bad Harveſt* after another, diminiſhed our *Ordinary Food* ? Let us Humbly Confeſs, our Sins have *Deſerved*, that the Earth which hath been thereby *Defiled*, ſhould have yielded us nothing at all.

Have Bloody, Popiſh, and Pagan *Enemies*, made very dreadful Impreſſions upon us, and Captived and Butchered multitudes of our Beloved Neighbours? Let us Humbly Confeſs, our Sins have *Deſerved*, that we ſhould be all of us, altogether given up, unto the will of our Enemies, to *Serve our Enemies in the want of all things, and have our Lives continually hanging in Doubt*, under their furious Tyrannies.

Have we been *Broken ſore in the place of Dragons, and Covered with the Shadow of Death* ? Say Humbly before the Lord, with them, in *Lam.* 3. 39. *Why ſhould a*
man

𝔴𝔦𝔱𝔥 𝔇𝔢𝔩𝔦𝔳𝔢𝔯𝔞𝔫𝔠𝔢𝔰.          13

*man Complain, for the punishment of his Sin ?*
And yet, we have had *Comforts*, to mi-
tigate and moderate, our *Troubles :* In the
*midst of wrath,* God ha's *Remembred Mer-*
*cy.* Now concerning all our *Comforts,*
on our Day of *Humiliation,* Let us Humbly make that *Confession,* in Lam. 3. 22.
*It is of the Lords mercies, that we are not*
*Consumed.*

Have we not the Tidings of *Salvation*
by our Lord Jesus Christ, Preach'd unto
us, to sweeten the *Bread of Adversity,* and
the *Water of Affliction,* which the Lord
hath given us ?   Let us Humbly Confess,
'Tis *of the Lords Mercies,* that this Countrey ha's the *Bread of Life,* and the *Wa-*
*ters of Life,* yet continued unto it, and that
it is not become a *Region of the Valley of*
*the Shadow of Death.*

Are our *Poor,* though greatly Increased
and Afflicted, yet more Comfortably provided for, than in many other parts of the
World ?  Let us Humbly Confess, 'Tis *of*
*the Lords Mercies,* that we are not all Scattered, and famished, and perished in our
Poverty.

Do we see less of the *Distress of Nati-*
*ons, and Perplexity, with the Sea, and the*
             B                       *waves*

*waves thereof Roaring*, than they do in a great part of *Europe* ? Let us Humbly Confels, 'Tis *of the Lords Mercies*, that all the Things, which the *fainting Hearts* of men any where do *fear, coming on the Earth,* are not come upon our felves.

Why do not our *Adverfaries* ufe the Advantages which they have to Confound us, but are themfelves in fuch Confufion, that we Endure not an Hundredth part of the Difturbance from them, which they might give unto us ? Humbly fay before the Lord, with him, in Gen. 32. 10. *We are not worthy of the leaft of all thefe Mercies !*

This, This would be the Language of a True *Humiliation.*

But a Second Admonition, muft be added unto *This.* What Signifies *Confeffion,* without Reformation ? 'Tis all but *Hypocrify,* all but *Impiety.* We are told in Prov. 28. 13. 'Tis *he that Confeffeth & Forfaketh, who fhall have Mercy.*

The Ancients, would well call the *Confeffion* of Sin, *The Vomit of the Soul.* But now, if we return, and proceed, unto the *Commiffion* of the Sins, which we have by our *Confeffion,* as it were *Vomited* up ; what
are

are we, but the *Dogs that Return unto their Vomit* ? When Sins are Sincerely Confef-sed, the Repenting Sinners, will fay, as in Hof. 14. 8. *What have we any more to do with them* ?

Come then ; We have now and then, that which we call, *A Day of Humiliation.* But, Sirs, *A Day of Reformation* ; Oh ! when fhall we fee fuch a Day ? *When fhall it once be* ! Behold, an Effential Piece of work, to be attended, when, *A Day of Humiliation,* arrives unto us Let every one of us, Earneftly Enquire with our felves, *What is there, that I am now fo Re-form in my own Heart and Life, and in the Family which I belong unto* ? and importu-nately implore, the Help of the Spirit of Grace, to purfue fuch a *Reformation.* But then, Let all that Suftain any *Publick Office,* whether Civil, or Sacred, further carry on the Enquiry : *What fhall we do to Reform any fpreading Evils in the Publick* ? Let the *Paftors* of the *Churches,* in their feveral Charges, Labour Watchfully to prevent all growth of Sin in their Vicinities ; and the *Churches* joyn with their *Paftors,* in Sharpening their Difcipline againft Offen-ces that may arife, and in preferving the

*Liberty,* and *Purity,* which they have heretofore been clothed withal.

And Let *Juftices, Grand Jury men, Conftables, Tythingmen,* have their mutual *Confultations,* to procure the *Executions* of Good Laws, and Remember the *Oath of God* upon them.

Were fuch an *Humiliation* once obtained, Then would our God fay, *I fee, they have Humbled themfelves, I will not utterly Deftroy them !* The Land of *Canaan,* is as much as to fay, in Englifh, The Land of the *Humbled.* Oh! if we were univerfally thus *Humbled,* our Land would foon be a *Canaan,* for the Reft, the Peace, the Plenty, which would be therein vouchfafed unto us.

*II.* The Exercifes of a Sacred Faft have a particular and peculiar Character of *Humiliation* in them, and we are to *Humble* our felves with *Fafting* before the Lord. Thus the Pfalmift of old manifefted his *Humiliation,* in Pfal. 35.13 *I Humbled my Soul, with Fafting.*

There is that Call *Now,* and *Often* [perhaps not *often* enough !] heard, thro' the Province, in Joel 1. 14. *Sanctify*

a

a Faſt, Call a Solemn Aſſembly, Gather the Elders; and all the Inhabitants of the Land, into the Houſe of your God, and Cry unto the Lord. And I perſwade my ſelf, that we generally concur in the General Princi-ple, hitherto Eſpouſed, by the Church of God, in every Generation, That a Religious Faſt, is a Needful Duty, (pro Temporibus et Cauſis, as Tertullian long ſince well ſtated it, ) on Juſt and Great Occaſions for it. That Merry Sect, who Explode Faſting, as a thing not Agreeable to our Goſpel Times, appear not among us. We know, that Faſting hath, in all Ages, been eſteem'd, a Duty incumbent on the People of God. We find ſuch Faſting uſed in Elder Times, [ Judg. 20. 26. and 1 Sam. 7. 6. ] Both more publickly, [ 2 Chron. 20. 30. and Ezr. 8 21 ] And more privately; [ 2 Sam. 12. 16 & Neh. 1. 4. ] What tho' theſe things were in the Dayes of the Old-Teſtament? I hope, the Old Teſtament is not become Apocry-pha, with any of us. But in the New-Teſtament alſo, we have a Prædiction, of our Faſting, [ Math. 9. 15. ]. Yea, and a Præſcription for it, [ Math. 6. 16. ] for doing it more publickly, we have a War-

B 3　　　　　　rant,

rant, [ Act. 14. 23. ] and more *privately*
too. [ 1 Cor. 7. 5. ] Yea, we are told,
that there are certain Bleſſings, which
cannot now be obtained, but in ſuch a
way. [Mar. 9. 29.] And I am ſure of one
thing more ; when the Apoſtles, and the
Believers in the Primitive Times, were
moſt *Filled* with the Holy Spirit of Chriſt,
*then* it was that they were moſt in *Faſt-*
*ing* before the Lord !

Now, if our **Faſt**, be *ſuch a Faſt as the*
*Lord hath choſen,* we ſhall therein *Humble*
our ſelves, moſt acceptably, moſt profitably, moſt efficaciouſly.   And becauſe, the
Right *Performance* of this Duty, is a thing
of great *Conſequence* in *Chriſtianity* ; 'tis
what is frequently required, and much
*Weal* or *Wo* will follow upon the management of it ; I will ſet before you, the
**Rules** of that **Sacred Faſt**, wherein
we are to *Humble* our Souls.

Having firſt, *Prepared* our ſelves for
our *Faſt*, as one would for an *Extraordi-*
*nary Sabbath,* we have theſe things to do.

Firſt ; There is the *Internal Humiliation*
of our Faſt ; The Duties of **Praying.**
**Repenting** and **Believing**, are the *Soul*
of that *Faſt* wherein we are to *Humble*
                                        our

our *Souls* ; and we are to Labour in thofe Duties. The Duties of a *Faſt*, are thofe, in 2 Chron. 7. 14. *My People ſhall then Humble themſelves, and Pray, and Seek my Face, and Turn from their wicked wayes.* For men to think, that they Serve God, by a *Faſt* wherein they do nothing but *Faſt* from Corporal Suſtenance, and they draw not near to God in *Devotions* all the Day long, 'tis a piece of Ignorance ; yea, more than one *Commandment* of God is broken, by this piece of Ignorance.

When we Celebrate a *Faſt*, we are in more than ordinary **Prayers**, to Acknowledge our own *Sinfulneſs*, and the *Greatneſs* and *Juſtice* of God, in Chaſtiſing our Sinfulneſs ; and we are to Supplicate thofe Favours of Heaven, which our *Sins*, our *Wants*, and our *Fears*, make Neceſſary for us. The Thing which we have to do, on a *Faſt*, is what the Praying *Daniel* did ; in Dan. 9. 3. *I ſet my Face unto the Lord God, to ſeek by Prayer, and Supplications, with Faſting.* And haing thus Quoted, the *Ninth Chapter* of *Daniel*, I may Remark, That there are Three **Ninths**, which admirably well deſcribe the Task of a *Faſt* unto us ; the
*Ninth*

20 **Humiliations follow'd**

*Ninth* Chapter of *Ezra*, the *Ninth* Chapter of *Nehemiah*, and the *Ninth* Chapter of *Daniel*. When the *Fast* comes, Remember, Christians, to consult those *Three Chapters*, with Lively Meditations thereupon. A Day of *Fast*, is to be a Day of *Prayer*. As in Act. 13. 3. so elsewhere, *Fasting* and *Praying*, are what *God has joyned*, and here, *Man may not separate them.* Would you *hear*, what you have to *Do*, when a *Fast* is to be kept? The words of an *Order for a Fast*, once ran so, in Jon. 3. 8. *Cry mightily unto God.* Prayer, 'tis That, whereof the Jewes in one of their Ancient Adagies, tell us, *Nulla est pulchrior virtus hac ipsa*; There is no *vertue* like it. It is beyond all *Oblations.* But **Repenting** and **Believing** as well as *Praying*, must signalize our *Fast. Reconciliation* with God, is the End of a *Fast*; without *Repenting* and *Believing*, this Reconciliation is not applied unto us.

A *Fast*, is but a *Form*, an Hungry and Empty *Form*, if we do not therein heartily **Repent** of our Miscarriages. Thus we are advised, in Isa. 58. 6, 7, 8. *Is not this the Fast, that I have chosen? To Loose the Bonds of Wickedness.* On a *Fast*, Let
us

us be thofe *Ephraimites*, who fhail *bemoan themfelves* ; *Thou haft Chaftifed me,* O Lord, *and I was Chaftifed, Turn thou me, and I fhall be Turned!* On a *Faft*, Let us take thofe *Directions*, in the midft of our *Lamentations, Let us Search and Try our ways, and Turn again unto the Lord.* A *Fafting* Day muft be a *Soul* grieving Day, and a *Sin* killing Day, or 'tis nothing. Our *Fafts* are to Slay our *Lufts* ; thofe are the *Beafts*, which are then to be flaughtered. Indeed, when-ever a *Faft* recurrs, we fhould go the whole *Work of Converfion* over again! Our *Faft* will notably be, *Cibus virtutis*, if we do fo.

Again; The *Satisfaction* and *Interceffion* of the Lord Jefus Chrift, muft on a *Faft* be Repaired unto ; and we muft 25c= lebe in it for our *Atonement.* It was the *Rite* appointed for a *Faft*, in Lev. 16. 27. *lo- The Blood of the Sin Offering, muft be brought in, to make Atonement ; On that Day fhall the Prieft make Atonement for you, to cleanfe you, that you may be clean from all your Sins before the Lord.* Our Lord Jefus Chrift is our *Prieft* ; What He hath done for our *Atonement*, muft be this Day, with a ftrong Faith Laid hold upon. A

*Faft,*

*Faſt* is a Day of *Expiation*; but we know it is only the Lord Jeſus Chriſt, that hath by His *Unknown Sufferirgs* ( as the Greek Church at this Day expreſſes it ) made *Expiation* for our Sins.  Hence on a *Faſt*, we muſt Renew the *Dependance* of our Souls, on the Obedience which our Lord Jeſus Chriſt, our *Surety*, hath yielded unto God for us.  Our *Sin* has procured the *Death* of our Lord Jeſus Chriſt ; In a *Faſt*, our *Faith* is to Feed upon it.  A *Faſting* Day, is with *Faith*, a *Feeding* Day. In our *Faſts*, we are to Imitate the Action of the *Moloſſians*, who ſeeking the Kings Good will unto them, took the Son of the King into their Arms, and preſenting themſelves thus before him, ſaid, *Syr, For the ſake of this your Son, we hope, you'l be favourable to us.*  Thus, Let us preſent our ſelves before the Eternal King of Heaven, on our *Faſt*, with His Only Begotten, His Dearly Beloved *Son*, in the Arms of our Faith, and plead, *Oh ! for the Sake of this thy Son, do Good unto us.* But then,

Secondly ; There is the *External Humiliation* of our *Faſt* ; when we *Humble* our ſelves in a *Faſt*, we are to Abſtain
from

from all our Secular Pleasures and Affayrs, that we may the better go thorough our Duties.    Like Silly Children,
we know not when to *Feed*, and when
to Forbear *Feeding*.    But our Good God,
in His Word ha's taught us !    We are
Taught, that we must sometimes have a
Day for *Fasting*, which must be a Day of
*Restraint* upon us ; and this *Restraint* must
Extend unto the Dimensions of a *Sabbath*.
Of a *Fast*, it is prescribed, in Lev. 23. 32.
*It shall be unto you, a Sabbath of Rest, and*
*ye shall Afflict your Souls ; from Evening un-*
*to Evening shall ye Celebrate your Sabbath.*
The Design of the *Abstinence*' thus to be
used on a *Fast*, is, not only that we
may be more *free* for the several Spiritual
Employments, which are then incumbent
on us, ( our Lord, like a wise Falconer,
will by keeping of us a little *Sharp*, fit us
for the *Highest Flights* in our *Prayers*! )
but also to *Show*, and *Speak*, the *Humilia-*
*tion* of our Souls in those Employments.
Tis a *Ceremony* of Gods Appointment, a
*Symbolical Ceremony*, which God Himself
hath appointed, and a part of Worship,
whereby we are to Signify, *That we term*
*our selves utterly unworthy of all those Bles-*
*sings,*

24 **Humiliations follow'd**

*ſings, which we now Deny unto our ſelves,
and therefore of all other Bleſſings whatſoe-
ever.* And the *Firſt Sin* of man, which
Lay in *Eating*, is to be conſidered, as very particularly herein referred unto.

Now, Firſt, A *Faſt* is to be kept with
an *Abſtinence* from the **Pleaſures** of
this Life. Our uſual *Diet* muſt on a
*Faſt* be Abſtained from. It was therefore ſaid, in Eſth. 4. 16. *Faſt, and neither
Eat nor Drink.* The very Term of a
*Faſt*, implies thus much ; and it hath
been of old ſaid, *They that will not ſo
Faſt with the Children of God, muſt Eat
and Drink of the Furious Wrath of God,
with the Wicked* There are indeed Caſes of Neceſſity, wherein our merciful God
calls for, *Mercy rather than Sacrifice* ; and
in thoſe Caſes, doubtleſs the *Abſtinence*
may be ſomewhat Abated and Relaxed.
Some cannot Encounter a ſevere and a
total *Abſtinence*, it would utterly Diſable
them, for the Service of the Day : the
Severity may then be mitigated. Yet
our *Abſtinence* muſt be ſuch as to produce our *Affliction*. Of a *Faſt*, it is ſaid,
in Iſa. 58. 5. *It is a Day for a man to
Afflict his Soul*; and it is ſaid, in Lev.
23.

23. 29. *Whatsoever Soul it be, that shall not be Afflicted in that same Day, he shall be cut off from among his people.* We may not Eat or Drink *so much,* nor may we Eat or Drink *so well,* on such a Day, as at another Time. In the *Fast* of a *Daniel,* we have this *Abstinence* observed, ch. 10. 3. *I ate no pleasant Bread, neither came Flesh nor Wine, into my mouth, neither did I anoint my self at all*: And in *Tertullians* Time, they had their *Xerophagiæ,* a Dry sort of Repast, for such as found that a *Rigid Fast,* was too hard for them. But by consequence, all other Delights of the *Senses,* are then also to be avoided. If you read, Joel 2.16. and I Cor.7.5. You'll find a particular prohibition of this Importance. Hence likewise, our *Sleep* is then to be Retrenched. If we are inclinable to *Sleep* so long on a *Fast,* as we do on another Day, we are to *Awaken* our selves, with such a Call from God, as that, *What meanest thou, O Sleeper, Arise, and Call upon thy God!* And it is not improper here to be noted, That our *Alms* are to be one Concomitant of our *Fasts.* It was said, in Isa. 58 7. *Is not this the Fast that I have Chosen? Is it not*

C

26    Humiliations follow'd

to deal thy Bread to the Hungry? When we
come to seek *Mercy* of God, we should,
in Thankfulness for our Hope to find
what we seek, show *Mercy* to men.  In
our *Fasting*, we *Deny* to our selves our u-
sual *Nourishments*; and we should then
*Bestow* on others at least as much as we
*Deny* to our selves, in Token of our Sense,
That we are more Undeserving of the
Divine Bounty, than any that we know
in our Neighbourhood.  Our *Alms* are
to go up with our *Prayers*, as a *Memorial*,
( we *Remember* who's did so! ) *before*
God.  But there is yet one thing more to
be added ; *Fine Cloathes* must in a *Fast*,
be *Abstained* from.  If there were no
*Scripture* for this, why might not meer
*Nature* teach it unto us, as well as unto
the *Ninivites*?  But we have *Scripture* for
it, in Exod 33. 4. *The people mourned, and
no man did put on him his Ornaments.*  I
have seen a Fault in this place, and *My
Neighbours, 'Tis utterly a Fault among you*;
That on a *Fast*, many people, will come
to the Worship of God, in  as Gay
Cloaths, as if they  were going to a
*Feast.*  Methinks, I hear, the Holy Angels of God thus uttering their Indignation

**with Deliverances.** 27

tion againſt ſuch Offenders ; *What ? will
thoſe vain people, never have any ſign of an
Abaſed, and an Afflicted Soul upon them ?*
Truly, to be arrayed in Gorgeous Apparrel on a *Faſt*, is very offenſive unto God.
*Rags* are fitter than *Robes*, for the Children
of men therein to appear as *Malefactors*
before *God the Judge of all.* They that
come to the Aſſembly, in a ſplendid, and
flanting Attire, on ſuch a Day, do but
*Affront* the God, whom they profeſs to
*Humble* themſelves before. Would you
Speed in a *Faſt* ? Then be able to ſay, if
not with him, in Pſal 35. 13. *My Cloathing was Sackcloth, when I Humbled my Soul
with Faſting,* yet, *My Cloathing is Sober,
Modeſt, Proper, and very Humble !*

And, Secondly, A *Faſt*, is to be kept
with an *Abſtinence*, from the Affairs of
this Life. The *Works* of our particular
Vocations are to be laid aſide, when a
*Faſt* is Indicted ; and *All Servile Labour on
the ſaid Day is Inhibited.* A *Faſt*, is to be
kept with the ſtrictneſs of a *Sabbath.* It
is Enjoined in Lev. 23. 28, 30, 32. *Ye ſhall
do no work in that ſame Day, for it is a Day
of Atonement. Whatſoever Soul it be, that
doth any work in that ſame Day, the ſame*
C 2 *Soul*

*Soul will I destroy from among his people. It shall be unto you a Sabbath of Rest; from Evening to Evening shall ye Celebrate it.* When the Services of the Congregation are over, we are not presently at *Liberty* to do what we will: Those persons do but help to Debauch the Land, who take such a *Liberty*. The Edicts of Heaven run so, in Joel 2. 14. *Sanctify a Fast*. The whole Day of the *Fast* is to be *Sanctified*, or, set apart, for Communion with God: When we *keep a Day*, we must *keep it unto the Lord*. The Expectation of our God, is intimated unto us, in Isa 58. 13. *Turn away thy Foot from the Sabbath*, (take no long Journeys on it ) *from doing thy pleasure on my Holy Day: Honour him, not doing thine own wayes, nor finding thine own pleasure, nor speaking thine own words.* Indeed, the *Weekly Sabbath* lays a claim to all the things here spoken of; nevertheless, I suspect that a *Fasting Sabbath* is here more peculiarly intended. A *Fast*, is no less than twice in one verse, Lev. 23. 32. called a *Sabbath* : and why may not that be the *Sabbath* more especially meant throughout the whole *fifty eighth* Chapter of *Isaiah* ? An Expression twice used in
the

the verse newly quoted, namely, *Doing thy pleasure,* and *Finding thy own pleasure,* on the *Sabbath,* occurs in the third verse, *In the Day of your Fast, you find pleasure;* which *finding of pleasure* is opposed unto the *Affliction,* both of *Spirit* and of *Body,* wherein we are to *Judge our selves* on such a Solemnity. Because we do not *Fast,* with a due conformity, to the *Edicts* of Heaven, therefore as of old, *Pompey* Siezed the Jewish Temple, on their *Fast-Day,* and *Sosius* on their *Fast-Day* took the City, so we in this Land, have on, or near our *Fast-Dayes* often felt such *Rebukes* of Heaven, that it has become the just *Astonishment* of many that have *wisely observed* it, and it should be the *Humiliation* of us all. But now, conform to this Expectation of Heaven, on your *Fast : Then shalt thou Delight thy self in the Lord, for the mouth of the Lord hath spoken it.*

III. That our *Humiliation* may be Quickened, Let us *Humbly,* Awfully and Mournfully, **Consider** the most **Humbling Circumstances,** which the *Mighty Hand of God,* hath brought us into. It was the **Counsel,** in 1 Pet. 5. 6. *Humble*

*your*

30 **Humiliations follow'd**

*pour selves under the Mighty Hand of God.*
*Wicked* and *Hurtful* men, have been called, *The Hand of God* : [ see Psal. 17. 14. ]
It may be, *Nero*, a *Mighty* man Raised by
God, for the Vexation of mankind, may
be more particularly designed, in that
passage, *The Mighty Hand of God.* And
by a French *Nero*, have we also been so
vexed, that we have cause to *Humble our
selves* under what we have Endured from
that *Mighty Hand.* But indeed, there is
the *Mighty Hand of God*, in all Afflictive
Dispensations of His Providence ; and
now, O Let us *Humble* our selves, by
*Considering*, how much the Dispensations
of His *Mighty Hand* have Humbled us.

The Circumstances of *Affliction* are *Humbling Circumstances.* It was said of the
*Afflicted*, in Psal. 107. 39. *They are brought
Low through Affliction.* It was said by
the Afflicted, in Psal 39 8. *We are brought
very Low.* An Afflicted people may say,
as the Afflicted *Paul* said, *My God Hum-
bles me.* *Afflictions* keep under our Aspi-
ring Spirits, and make us feel and own
our own wretchedness. But Oh ! what
*Afflictions* has this poor people, been Humbled withal !

It

It was a Prophecy concerning, *The Daughter of Zion*, in Isa. 3. 26. *She being Desolate, shall sit upon the Ground.* When Zion was *Desolate*, by the Roman Conquest, ( unto which this Prophecy might Extend ) there were Coins made in Commemoration of that Conquest, and on those Coins there was a Remarkable Exposition of this Prophecy. On the Reverse of those Medals, which are to be seen unto this Day, there is, *A Silent Woman sitting upon the Ground, and leaning against a Palm-tree, with this Inscription* IUDÆA CAPTA. Nor was any Conquered City or Countrey, before this of *Judæa*, ever thus drawn upon Medals, as, *A Woman sitting upon the Ground.* Alas, If poor *New-England*, were to be shown upon her old Coin, we might show her *Leaning* against her Thunder-struck *Pine tree, Desolate, sitting upon the Ground.* Ah! *New England!* Upon how many Accounts, mayst thou say with her, in Ruth 1 13. *The Hand of the Lord is gone out against me!*

An Excellent Minister, who dyed among us, a Young Man, Considerably more than Twenty years ago, [ It was Mr. *John Eliot*, the younger, ] when he lay

32 𝕳𝖚𝖒𝖎𝖑𝖎𝖆𝖙𝖎𝖔𝖓𝖘 𝖋𝖔𝖑𝖑𝖔𝖜𝖉

lay on his Death-bed, and was Drawing his *Profagious Breath*, had thefe Memorable Expreffions. ' My Lord Jefus Chrift, hath
' been a Great while, preparing a *Manfion*,
' which is now ready for me. He will
' quickly take me, as He did *John*, by the
' Right Hand, and prefent me unto the
' Father, who has *Loved me, with an Ever-*
' *lafting Love.* As for *New England*, I
' believe, that God will not *Unchurch* it;
' but He will make a *Poor and Afflicted*
' *People in it* Bofton, and the *Maffachufet*
' Colony, is Coming *Down*, Coming
' *Down*, Coming *Down* a pace! Expect
' fad and fore Afflictions; but Oh! Get
' an Intereft in the Lord Jefus Chrift, and
' you may Live on *That*, all the World
' over. So fpoke an Eminent Servant of the Lord Jefus Chrift, when he was juft Entring into the *Joy of His Lord.* Now this Prædiction, we have feen very terribly Accomplifhed; It has been Strangely and Sadly Accomplifhed, ever fince the Time that it was uttered: And in almoft all our Concerns, our Story hath been that in Judg 2. 15. *Whitherfoever they went out, the Hand of the Lord was againft them for evil, as the Lord had faid, and they were greatly Diftreffed.* We

We have been *Humbled*, with an *Annual Blaß* upon our *Daily Bread*, until at laft, the very Staff of the Countrey ha's been broken for Two years together, and an horrible Cry, for *Bread, Bread*, hath been heard in our Streets.

We have been *Humbled*, with such *Loffes* by Sea & Land, that Strangers afar off, take notice of it, Concluding, *Surely Almighty God is in ill Terms with that Country?*

We have been *Humbled* by the *Angels of Death* shooting the *Arrows of Death*, with direful Repetitions of Mortality, in the midft of us *!*

We have been *Humbled* by a Barbarous Adverfary once and again let loose to *Wolve* it upon us, and an unequal Conteft with such as are *not a People, but a Foolifh Nation.*

We have been *Humbled* by *all Adverfity vexing* us, in our Going out, & our Coming in, and in the *Conftant Mifcarriages* of our moft *Likely Expeditions.*

We have been *Humbled* by the *Wrath of the Lord of Hofts Darkning our Land*, when *Evil Angels* broke in among us, to do those Amazing Things, of which no *Former Ages* give a parallel.

We

We have been *Humbled*, by the Ireful, and the Direful Rebukes of Heaven, upon all our *Precious and Pleasant Things* : But above all, by *Spiritual Plagues* whereto we are abandoned. The *Plagues* of a *Blind Mind*, and an *Hard Heart*, and an Asto-nishing *Unfruitfulness* under all the Means of Grace ; and a Stupid *Insensibility* of the *Causes* for which, & the *Manners* in which, the Almighty God is *Contending with us*, have Siezed upon us. Some of our *Seers* have a mist before their Eyes ; Some of our *Churches* fall asleep till they are stript of their Garments ; under the Sharpest Chastisements of Heaven, we *grow worse and worse*, with such a *Swift Apostasy*, that if we Degenerate the *Next Ten Years*, as the most Impartial observers do say, that we have done the *Last*, *God be Merciful unto us !* What a *Swift Destruction* are we like-ly to be overwhelmed withal ?

Now there is a Loud *Voice*, in all these things ; the Voice of them is, *Be Humbled,* O New-England ; *Humble thy self, Lest a fiercer Anger of the Lord yet come upon thee !* Oh ! Let not that be written on our Doors, in Jer 44. 10. *They are not Humbled unto this Day !* Sirs, We

are

are every Day *Coming down* moſt wonderfully ; But let us then *Fall down* moſt
*Humbly*, in the Conſideration thereof, and
let our Lamentation be *That*, in Lam. 3.
19, 20. *Remembring my Affliction and my
Miſery* ; *my Soul has them ſtill in Remembrance, and is Humbled in me* !

*IV.* What will our *Humiliation* Signify,
if it carry us not unto our Lord Jeſus
Chriſt ? Wherefore, when we *Humble*
our ſelves, Let us *Humbly* Rely on our Lord
Jeſus Chriſt alone, for our Acceptance
with God. So are we Directed, in Jam.
4 10. *Humble your ſelves in the ſight of the
Lord* : That is to ſay, With an Eye to the
*Lord Jeſus Chriſt*, in all you do.

That the *Humiliations* of men, are of
no Account, with God, while the Lord
Jeſus Chriſt is not therein referred unto, the poor Jewiſh Nation have given to
us, a doleful Experiment : related in a
Book Tranſlated by one *Paul Iſaiah*, a
Jew, by that among other motives, converted unto the Faith of our Bleſſed Jeſus. After many former *Humiliations*,
that the End of their Captivity might be
Revealed unto them, they did in the year
1502,

1502. make a *Publick Repentance*, thro' all
their Habitations, all over the face of the
whole World, and both old and young,
men, women and children, spent almost
a year together in such marvellous Devotions as were never heard of in the
world before. But all signified nothing;
why? Because they do as the Prophet
*Isaiah* foretold that they would; they
still *Reject* our Lord Jesus Christ, through
whom alone it is, that any of our *Humi-*
*liations* have Acceptance with the God
of Heaven. The Great God has promised, That He will be favourable unto
that Nation, in Lev. 26 41. *When their*
*Uncircumcised Hearts be Humbled, and they*
*then Accept the punishment of their Iniquity.*
The *Sacrifice*, upon whom the *punishment*
*of our Iniquity* does fall, [ Isa. 53. 6. and
2 Cor. 5. 21. ] is that of the *Messiah*;
and the *Messiah* therefore is by that Name
intended. When the Jews come to leave
off their Thoughts and Hopes, of any o-
ther *Sacrifice*, or their Dreams of making
Satisfaction by *bearing the punishment of*
*their own Iniquity*, but *Accept* the *Messiah*,
as the only Help of their Souls against
all the Guilt of their Sins; THEN
God

God *will Remember His Covenant.* O
That they would at Laſt, and at Leaſt
come to ſuch Thoughts, as were in the famous Rabbi *Samuel Marochianus,* who upon that Prophecy of *Amos,* where the
Lord threatens to puniſh *Iſrael* for Selling the Righteous for Silver, has
theſe Memorable words ; *The Prophet A-
mos, Expreſly declares the Wickedneſs, for
which we are in our Captivity : It manifeſtly
appears to me, that we are juſtly puniſhed,
for that Sin of Selling the Righteous. A
thouſand years and more, are ſpent, in all
which Time our condition among the Gentiles
is not minded, nor have we any Hopes of
mending it.* O My God, I am afraid,
I am afraid, Leſt the JESUS, whom
the Chriſtians Worſhip, ſhould be the
Righteous One, whom we have Sold
for Silver! In the mean time, Let us
that *own* our ſelves *Chriſtians,* now *prove*
our ſelves to be ſo, by our *Humbling* our
ſelves before God, but Looking for the
Succeſs of it, only from and thro' our
Lord Jeſus Chriſt, our only Mediator.
Let the *Humiliation* of our Lord *Jeſus
Chriſt,* be our *Meditation,* and our *Conſolation.* Of Him 'tis ſaid, in Phil. 2. 8. *He*

D                              *Humbled*

*Humbled Himself.* And let it provoke our *Humiliation,* when we meditate on what our Lord Jesus Christ suffered, when *God Laid no Him the Iniquity of us all.* But when we have *Humbled* our selves never so much, Let us count that we have cause to be *Humbled* over again, for the defects of our own *Humiliation.* As he of old said, *Lava meas Lachrymas Domine ;* Lord, *My very Tears want washing !* So let us be sensible, *There is enough in our best Humiliations, to call for more Humiliations.* Fly then to the Lord *Jesus Christ,* whose *Prayers* were alwayes perfect, and whose *Fasts* were ever Faultless, and whose *Blood* being Sprinkled upon our *Humiliations,* is that, which alone, can render such Defective Things Acceptable unto the *Holy, Holy, Holy, Lord God Almighty.* Put all into the Hands of the Great *Angel of the Covenant :* His *Incense perfuming* of them, they will *Ascend before God,* with glorious Effects following thereupon.    Among some of the *Americans,* 'tis reported, they have a strange Usage, when they are *Humbling* themselves before their Gods, to bring their *Sheep* into their Assemblies, that by the Bleats and Cries of their *Sheep*

they

they may move the compassion of their *Gods.* We are better taught than so! when we are *Humbling* our selves, we are to bring before our God, *that Lamb of God, which takes away the Sins of the world.* Syrs, There was a *Sacrifice for the Congregation,* which was on a *Day of Humiliation* of old Commemorated. Our Lord Jesus Christ, is to be on our *Day of Humiliation,* Look'd unto, as the *Sacrifice for our whole Congregation.* Our *Faith* is to Argue it, That God has had more Honour from the *Sacrifice* of our Lord Jesus Christ, than if all our *whole Congregation,* were destroy'd for ever. Our *Faith* is to Resolve it, That whatever Salvation is vouchsafed unto all our *whole Congregation,* the *Sacrifice* of our Lord Jesus Christ shall have the Honour and the Merit of it all, ascribed thereunto. Now, who can tell, how far one *Humble Soul,* may prevail, that shall put in Suit, the *Sacrifice for the Congregation?* The Faith of one *Moses,* of one *Samuel,* yea, of one *Amos,* one poor, obscure, honest Husbandman, Oh! how far, may it go, to obtain this Answer, from the Great God, *They have Humbled themselves, I will not destroy*

40        *Humiliations follow'd*
*them, but grant them some Deliverance!*

¶ AND, I suppose, there happens to
be at this very Time, in this Assembly,
an *Example,* full of Encouragement unto
those *Humiliations,* which have been
thus called for.

In our Solemn *Humiliations* before the
Lord, we have with a very particular
*Fervency* besought His Mercy for our
poor *Captives,* that were become the *Prey
of the Terrible;* Yea, we have done it, with
some *Assurance,* that the Glorious *Hearer
of Prayer,* would Vouchsafe of His Mercy
to some of those *Miserables.*

Now, I think I see, among you, at
this Hour, *Three Persons,* namely, Two
Women, and one Youth, who have just
now, Received a Deliverance from a Captivity in the Hands of horrid Indians,
with some very Singular Circumstances;
And therefore, Let it not seem an Un-
suitable or Unseasonable Digression, it I
Conclude, this Discourse, with making
this unexpected occurrence, to be Subser-
vient unto the main Intention thereof.

## with Deliverances. 41

[ *A Narrative of a Notable Deliverance from Captivity.* ]

'ON the fifteenth Day, of the Laſt
' *March*, *Hannah Duſtan*, of *Haver-*
' *bil*, having Lain in about a Week, at-
' tended with her Nurſe, *Mary Neff*, a
' Widow a Body of Terrible *Indians*,drew
' near unto the Houſe where ſhe lay,with
' Deſigns to carry on the bloody Devaſta-
' tions, which they had begun upon the
' Neighbourhood. Her Husband,haſten-
' ed from his Employments abroad, unto
' the Relief of his Diſtreſſed Family ; and
' firſt bidding *Seven* of his *Eight* Children
' ( which were from Two to *Seventeen*
' years of age, ) to get away as faſt as
' they could, unto ſome Garriſon in the
' Town, he went in, to inform his Wiſe,
' of the horrible Diſtreſs now come upon
' them. E're ſhe could get up, the fierce
' *Indians* were got ſo near, that utterly deſ-
' pairing to do her any Service, he ran
' out after his Children ; Reſolving, that
' on the Horſe, which he had with him,
' he would Ride away, with *That*, which
' he ſhould in this Extremity find his Af-
' fections to pitch moſt upon, and leave
' the Reſt, unto the care of the Divine

D 3                                        ' Pro-

'Providence. He overtook his Children,
' about Forty Rod, from his Door ; but
' *them*, such was the *Agony* of his Parental
' Affections, that he found it Impoffible
' for him, to Diftinguish any one of them,
' from the Reft ; wherefore he took up
' a Courageous Refolution, to Live & Dy
' with them All.    A party of *Indians*
' came up with him ; and now, though
' they Fired at him, and he Fired at them,
' yet he manfully kept in the Reer of his
' *Little Army* of unarmed Children, while
' they March'd off, with the pace of a
' Child of Five years old ; until, by the
' Singular Providence of God, he arrived
' fafe with them all, unto a place of Safe-
' ty, about a Mile or two from his Houfe.
' But his Houfe muft in the mean Time,
' have more difmal *Tradegies* acted at it !
' The Nurfe, trying to Efcape, with the
' New born Infant, fell into the hands of
' the formidable Salvages ; & thofe furi-
' ous Tawnies, coming in to the Houfe, bid
' poor *Duftan*, to Rife immediately.  Full
' of Aftonifhment, fhe did fo ; and Sitt-
' ing down in the Chimney, with an heart
' full of moft fearful Expectation, fhe faw
' the Raging Dragons rifle all that they
                                                could

' could carry away : and set the House on
' Fire. About Nineteen or Twenty *In-*
' *dians,* now led these away, with about
' Half a score other, English *Captives* :
' but e're they had gone many Steps, they
' dash'd out the Brains of the *Infant,*against
' a Tree, and several of the other *Cap-*
' *tives,* as they begun to Tire in their sad
' Journey, were soon sent unto their long
' Home, but the Salvages would presently
' bury their Hatchets in their Brains, and
' leave their Carcases on the ground, for
' Birds & Beasts, to feed upon. [ Christians,
' A *Joshua* would have *Rent his Clothes, &*
' *fallen to the Earth on his Face,* and have
' *Humbled* himself Exceedingly upon the
' falling out of such doleful Ruines upon
' his Neighbours ! ] However, *Dustan*
' ( with her Nurse,) notwithstanding her
' present Condition, Travelled that Night,
' about a Dozen Miles ; and then kept
' up with their New Masters, in a long
' Travel of an Hundred and fifty Miles,
' more or less, within a few Dayes Ensu-
' ing ; without any sensible Damage, in
' their Health, from the Hardships, of
' their *Travel,* their *Lodging,* their *Diet,*
' and their many other Difficulties. These
' Two

'Two poor Women, were now in the Hands
'of those, *Whose Tender Mercies are Cruelty:*
'but the Good God, who hath all *Hearts*
'*in His own Hands,* heard the Sighs of
'these *Prisoners* unto Him, and gave them
'to find unexpected Favour, from the
'*Master,* who Laid claim unto them.
'That *Indian Family* consisted of Twelve
'persons, Two stout men, three women,
'and seven Children; and for the shame
'of many a *Prayerless Family* among our
'*English,* I must now publish what these
'poor women assure me; 'Tis *This;* In
'Obedience to the Instruction which the
'French have given them, they would
'have *Prayers* in their Family, no less
'than Thrice every Day; In the *Morn-*
'*ing,* at *Noon,* and in the *Evening;* nor
'would they ordinarily let so much as a
'Child, *Eat,* or *Sleep,* without first saying
'their *Prayers.* Indeed, these *Idolaters,*
'were, like the rest of their whiter Bre-
'thren *Persecuters,* and would not Endure
'that these poor *Women* should Retire to
'their *English Prayers,* if they could hin-
'der them. Nevertheless, the poor Wo-
'men, had nothing but fervent *Prayers,*
'to make their Lives comfortable. or
　　　　　　　　　　　'tolerable;

' tolerable ; and by being daily sent out,
' upon Business, they had opportunities
' together and asunder, to do like another
' *Hannah,* in *pouring out their Souls before*
' *the Lord* : Nor did their PrayingFriends
' among our selves, forbear to *pour out*
' Supplications for them. Now, they could
' not observe it, without some wonder,
' that their Indian Master, sometimes,
' when he saw them Dejected, would say
' unto them ; *What need you Trouble your*
' *self ? If your God will have you Delivered,*
' *you shall be so !* And it seems, our God,
' would have it so to be !

　　' This Indian Family, was now Tra-
' velling with these two Captive women,
' ( & an English Youth, taken from *Wor-*
' *cester,* last *September* was a Twelve month,)
' unto a Rendezvouze of Salvages, which
' they call a *Town,* somewhere beyond
' *Penacook* ; and they still told these poor
' women, that when they came to this
' Town, they must be Stript, & Scourg-
' ed, and Run the *Gantlet,* through the
' whole Army of *Indians.* They said,
' This was the *Fashion,* when the Captives
' first came to a Town ; and they deri-
' ded, some of the faint hearted English,
　　　　　　　　　　　　' which,

'which, they said, fainted and swooned
'away under the *Torments* of this Disci-
'pline.  [ Syrs, can we hear of these
'things befalling our Neighbours, & not
'*Humble* our selves before our God! ]
'But on this Day Se'night, while they
'were yet it may be, about an hundred
'and fifty miles from the Indian Town,
'a little before Break of Day, when the
'whole Crew, was in a *Dead Sleep*, ('twill
'presently prove so! ) One of these wo-
'men took up a Resolution, to Imitate
'the Action of *Jael* upon *Sisera*, and
'being where she had not her *own Life*
'secured by any *Law* unto her, she thought
'she was not forbidden by any *Law*, to
'take away the *Life*, of the *Murderers*,
'by whom her *Child* had been butchered.
'She heartened the *Nurse*, and the *Youth*,
'to assist her, in this Enterprise ; & they
'all furnishing themselves with *Hatchets*
'for the purpose, they struck such Home
'Blowes, upon the Heads of their *Sleep-
'ing Oppressors*, that e're they could any
'of them struggle into any effectual Re-
'sistance,  *at the Feet* of those poor Pri-
'soners, *They bowed, they fell, they lay
'down ; at their feet they bowed, they fell ;*
                        ' *where*

' *where they bowed, there they fell down*
' *Dead.* Onely one *Squaw* Escaped fore-
' ly wounded from them, and one *Boy,*
' whom they Reserved Asleep, intending
' to bring him away with them, suddenly
' wak'd and stole away, from this Deso-
' lation. But cutting off the Scalps of
' the *Ten Wretches,* who had Enslav'd 'em,
' they are come off; and I perceive, that
' newly arriving among us, they are in
' the Assembly at this Time, to give
' Thanks unto, *God their Saviour.*

[ *An Improvement of the foregoing*
*Narrative.* ]

IF we did now *Humble* our selves
throughout the Land, who can say,
whether the *Revenges on the Enemy,* thus
Exemplified, would not proceed much
rather unto the Quick Extirpation, of
those *Bloody and Crafty men.*

However, I may not Conclude, until I
have said Something unto YOU, that I
see, now stand before the Lord, in this
Assembly, the Subjects of such a Wonderful *Deliverance,* from your *Captivity ;* a
*Deliverance* which hath been Signalized
with

48 Humiliations follow'd

with such *Unusual Circumstances.* Words
that are spoken in an *Ordinance* of the
Lord Jesus Christ, carry with them a peculiar Efficacy and Authority. The
Lord Jesus Christ, hath by a Surprising
*Providence* of His, brought you this Day,
to wait upon Him, in that Great *Ordinance,* which is *His Power for the Salvation
of our Souls.* Hear a Servant of the Lord
JESUS CHRIST, in His Name, now
Publickly & Solemnly calling upon you,
to make a Right use of the *Deliverance,*
wherewith He ha's Highly favoured you.
The *Use,* which you are to make of it,
is, To *Humble* your selves before the
Lord Exceedingly. As you have had the
Extraordinary *Judgments* of God upon
you, to *Humble* you, so, Except His Extraordinary *Mercies* do likewise *Humble*
you, you do but Exceedingly *Abuse*
them : The *Rich Goodness of God unto you,*
is *to Lead you unto Repentance !*

When you were Carried into *Captivity,*
We did not say, *That you were greater
Sinners, than the rest that yet Escape it.*
You are now Rescued from *Captivity,*
and must not think, *That they are greater
Sinners, who are Left behind in the most*
barbarous

*barbarous Hands* imaginable. No, you, that have been under the *Mighty Hand of God*, are to *Humble* your selves, under that *Hand*. But if you do indeed so, I know, what you will do. You will seriously consider, *What you shall render to the Lord for all His Benefits?* And you will sincerely *Render* your very *Selves* unto the Lord. You are not now the Slaves of *Indians*, as you were a few Dayes ago ; but if you continue *Unhumbled*, in your Sins, you will be the Slaves of *Devils* ; and, Let me tell you, A Slavery to *Devils*, to be in *Their* Hands, is worse than to be in the Hands of *Indians! I beseech you then, by the Mercies of God, that you present your selves unto the Lord Jesus Christ* ; Become the sincere *Servants* of that Lord, who by His *Blood* has brought you out of the *Dungeon*, wherein you were lately Languishing ; *Oh! Deny not the Lord*, who has thus *Bought you*, out of your *Captivity*. I tell you truly, The Lord Expects great Returns of *Humiliation*, of *Thankfulness*, and of *Obedience*, from you ; and I therefore Leave with you, one Sentence of Scripture to be often

E thought

## 50  Humiliations follow'd &c.

thought upon; 'Tis That, in Exra 9. 13, 14. *After all that is come upon us, for our Evil Deeds, seeing thou, our God, hast given us such Deliverance as this, should we again break thy Commandments, wouldest thou not be angry with us, till thou hadst Consumed us?*

Now, Let all *Consider what hath been said, and the Lord give us Understanding in all things!*

Appendix

# Advice from TABERAH.

# A SERMON

### Preached
### After the Terrible

# FIRE,

Which, ( attended with Some very
Lamentable and Memorable cir-
cumstances, On *Oct.* 2, 3. 1711.)
Laid a Confiderable Part of BOSTON,
in Afhes.
Directing a Pious Improvement of Every
Calamity, but more Especially of fo
Calamitous a Defolation.

## By COTTON MATHER, D.D.

Numb. XI. 3.
*And he called the Name of the Place* TABERAH;
*becaufe the Fire of the Lord burnt among them.*

BOSTON in N. E. Printed by B. Green :
Sold by *Samuel Gerrifh,* at his Shop at the
Sign of the Buck over againft the South
Meeting-Houfe. 1 7 1 1.

# The Occasion.

**B**Eginning about Seven a Clock in the Evening, and Finishing before Two in the Morning, the Night between the *Second* and *Third* of *October*, 1 7 1 1. A terrible F I R E Laid the Heart of B O S T O N, the *Metropolis* of the *New-English America*, in Aſhes. The Occaſion of the *Fire*, is ſaid to have been, by the Carelesſnesſ and Sottiſh-neſs, of a Woman, who Suffered a Flame which took the Okum, the Picking whereof was her Buſineſs, to gain too far, before it could be maſtered. It was not long before it reduced *Corn-hill* into miſerable Ruines, and it made its impreſſions into *King-Street*, and *Queen-Street*, and a great Part of *Pudding-Lane* was alſo Loſt, before the Violence of it could be Conquered. Among theſe Ruines, there were Two Spacious *Edifices*, which until now, made a moſt Conſiderable Figure, becauſe of the Publick Relation to our greateſt Solemnities, in which they had ſtood from the Dayes of our Fathers. The One was, the TOWN-HOUSE: the Other, the

the OLD MEETING-HOUSE. The Number of Houses, and Some of them very Capacious Buildings, which went into the Fire, with these, is computed near about an hundred, and the *Families* which inhabited these Houses, cannot but be very many more. It being also a Place of much Trade, and fill'd with well-furnished Shops of Goods, not a little of the Wealth of the Town was now consumed. But that which very much added unto the Horror of the *Dismal Night*, was the Tragical *Death* of many Poor Men, who were killed, by the Blowing up of Houses; or by Venturing too far into the Fire, for the Rescue of what its fierce Jaws was ready to Prey upon. Of these, the Bones of Seven or Eight are thought to be found; and it is feared, there may be some Strangers, belonging to Vessels, besides these, thus buried, of whose unhappy circumstances we are not yet apprised; And others have since died of their Wounds.

Thus the Town of BOSTON, just going to get beyond *Fourscore years* of Age, and conflicting with much *Labour* and *Sorrow*, is, a very Vital and Valuable part of it, *Soon Cut off and flown away* !

A 2 And

## The Occasion.

And yet in the midst of these *Lamentations* we may say; *Tis of the Lords Mercies, that we are not Consumed.* Had not the Glorious Lord who has *gathered the Wind in His Hands*, Mercifully kept under the *Wind* at this Time, *He* alone knows, how much more of the Town must have been *Consumed*!

A Great Auditory of the Inhabitants, with many from the Neighbouring Towns, coming together, on the Ensuing *Thursday*, that they might hear the *Instructions of Piety*, which might suit the present & grievous Occasion : One of the Ministers, who is also a *Native*, of the Town, entertained them with the Ensuing *Sermon*, which is now by the way of the Press, made a more Durable, and a more Diffusive MEMORIAL, of a Divine Dispensation, which may not quickly be Forgotten.

I remember, *Dion Cassius* relates an odd circumstance attending the Burning of Mount *Vesuvius* ; *Quod clangor Tubarum audiretur.* If we may devoutly apprehend the *Trumpets* of God, Sounding to us from the *Fire*, wherein we have seen so much of *Boston* burned, the Essay before us, is that they may not *give an uncertain Sound* ; that the Voice thereof may be Articulate and Intelligible.

The

# The Voice of GOD, Crying to the City.

At a Lecture, held in the *South-Meeting-House*, of BOSTON. 4 *d.* 8 *m.* 1711.

### Jeremiah V. 3.

*Lord, Thou haft Confumed them, but they have refufed to receive Correction.*

OUR *Eyes*, which ought to *Affect* our *Hearts*, have newly been Entertained with a very *difmal Spectacle*. Our *Cares*, and Oh, how *Hearty* ones *!* muft now be, that it be not followed, with a much *more difmal* one. Such a *Spectacle* there is, very Frequent in the World. And *fuch* an One it is, that the *Text* now-read, complaineth of.

The *Weeping Prophet*, had Preached unto a People, very *Obftinate* in their Wandrings from God. It is a very Emphatical and Pathetical Rebuke upon their Obftinacy, that he turns from *Them*,

to

2      *The Voice of G O D,*

to GOD. *They* were, it feems, no longer to be
Spoken to. It Seems in vain, to Speak unto
*Them* any more. He *Pours out His Complaint un-*
*to GOD* ; Yea, *He Mourns in His Complaint and*
*makes a Noife* : That they were an *Incorrigi-*
*ble People.* Behold, the Difcovery of their being
fo !

Firft. We have the *Condition* of the People.
They were *Stricken* of God ; Yea, *Confuming*
*Strokes* were difpenfed unto them.

Secondly ; We have their *Behaviour* in this
Condition. Tis a flaming *Impenitency.* There
are Two Expreffions of it. Firft ; *They have*
*not grieved.* That is, with a *Godly Sorrow that*
*works Repentance.* This was the Αναλγησια, the
*Indolence,* into which they were Stupified. O-
therwife, no doubt, as *Calvin* fayes, They felt
the Plagues of Heaven, with Grief and Pain E-
nough, and cried out of their Afflictions. Tis
the very fame that is elfe-where called, *A being*
*Smitten in Vain.*

Secondly ; *They have refufed to receive Correction.*
That is, They were not mended, by the Blows
wherewith God had corrected them : To *receive*
*Correction,* is, as it has been of old Paraphrafed ;
*Ex Tribulatione Proficere, emendando mores ;* To
mend our Manners upon *Correction.* The want
of fuch a *Senfibility* is here propounded, as a very
deplorable Thing. Even an Aphorifm of *Hip-*
*pocrates* will tell you, when men have no fenfe of
their Painful circumftances, *Certum eft Signum men-*
*tem ægrotare,* the Mind is deplorably diftempered.

                    The

The DOCTRINE which I am now to bring unto you, I do not only bring from the 𝕿𝖊𝖝𝖙 which I have read among you, but also from the midſt of the Devouring Flames, which a few Hours ago ſo dreadfully *Conſumed* our Neighbourhood. Sirs, *Our God has come,* and *has not kept Silence,* when the *Fire Devoured* before Him. I am now to *Repeat* what the *Mighty God,* the Lord hath Spoken, in the Deſolation wherein ſo many Perſons and Eſtates, were the Night before laſt, ſo horribly *Conſumed.* My *Sermon* is but a *Repetition ;* It is the Thundring Voice of our Glorious GOD, that is to be heard over again ; in the Operation of this 𝕯𝖔𝖈𝖙𝖗𝖎𝖓𝖊 at this time among you.

> *It is a very Sad Character, and it will be of a very Sad Conſequence, for men, to have the Strokes of Affliction thrown away in Vain upon them ; to be Conſumed with Afflictive Strokes of God, and be nothing the better for them.*

It is a very ſad thing, when a People are ſo to be complained of : Jer. II. 30. *In vain have I Smitten your Children, they have received no Correction.* A very ſad thing, when it may be complained of a Perſon ; 2 Chron. XXVIII. 22. *In the time of his Diſtreſs, did he Treſpaſs yet more againſt the Lord.* My Hearers, Be attentive to theſe things ! To *Suffer much Evil,* and *Get no Good* by it ; This is a very Sad Thing ! A Sad Thing it is, when any *Means of Good,* are loſt upon men ;

A

4                      *The Voice of GOD,*

A very Sad Thing, When *Evil* is inflicted on them for their Good, and yet they *Get no Good.* It is a thing that has a very fad Aspect upon us, when the *Words* of God, have no Good Effect upon us. But when from *Words,* He comes to *Blows,* and thefe alfo do us *no Good,* This has the Saddeft Afpect of all. If we are not the *Better* for *Prosperity,* we are very *Bad.* It looks very *Ill,* when *Good Things* do us *no Good.* But then, it may be *worfe* upon Some Accounts, if we are not the *Better* for *Adverfity* neither. To undergo much *Evil,* and be no Gainers by it ; Oh ! It is Lamentable ! It is Lamentable !

> We are to Enquire; Firft ; *Who are they, that have the Strokes of Affliction thrown away in Vain upon them ?* Who, they *that when they are Confumed, refufe to receive Correction ?*

*I.* When *Afflictive Strokes,* do not Cure a man of his *Miftakes,* but leave the *Follies* of a carnal Mind uncured in him ; Then the Strokes are *in Vain, in Vain* ! thrown away upon him. He *receives not Correction,* when his miftakes are not *Corrected* by His Affliction. Truly, Sirs, The *Strokes* of God have Afflicted you in Vain, if under and after much Affliction, you take up no *Truer Apprehenfion* of Things, than you had before. Affliction, tho' we call *Sorrow* by the Name of *Darknefs,* yet comes to *Enlighten* us. We read, Prov. XXIX. 15. *The Rod and Reproof give Wifdom.* If we are no *Wifer* for being Afflicted, then we
are

are no *Better* for it. The *Strokes* which *Correct* us
and *Consume* us, are thrown away upon us. Our
*Correction* is for our *Instruction.* We read, Pſal.
XCIV. 12. *Bleſſed is the man, whom thou Chaſtneſt, O
Lord, and Teacheſt him out of thy Law.* The *Strokes*
given to us in our Affliction, are to *Awaken* us
out of our *Dreams.* If we Dream on Still, and
have our *Vain Thoughts Lodged in us,* then, *My
Strokes are in Vain thrown away upon them ; they re-
fuſe to receive Correction,* Saith the Lord. Thus
the matter lies. The *Miſtakes* of a *Carnal Mind,*
are Many, are Deadly. A Carnal mind makes
Light of Sin ; The *Fool makes a mock at Sin.* A
Carnal mind will hope and graſp for Happineſs
in Earthly Enjoyments. It *Minds Earthly Things.*
A Carnal mind has a mean Opinion of Zeal in
Religion. It is no Friend unto Zealous Dili-
gence, *Always abounding in work for the Lord.* An
Afflicted Perſon, yet Continuing under ſuch
miſtakes of a *Carnal mind ;* Such an one moſt
certainly is nothing the better for his Affliction.
*This World* is nothing but *Vanity.* The *Grand
miſtake* of men, is that they will not reckon it ſo.
The *Strokes* of Affliction, are *in Vain* thrown away
upon us, if we are not Convinced of this
miſtake ; if the *World* appear not unto us, all
*Vanity.* Tis *Vanity* and *Vexation.* Our *Vexation* is
in *Vain,* if we are not brought thereby to ſee the
*Vanity.* There is a *Vain mind* The Afflicted
muſt be reſcued from the Follies of a *Vain mind,*
Elſe Afflictive Strokes are thrown away in *Vain*
upon him. O you *Stricken of God, and Afflicted ;*
B It

6       *The Voice of GOD,*

It is all in *Vain*, if you don't come now to see
all things, just as the *Word* of God has represented
them. You must be able to say ; ' *Before I was*
' *afflicted I went astray* ; but NOW, I see *Sin* is
' Odious ; NOW, I see *Christ* is Precious ; Now,
' I see *this World* must not be my Resting place ;
' NOW I see, that I am a Poor, Frail, Vile Crea-
' ture ; NOW, I see, that the *Salvation of my Soul,*
' is the main Thing I am to be Concerned
' about. All the *Strokes* are in vain, I say, *All in*
*Vain !* if your Thoughts are not thus *Rectified* ; if
you do not come to these *Right Thoughts of the*
*Righteous !*

II. When *Afflictive Strokes* do not *Reform* a man,
but such Evil Practices as it found him in, remain still unreformed ; then, *In Vain, In Vain !*
are the Strokes thrown away upon him. He is
*Corrected,* that he may be *Reformed* ; he *refuseth to*
*receive Correction,* till he be so. Afflictive Strokes
come with a *Message* from God ; The Message
and Language of them, is, *Repent, O Sinful Man,*
*Repent of thy Miscarriages !* *In vain* are those Afflictive Strokes Employ'd upon us, which do not
bring us to *Repentance.* Of *Affliction* we read ;
Isa. XXVII. 9. *By this, Iniquity shall be Purged, and*
*all the Fruit is to take away Sin.* We are not the
*Better* for Afflictive Strokes, if our *Iniquity* be not
*Purged,* and our *Sin taken away* ; if we come not
*as Gold out of the Fire* : Not the *Better,* if not im-
proved in *Goodness.* Our Comforts are *Consumed,*
altogether *in Vain,* if our *Corruptions* be not also
*Consumed.* Our *Sins* make Affliction to be so

                        Need-

*Needful* for us; that there is *Need* we fhould be *in Heavineß.* But it is *in Vain* thrown away upon us, if we are not brought thereby, to *Mourn* for our *Sins*, to *Turn* from our *Sins*, to loath 'em with a growing Deteftation. Thus we read ; Job XXXIV. 31, 32. *Surely, It is meet to be faid unto God, I have born Chaftifement, I will not Offend any more. That which I fee not, Teach thou me ; if I have done Iniquity, I will do no more.* Among the *Ifraelites*, while they *Scourged* a Malefactor, there were certain Portions and Leffons of the *Law*, Read unto him. Under the *Scourges* of God, the Leffons and Maxims of His *Law*, are to be laid before us ; and we muft *Reform* our Violations of it. If we have committed any *Trespaß*, our Affliction muft bring us to fay, *I am Sorry for my Trespaß ! I will not go on ftill in it !* If we have Omitted any *Duty*, our Affliction muft bring us to fay, *I will no longer Neglect my Duty; I will Perform it, as foon and as well as I can !* Tis all thrown away *in Vain*, if *this* be not the iffue of it. *Stricken in Vain* is that man, whofe Affliction does not bring him to an *Amendment* of his ways : *To no Purpofe!* Except it bring a Man to *Purpofe* more Piety, than has been in his former wayes. It muft *Work* at this rate, ' Since the Holy One hath been *Striking* of me, I will be more Afraid of *Sinning* a-
' gainft Him than formerly. I will be more
' weaned from the *Love of the World*, fince I find
' it fuch an *Evil World.* Since I have fuch an
' *Afflicted* Life, it fhall be a more *Prayerful*, a more
' *Fruitful*, a more *Heavenly* Life ; A Life of more

' Com-

8 *The Voice of GO D,*

' Communion with God. My Friend ; *Hear the Rod* ; Thou doft not *Receive Correction*, if the Rod be not heard. And, This, This, is the Cry of it !

*III.* My Third Article, in my Proceeding to find out the Delinquents, will be alfo an *Inference* from the Premifes. *Afflictive Strokes* are beftow'd *in Vain* on *them*, and they *refufe to receive Correction*, who after their *Affliction* remain ftill in their *Unregeneracy.* Every *Unregenerate* is led away with the *Miftakes* & *Follies* of a *Carnal Mind.* Every *Unregenerate* Reforms not, but *Retains,* many *Evil Practices. Therefore!* it follows, That the *Afflicted* who continue *Unregenerate,* may have that charge brought in againft them. *God ftrikes them, and they are not grieved ; He confumes them, and they refufe to receive Correction* ! We read, Pfal. CXIX. 71. *It is Good for me, that I have been Afflicted, that I might learn thy Statutes.* An *Unregenerate* has not *Learn't the Statutes* of God ; he *Knows* them not, he *Loves* them not, he *Does* them not. Therefore, 'tis *not Good for him, that he has been Afflicted ;* he has got *no Good* by his Affliction. My Hearers, call your felves to a ftrict Account. You have had *Afflictive Strokes* laid upon you ; you have been *Confumed* with them. Can you fay ? *I am a New Creature! Since I have been Afflicted, I am quite another Creature, than what I was before !* Are you now able to fay ; ' Since my ' *Affliction,* I find, That I am come into the *Cove-* ' *nant* of God, and of His Grace ; that I have ' confented unto all the Propofals of it. I find,
' That

## Crying to the City.

' That I have Embraced a Precious CHRIST
' in all His Offices, and made sure of all His Be-
' nefits. I find, That all my *Sins* are become A-
' bominable to me ; and that every thing that
' Saves me from my Sins, is therefore so far
' Acceptable to me. I can Bless God, in that He
' has Afflicted me ! If thou art still a Stranger
to these Attainments, Ah, my Afflicted Neighbour, Thou art yet in thy Sins. Unregenerate,
*In Vain* ! *In Vain,* hast thou been *Stricken* ! *Consumed,* but not *received Correction* ! O Sad Condition ! O Condition of One Sitting *in Darkness,
and in the Shadow of Death* !

But the Sadness of it, is what we now proceed
unto.

We are to Enquire, Secondly. *Wherein appears the Sadness of the Character and the Consequence, of being so Incorrigible under Afflictive
Strokes ; Consumed, but refusing to receive Correction* ?

I desire to know, first of all ; Whether a *Thief
on a Cross,* Rejecting, Reviling, Blaspheming the
only Saviour, were not a *Sad Spectacle* ; and what
became of him ? Why, This is the case now
before us. But it must be further answered.

I. A *Divine Husbandry* is defeated, yea, a *Divine Patience* is affronted in it, when *Afflicted* People prove *Incorrigible.* The Great God may Reasonably expect this from those that are under the
Afflictive Strokes of His Hand ; Zeph. III. 7. *I
said, Surely, Thou wilt fear me, thou wilt receive Instruction.*

*ſtruction.* Who is there willing to *Labour in Vain!* Affliction imploy'd upon an *Incorrigible* Sinner, is *Labour in Vain;* And yet it is the *Labour of Hea-ven* about the Sinner. The *Incorrigible* do their worſt, that God may *Strike in Vain,* and fail of His juſt Expectation. When we are under Af-fliction, we are under the *Husbandry* of God. It is a Digging, and a Dunging, and a Pruning ; an hopeful *Cultivation* that is imploy'd upon us. Oh ! That you were ſenſible of This ! Every Affliction upon us, is the Fulfilment of that word ; Joh. XV. 1, 2. *My Father is the Husband-man ; Every branch that beareth Fruit, He Purgeth it, that it may bring forth more Fruit.* In the mean time, the *Patience* of God, waits to ſee the Fruits of His *Husbandry.* Yea, *The Lord waits that He may be Gracious.* Inſtead of *Afflicting* us, the Holy God might juſtly have *Deſtroyed* us. We have deſer-ved nothing leſs than Total and Final *Deſtruc-tion ;* the *Deſtruction from God,* which may be a *Terror* to us. There is the *Patience* of a Good God Exerciſed in every *Affliction* upon us. God is Exerciſing of His *Patience,* while He puts us on the Exerciſe of ours. Oh ! that the *Afflicted* were duely *Affected* with it ! Is it a *Night of Affliction* with thee ? Child, It is a *Day of Patience* with thee. It may be ſaid, as 'tis in 1 Pet. III. 20. *The Long-ſuffering of God has Waited.* Well ; But now, ſhould this *Husbandry* be defeated : Should this *Patience* be affronted ? *Affliction* upon a Man, and he not the *Better* for it, is, in ſhort, *The Waſhing of the Ethiopian.* But is it not a Sad Thing, that the

Great

*Crying to the City.*  II

Great GOD ſhould be put upon ſuch a Thing? *Judge, I Pray you, between me and my Vineyard, ſayes the Lord?* He is Diſpleaſed ; and ſo does He Speak in His *Diſpleaſure.*

*II.* What are the *Cauſes* of it? Of *Incureablenefs* and *Unreformablenefs* under Afflictive Strokes from Heaven : They are very Sad Ones. When People *Get no Good* by Affliction, there are *no Good Cauſes* to be aſſigned, for their being ſo Incorrigible. Firſt, It proceeds from a Vile *Atheiſm* in the Heart. *The Fool ſaith in his Heart,* His Affliction is not from GOD ; GOD never ſent it upon him. This is to ſay, *There is no God.* If People did believe, That they have to do with GOD, when they have *Afflictive Strokes* laid upon them, their Affliction would make them Turn to GOD, Fly to GOD. We read, Job V, 6, 8. *Affliction comes not forth of the Duſt, nor doth Trouble ſpring out of the Ground. I would ſeek unto GOD.* If men do not *Seek unto GOD* in their Affliction, as they will do, if they be not *Incorrigible,* 'tis becauſe they believe, it only *Comes forth of the Duſt,* it only *Springs out of the Ground*; They look no Higher than *Second Cauſes.* Again ; There is a *Stupidity* of Soul in this Wretchedneſs ; A worſe than *Brutal* Stupidity. The *Bruit* will mend his Pace, for the *Whip.* Ah, worſe than *Bruitiſh* Impenitent ; Thou doſt it not. A *Beaſt* that has *felt* the Fire, will *dread* the Fire. The Sinner not the better for Affliction, runs into the *Fire,* and cares not tho' he ly there. So we read ;

Iſa,

Ifa. XLII. 25. *He hath Poured upon him the Fury of His Anger, and it hath fet him on Fire round about; yet he knew it not; and it hath burned him, yet he laid it not to heart.* Once more ; It argues, that *Sin* is very dear to a Man, when *Affliction* won't compel him to part with his *Sin.* To be afflicted in One Interest, and then Perhaps in Another ; but still, to *Sin on!* Tis an Argument, that *Sin* is more beloved by these People, than that *Interest* in which they are afflicted. We read, 1 King XVI. 34. *Hiel the Bethlite, built Jericho ; He laid the Foundation thereof in his First-born, and set up the Gates thereof in his Youngest Son.* There was a Curse to befal him that should Rebuild the *Walls* of *Jericho* ; ( For to *that,* I Suppose the Curse confined: ) *Maimonides* notes, *This Anathema was pronounced, that the Miracle of the falling and sinking of the Walls of that City by an Earthquake, might be kept in Perpetual Memory. For whoever saw the Walls sunk into the Earth, would clearly discern that it was not the Form of a Building destroy'd by men, but miraculously thrown down by God.* Hiel would persist in Rebuilding these Walls, tho' it cost him the Lives of all his Children, one after another. His Ambition was dearer to him than the *Lives* of all his Children. *Sin* is dearer to the Afflicted and Unmended Sinner, than all those *Enjoyments,* which his Affliction falls upon. O *Confirmed* Wickedness ! O *Confummate* Wickedness !" Finally ; The Dominion of *Satan* has a Sad Influence in the matter. If People are not *Bettered* by Affliction, or *turned from Darkness to Light,*

*Light,* 'tis becaufe they are under the *Power of Satan.* If People in Affliction are ftill *Enflaved* unto their *Lufts,* it is becaufe they are *Led Captive by Satan to do his Will.* When People in the *Chains of Affliction,* have the *Chains of their Sins* lying ftill upon them, *Satan* holds them in thofe heavy, iron, direful *Chains.* Alas, Is it poffible to be more fadly circumftanced *!*

*III.* What will be the *Effects* of it ? Of being *Incurable,* and *Unreformable,* under thefe Afflictive Strokes ? They cannot but be very Sad Ones. One Effect will be This. If the *Affliction* which you already Endure, Do you *no Good,* you may look for *more Affliction to come.* Thus we read; Ifa. I. 5. *Why fhould ye be Stricken any more ? Ye will Revolt more and more.* You fhall be *Stricken more,* if after you are Stricken, you will *Revolt* ftill, and Rebel more and more. Yea, The Threatenings of God Speak of fuch a thing as this, for them, who being Afflicted, Go on in a Sinful walk ; *I will go on, and Punifh you yet Seven times for your Sins.* Thus, While the Lord in a way of Special Difpenfation, held the *Leprofy,* as a *Peculiar Scourge* in His Hand, for the People in the *Holy Land,* this was no rare thing ; Firft He fmote a Mans *Houfe* with the *Leprofy* : [ a Plague unknown in our Dayes! ] If the man went on in Sin, He came nearer, and Smote his *Clothes* with the *Leprofy.* If the man ftill went on, He came nearer ftill, and Smote his *Flefh* with the *Leprofy.* He was then chafed out from the Con-

C gre-

gregation of God !  A Sad Progreſs of Calamity !
Be ſure, If you do belong to God, *Affliction* muſt
then Do you *Good*.  And, I Pray take a due Notice of it.  *If One Affliction won't, another ſhall* !
God will *go on* Afflicting of you, till He has
broke your *Wills*, and brought your Hearts to
be *after His own Heart*.  Look for it, O Children
of God ; Children, *Whom He Loves, and therefore
will Rebuke and Chaſten* !  But then, Another Effect will be this.  If no Affliction in *This World*
will do People any Good, what can Succeed, but
the horrible Puniſhment in *Another World* ?  A
*Strange Puviſhment* for the Obdurate *Workers of Iniquity* ; A Strange one, and a Sad one !  To be
ſo ſet upon Ungodlineſs, as to be Reduced by no
*Afflictive Strokes* !  Oh ! Tis a Black Mark !  It
proclames an Hideous *Hardneß of Heart*.  So,
when we read, *They have refuſed to receive Correction*, it follows, *They have made their Faces harder than a Rock; they have refuſed to return*.  I will
fetch one Stroke more at the *Rock*, with telling
you ; There is a Strong Scent of the Fire and
Brimſtone of the Devouring Pit, in this *Obdura-
tion* !  The *Lion* ſhall roar, and, Sinners, will not
you *Tremble* at it ?  I am to tell you a dreadful
Thing.  There cannot be a blacker Mark of
*Reprobation*, than to be afflicted many ways for
your Sins, and after all, to remain *Incorrigible*.
We read, Rom. II. 5. *After thy Hardneſs and Impenitent Heart, thou treaſureſt up unto thy ſelf Wrath
againſt the day of Wrath, and Revelation of the Righteous Judgment of God*.  It ſhows a fearful *Hardneß*
*of*

*of Heart*, when People are *Impenitent* under Affliction. And, O *Impenitent*, what art thou doing ? *Treasuring up wrath against the Day of wrath* ?
Ripening, Ripening for the everlasting Vengeance of God. A *Pharaoh*, that *hardens his Heart*,
and is nothing the better for all the Plagues of
God upon him ; what becomes of him ? He is a
*Vessel of Wrath ;* a *Vessel fitted for Destruction*. And
it comes upon him ! O my Poor Friend, Be-
ware, Beware, Lest all thy *Affliction*, be only the
*Prison*, the *Dungeon*, the uneasy *Fetters*, of a Malefactor, to be afterwards brought forth unto an
astonishing Execution ; To *be burnt Alive* !

## A P P L I C A T I O N.

But now, Let them that are *Consumed*, or in
any measure *Visited*, with the *Afflictive Strokes* of
Heaven, hearken to the Counsils of God.

*I.* And, first, there is a more *General* Addrefs
to be made, and Advice to be giv'n, unto *All* the
Auditory, and with regard unto *All* the Affliction
that has been ever undergone, by every one in
the Auditory. Oh ! See that it be not all *Thrown
away in Vain* upon you ! There are enow of us
that may fay with him ; Lam. III. 1. *I am the
man that have feen Affliction by the Rod of His wrath.*
But, where, Oh, where is the man that can fay,
*I have got all the Good, that I should have got by my
Affliction !* It was a Good Speech of a Good
Man ; *'Tis a Great Lofs to Lofe an Affliction.* Truly,

16      *The Voice of GOD,*

Tis a Time of Affliction ; we are Afflicted with many Losses.  I am afraid, I am afraid, That of all our *Losses,* this is the moft *Common ;* tho' it be of all the moft *Woful* one ; To *Lose the Benefit, which we should have got by our Affliction.*  Tis to be feared, that this word, 𝕮𝖔𝖓𝖘𝖚𝖒𝖊𝖉, 𝖇𝖚𝖙 𝖗𝖊𝖋𝖚𝖘𝖎𝖓𝖌 𝖙𝖔 𝖗𝖊𝖈𝖊𝖎𝖛𝖊 𝕮𝖔𝖗𝖗𝖊𝖈𝖙𝖎𝖔𝖓, does too much defcribe the *General Case* of our People. *I am diftreffed* for you, my Brethren, *I am diftreffed* for you !  What ?  Meet with fuch Sad Things, and Get no Good by them ?  Yea, meet with *Sad Things* here, and, O Unregenerates, Meet with *Worfe Things* hereafter !  No Tongue is able to exprefs the Sadnefs of fuch a cafe.  But, My Neighbours, If you have hitherto *Loft* your Affliction, I am now come unto you with Methods to fetch up your *Loffes* !

I Prefs thefe things upon you.

Firft.  We cannot be Satisfied, Except you Every One of you *Examine* your felves, *What Good have I gained by my Affliction ?*  O you, *Afflicted and toffed with Tempeft ;* I come to you with this demand ; Hag. I. 5. *Thus faith the Lord of Hofts, Confider your Wayes.*  Confider and Examine, *Whether* after all the *Affliction* that has been upon you, You are yet Converted unto God ; or, yet *Children of Wrath ?*  After all the *Bitternefs* of your Affliction, yet in the *Gall of Bitternefs !*  After all the *Bonds* your Affliction has laid upon you, yet in the *Bonds of Iniquity !*  Confider and Examine ; *Whether* you are at all advanced in *Piety* by your *Affliction ?*  More Fervent in
*Pray'r ?*

Pray'r ? More Wean'd from *Earth* ? More Fit for
*Heav'n* ? And more *Fruitful in every Good Work* ?
My Friend ; Haft thou been *Sick* and *Weak ;* but
no Health of *Mind,* no Strength of *Grace,* attain'd
by thy Sickneſs & Weakneſs ? Has *Death* ſnatched
away thy neareſt Relatives ; and art thou not
Prepared the more for thy own *Death* ? Has thy
Family had *Coffins* in it ; and has thy Family yet
no *Prayers* in it ? Haft thou met with *Loſs* upon
*Loſs ;* and art thou not a jot the more ſolicitous,
that thy *Soul* may not be *Loſt* ? Haft thou been a
*Captive* with the Enemy ; and is thy *Soul* ſtill in
Captivity to thy *Sin,* and to the *Powers of Dark-*
*neſs* ? Oh ! Put the Queſtion. Be not put off
without a *Certain Anſwer* to the Queſtion !

But, Secondly ; If this be your Condition, that
you can tell of, *no Good gain'd by your Affliction ;*
Oh, be afraid of going on ſtill in ſuch a Condition ; of *Going on ſtill in your Treſpaſſes :* God will
*Wound* them who do ſo ! I beſeech you, to deprecate Exceedingly, that forlorn Brand; Prov.
XXVII. 22. *Bray a Fool in a Mortar, yet will not his*
*Fooliſhneſs depart from him.* That you may be de-
livered from it ; Firſt, Conſider the *Errand* of
every Affliction. Beg of the Glorious One ; Job
X. 2. *O ſhew me, wherefore thou Contendeſt with me !*
Hereupon, Set your ſelves to think ; *What does this*
*come for ? Good* is already got, if you are got thus
far. And it will ſoon lead you to *more Good.*
The Next Thing you have to do, is, To *Repent*
of the Miſcarriages, for which you have been
Chaſtiſed of the Lord. So tis required ; Rev.
III. 19.

18 *The Voice of GOD*,

**III.** 19. *I Rebuke and Chaften ; Be Zealous therefore and Repent.* And then, Finally ; Endeavour to Comply with the Demands of a *Better Carriage.* But in fo doing, Let your Compliance carry as much of *Suitableness* to your Affliction as may be   There may be fuch *Signatures* upon your Affliction, as may carry *fpecial Intimations* in them. Sleight not fuch *fpeaking Intimations.* In fhort, Be more Sollicitous to *get Good* by Affliction, than to *get Out* of Affliction. Oh, Be Reftlefs, till you can fay, of whatever Affliction comes upon you ; *I am a Gainer by this Affliction! A Sanctified Affliction;* Oh! My Brethren, You will Blefs God for it, unto Eternal Ages.

*II.* But it is now Time for us to beftow our more *Particular Thoughts* on a very *Sad Occafion;* which among other Circumftances, ha's altered this Day, the very *Place* of our Affembly.

Methinks, I find my felf Preaching a 𝕱𝖚𝖓𝖊𝖗𝖆𝖑 𝕾𝖊𝖗𝖒𝖔𝖓, for that ancient and famous EDIFICE, which had from the Dayes of our Grand-fathers [ I fuppofe, *mine* Preach'd the firft Sermon in it, Sixty five or fix years ago! ] been the Place of our moft confiderable Solemnities. *Ah Lord, The Houfe wherein our Fathers praifed thee, is burnt up with Fire!* May we all, even with a Strain unto the very uttermoft of our Ability, in our Liberality on Pious Ufes, do all that is poffible, as foon as we can, to Raife that *Edifice* out of its Afhes. Tis not the *Bereaved Church* a-lone, but the whole Town, that owe their Li-
<br>beral

beral Contributions unto such a Service of GOD.

In the mean time, and even before I mention the *Improvements,* which I shall presently propose, to be made of the *Confuming Stroke,* wherewith our God ha's newly afflicted us, I will say Two Things, upon that Article of our being driven out this Day, from that most Memorable of all the *Synagogues of God in the Land.*

The *First* is; That the Holy One seems to put us in mind of that Shameful Negligence, with which too many People in this Town treated the Weekly *Lecture* there. I might say unto you, It was not attended, as it ought to have been. And God calls the Town this Day to be Humbled for it.

The *Second* is; That the Well-affected People, who did frequent the *Lecture,* Should now call to mind the Holy *Instructions* which they heard inculcated in it. Oh! *Remember what you have received and heard,* in that House; Call to mind what you have been Exhorted unto, and be humbled for all Unfruitfulness.

I could not pass by the Honourable Rubbish of that Building, without making these *Two Reflections.*

But I proceed now to urge for this Thing. A most *Confuming Stroke* of God has been upon us. The Glorious GOD ha's *Corrected* us, and very dreadfully *Confumed* us. The *Ruines* brought upon us, are very Dreadful ones, and not Easily or Speedily to be repaired, That among these
awful

awful Ruines, both our 𝔖tate-𝔋oufe, and
the 𝔉irᵴt-boᵲn of our 𝔐eeting-𝔋oufes,
are made a Defolation ; Verily, it looks awfully enough, to make one cry out, *God Avert the
Omen !* The Great GOD ha's fired a couple of
*Becons,*which call the whole Province to takeNo-
tice of them ; and toConfider, how far they may
be*Alarms* to us,in regard of our greateft Interefts.
Unhappy we, Oh ! moft unhappy ! If after we
have been fo long *Incorrigible,* we ftill *refufe to
receive Correction.* Oh! Let our Behaviour be
that of a People duely *Awakened* by the *Confuming* Difpenfations of God. If the *Fire* will
not *Awaken* us, what will ? God forbid that it
fhould be faid of us, *I have overthrown fome of
you by Fire, and the reft of you are as a Fire-brand
pluck'd out of the Burning, yet have ye not returned
unto me, faith the Lord.* God forbid, that it fhould
be faid ; *Lord, when thy hand is lifted up, they will
not fee, but go on, till the Fire that belongs to thine
Enemies fhall devour them!* Oh ! Let us *Glorify
the Lord in the Fires ;* and while we are yet fo much
in the *Heat* thereof as to receive Impreffion, [ For,
but *One Day* has paffed fince the *Fire !* ] Hearken
to the Voice of God ; Hearken to thofe things, at
which, O *Cold Hearts* indeed, if our *Hearts* do not
*burn within us !*

    Firft, We fhould Serioufly *Examine,* Whether
the 𝔖ins, which ufe to be Punifhed with *Confuming Fires,* are not fo found among us, as to call
for a very Deep Repentance. Verily, As we
pafs along, by the adjacent *Ruines,* we may make
the

the Remark, and the Outcry, which the Devout Spectator of thofe in *Germany* did ; *Hic fu-*
*it Iniquitas !* -- Behold the *Mifchiefs* & *Ruines* that
our *Sins* have brought upon us. The *Ruines*
which have now come on *the Heart* of this Town,
and by confequence *the Heart* of the whole Province, do feem to flafh thefe Rebukes in our
Faces, *Thy Way & thy Doings have procured thefe things*
*unto thee ; this is thy Wickednefs,becaufe it is bitter, be-*
*caufe it reacheth unto thine Heart.* God has rendred his
*Rebukes* in the *Flames* of this *Fire.* Oh, be In-
quifitive into the Controverfy : Tis true, all
*Wickednefs* does *burn like Fire ;* and will *bring a*
*Fire.* But there are fome forts of *Wickednefs,*
which are peculiarly branded by God, as the
*Burners* of the Places in which they are practifed and indulged.

I will deal Faithfully. *Profanations* of the *Sab-*
*bath,* I am to tell you, They are *Burning Abomi-*
*nations.* He that of old forbad His people to
Kindle a *Fire* on the *Sabbath-day,* fometimes
does kindle a *Fire,* to Revenge our *Profanations*
of the *Sabbath-day.* It comes from the *Secret*
*place of Thunder,* and is *It,* what we read. Jer. XVII.
25. *If ye will not hearken unto me, to Sanctify the*
*Sabbath-day, and not to bear a Burden on the Sabbath*
*day ; Then will I kindle a Fire, and it fhall devour*
*the Palaces of Jerufalem, and it fhall not be quenched.*
Some Late Things among our felves have made
that Scripture very much to run in the minds
of fome Servants of God ; They told us, *They*
*fear'd a terrible Accomplifhment !*

**D** Again ;

22     *The Voice of GOD,*

Again; The Neglect of *Divine Worship*; A *Fire* sometimes breaks forth upon them that are Guilty of it. It is an observable passage, Amos V. 6. *Seek the Lord, lest he break forth like Fire, in the House of Joseph, and devour it.* *Prayerless Houses,* My Friends, You must not wonder at it, if they lay a whole Neighbourhood in Ashes. And if the *Houses of God* are not visited, no wonder if God also take them away, together with ours, and Lay them in Ashes. If men *break the Everlasting Covenant,* and slight the Ordinances of it ; Can you wonder, that a Fiery *Curse devours* them ? Our Bible tells of such a thing.

Yet more ; *Dishonesty* in Dealings ; God by *Fire* often makes very just *Reprisals* upon it. The passage is worthy to be observed : Job XX. 19, 26. *Because he hath Oppressed, and hath forsaken the poor, because he hath violently taken away an House, which he builded not ; A Fire not blown shall consume him.* For men to *Engross* what they ought not, & *Possess* what is none of their own ; 'tis to carry *Burning Coals* into their *Nests.* The Justice of God makes *Fiery Confiscations* on them. And, I pray, what befals the *Tabernacles of Bribery?*

Once more ; The Crimes of *Intemperance* and *Unchastity*; they plunge men into *Eternal Burnings* ; and sometimes also into *Temporal.* In *Drunkenness,* men *Drown* themselves. Their Doom has a kind of *Antiperistasis* in it ; God *Burns* them for it. I am very much misinformed, if the Destruction just now come upon us,
had

had not fome things attending it, that ought mightily to raife an horror and hatred of *Drunkennefs* in all that fhall hear of them. In *Uncleannefs* the filthy Children of men, do cherifh forbidden Flames, in their *Breafts.* But how avenged of God ! The Saint of old faid; Job XXXI. 12. *It is a Fire that confumeth to Deftruction.* There were fome Towns Long fince, that were Infamous for *Uncleannefs.* There were *Bawdy Houfes* in thofe Towns. But God fent *Fire* from Heaven upon them. If you Read the XIXth Chapter of *Genefis,* you will know the Names of the Towns, I refer unto.

[ My Catalogue is not yet perfect; nor at this Time like to be; nor will it be, when I have added, That *Proud Exceffes,* either in *Habits* or *Dwellings,* or any other points of Living ; Difagreeable to the *Religion of the Crofs,* which we make profeffion of ; thefe provoke the moft High God by *Fires* to *Abafe them that walk in Pride* ; He brings them down by laying their *Pride in Afhes.* Even the *Daughters of Zion,* may fo overdo in fome Vanities, that God may fend a *Burning* on the Place for their Exorbitancies, and Extravagancies. And if I add, That *Fiery Contentions* do fometimes call for *Fiery Confufions. Fires* are punifhed with *Fires.* How Suitably, How Terribly ! Or, if I add, That an immoderate *Love of this World* may bring the Sons of *Lot,* to be *Burnt out of all.* O *Remember* him ! If you make an *Idol* of *This World,* God will throw your *Idol* into the *Fire!* Whither, Sirs,

D 2                                      whither

24      *The Voice of* GOD,

whither fhould the *Images of Jealoufie* go, but thither ! ]

Sirs ; Let us bring our felves under an Impartial *Examination.* And if fuch 𝕾𝖎𝖓𝖘 as thefe are found among us, Let us Judge and Loath our felves before the Lord. Verily, The *Voice of the Lord Cries to the City.* O you that would Approve your felves *Men of Wifdom,* Hear His Voice ; *Take heed, yea, Take pains, that there be no more fuch Doings among you* !

Secondly. The *Repentance* on fuch an Occafion, fhould be very *Univerfal* ; and therefore very *Particular.* Every Man, *Every One* ! fhould avoid that Cenfure ; Jer. VIII. 6. *No man Repented him, faying, What have I done* ? Oh, Let every one of us think, *What have I done, to Enkindle the Flames of the Indignation of God againft the Neighbourhood* ? *Repent* every one of us, of all we can find *Amifs* in our own Hearts and Lives, and form agreeable *Refolutions.*

I believe, the *Burning* of the 𝕿𝖔𝖜𝖓-𝖍𝖔𝖚𝖘𝖊, and of fuch an adjoining 𝕿𝖊𝖒𝖕𝖑𝖊, calls the *Two* Superior Orders among us, to be very Thoughtful ; *O our Good GOD, Show us, Show us, what we have been defective in* ! But, *all Orders* have a fhare in the Duty ; *All Perfons* have fo. And *above all,* O you our dear Brethren, that are the more Immediate Sufferers ; You *above all* are concerned in it. Oh *!* that *you* would each one of you, fet your felves now more than ever, to think, *What, what is there, in my Heart & Life to be Repented of* ? God has caft you into a

*Fire.*

*Fire.* By this *Repentance,* you will *come forth as* Gold!

Thirdly. Can't we read, 𝕿𝖍𝖊 𝖁𝖆𝖓𝖎𝖙𝖞 𝖔𝖋 𝖙𝖍𝖎𝖘 𝖂𝖔𝖗𝖑𝖉, by fuch a *Fire-light?* The *Fire* fhall be our *Ecclefiaftes.* O thou *Flaming Preacher,* fhall we not hearken to thee? Surely, we may hear the Great GOD fpeaking to us, from the midft of the *Fire,* and the *Smoke* that we have feen *afcending like the Smoke of a Furnace;* yea, the voice of the *Trumpet waxes Louder and Louder* unto us: Tis That; Jer. XLV. 5. *Seekeft thou Great Things for thy felf? Seek them not; for behold, I will bring Evil upon all Flefh, faith the Lord.* Tis that; Prov. XXIII. 5. *Wilt thou fet thine Eyes upon that which is not? For Riches certainly make themfelves wings; they fly away as an Eagle towards Heaven.* Sirs, You fee *Fine Eftates* Loft in *Half an Hours* time; *Fine Buildings* in *Half an Hours* time rendred an Heap of Rubbifh; But *Half an Hour* between Rich Revenues, and none at all. Oh! What was done in about *Seven Hours* time the Night before laft among us! To labour infatiably for thefe things, is you fee, to *Labour in the Fire;* perhaps for it; it is to *weary your felves for very Vanity.* O *Uncertain Riches!* O *Deceitful Riches!* What *Fool will Truft in you!*

Tis not only *here* that you read thefe *Lectures* of the *Preacher;* They are *every where* to be met withal: The world is full of them; grows fuller than ever of them. The *Third Wo,* to which we are now arriving will fill the world more than ever

with

26        *The Voice of GOD,*

with them. The *Angel* that has *Power over the Fire,* will Execute part of that *Wo ;* pour out a *Vial* which belongs to that *Wo.* There is a Day at hand, when, Iſa. LXVI. 15, 16. *Behold, the Lord will come with Fire ; For by Fire &by HisSword, will the Lord plead with all Fleſh, and the Slain of the Lord ſhall be many.* O People of God, There is a **Conflagration** to come. This *Bewitching World* is to be *Burnt* in that horrendous *Conflagration.* Perhaps, the prodigious multiplication of *Deſtructions by Fire* in our Dayes, is to warn us in-to an Expectation of, *That Great and Terrible Day of the Lord.*

However,You ſee,To be put off with a *Portion* in theſe things: -- Oh,Tis anInſignificantPortion, a Miſerable Portion! This, This is the **Uſe** to be made,of what we have Seen. Oh! Let us take off ourHearts from *Such a World.*Upon theLeaſt Suſ-picion that *Such a World* may prove our Portion, Cry out with unſpeakable Agony : *O Lord, I be-ſeech thee to deliver my Soul !* Oh ! Let us be more Zealous, have a more *Flaming Zeal,* in our Eſſays to make ſure of a part in a Better World ! Put our ſelves under the Conduct of the dear JESUS, who has aſſured us, With *me are Durable Riches !*

Fourthly. If the *Fire* be ſuch a fearful *Conſu-mer,* Oh ! what is the wrath of a Righteous and a Terrible GOD ! Our GOD, who is a *Conſu-ming Fire !* We read : Nah. I. 6. *Who can ſtand be-fore his Indignation ! and who can abide the Fierceneſs of His Anger ! His Fury is poured out like Fire, and the Rocks are thrown down by Him.* The wrath

of

of an Infinite GOD! Oh, No *Fire* so formidable. Sinners, I bring you this warning from the *Taberah* in the Neighbourhood ; *It is a fearful Thing to fall into the hands of the Living God!*

We think with a Shuddering Horror, on the Fate of the poor men, who Lost their Lives in the *Fire,* the Night before Last. Most of them, no doubt, by the Blowing up, and Falling down of Houses, when we had *Brimstone,* without a metaphor, *Scattered on our Habitations*! I am willing to have that Thought Profecuted and Profitable. You have read of a *Dead Person* Enlivened by touching the *Bones* of a *Dead Prophet.* Oh, that the *Bones* of the *Dead Peeple,* Every Hour more and more of them coming to Light, may convey *Lively* Admonitions to the *Dead Souls* of them that are yet *Alive.* Surely, Those *Bones* are Speaking Things, and they Speak at Least, this unto you ;
' Sinners, while you are by Sin Expofing your
' felves to the *Wrath* of a Righteous and a Terri-
' ble GOD, you are but Running into an Hor-
' rible *Fire* ; *Briars and Thorns* are engaging a *Fire,*
' that will *Burn them together* ; a *Fire* that will ne-
' ver be *Quenched!* Oh ! be afraid of *Sinning* ;
' Tremble to *Dy in your Sins!*

I must bring home the Admonitions yet more Livelily to one Tribe among you. They were mostly *Young men,* that were Lost in the *Fire.* It has been most Literally fulfilled upon us, that word, Psal. LXXVIII. 63. *The Fire Consumed their Young men.* Children, Those *Young men* do cry to you the Survivers from the *Flames* in which they

they Perifhed ; *Oh ! Get into Good Termes with Hea-*
*ven ; Forfake your Sin, and Follow your Saviour ; &*
*Flee from a more dreadful Fire, which until you do*
*That, you are in danger of !* I am to tell you, yea,
as from *Them,* I am to tell you ; For could *they*
now Speak, as *I* now do, this is what they would
tell you : if you remain Defpifers of Serious Religion, *Alienated from the Life of God,* not Living
to God, nor as God calls you to Live ; I do not
know, That you are to *Dy by Fire ;* any more
than you know, *how Soon* you are to Dy ; But
this we both know ; At your *Death,* you will drop
into an *Everlafting Fire.* The *Fiery Cellars* in
which you find the *Bones* of your *Young* Brethren,
are nothing, nothing, not fo much as a *Meta-*
*phor,* to that *Fiery Oven,* into which the Wrath
of the Glorious God will banifh you. I wifh
you may be *Saved as by Fire,* in this regard,
that what has been done in the late *Fire,* may
inflame your Agony to look after your Salvation.

That which may fet a very cutting Edge on
thefe Admonitions, is ; The Confideration of the
*Sudden Contingencies* to which, you now fee, you
may be liable. The *Young men* that were Loft,
Little did they forefee an *Hour* before, what a
Death was juft coming upon them. When the
*Bells* began to Ring, Little did they forefee, that
it was to call them unto the *Death,* for which
the *Decretory Hour* was now come upon them.
*Young men,* Will you think on that Word, Eccl.
IX. 12. *Man knoweth not his Time ; The Sons of*
                                                    *men*

*men are Snared in an Evil Time, when it falleth*
*Suddenly upon them.* Will you think on that
word ; Prov. XXVII. 1. *Boaſt not thy ſelf of To*
*Morrow ; for thou knoweſt not, what a Day may*
*bring forth.* Oh ! Conſider This, and put not off
your Converſion to God. A matter of ſuch
Moment ; It is a *Madneſs* to put it off a Moment.
*Conſider this, ye that forget God, Leſt he tear you*
alſo *to Pieces, and there be none to deliver you.*

Fifthly. You that have Loſt your Intereſts,
by the *Conſuming Fire ;* Oh, Let your Behaviour
be very Conformable to the Expectations of
God. I can tell you of ſome, who *fell by*
*Flame,* and, [ Dan. XI. 33, 35. ] it was to *Try*
them. and to *Purge* them, and to *Make* them
*White.* Oh ! ſhall this be the Event of the *Flame*
in which you are ſo *Fallen,* and brought down
before the Lord. Be very *Humble,* very *Humble ;*
Have a Spirit Reconciled unto *Humiliations.*
Take that Counſel ; 1 Pet. V 6. *Humble your*
*ſelves under the mighty Hand of God, that He may*
*Exalt you in due time.* Yea, There is a Flight of
*Heroick Piety,* now to be aſpir'd unto ; Bear *Humi-*
*liations,* and *Eximanitions,* with ſome Satisfaction,
becauſe they reduce your State, into ſome
*Reſemblance* of that wherein your admirable Savi-
our was once Exhibited. How few, how few,
underſtand the meaning of that word ! Jam. 1. 10.
*Let the Rich Rejoyce in that he is made Low.* But,
Ee the Chriſtians I Speak to, of whatſoever
Form, *this* I will urge upon them. Give not
way to *Diſcouragements,* to *Deſpondencies.* Be full
E                                of

of *Refignation* to the Will of God. Offer up, with
a *Sacrificing Difpofition*, unto the Lord, all that the
*Fire has Confumed.* Be not now in the Dejections of
people that have Loft their *All*. When the Venerable Minifter of *Nola*, had his Houfe laid in
Afhes, he Stood by the Ruines, and Lifting up his
Eyes to Heaven, Said ' *Ubi Omnia mea, Domine,*
' *Tu fcis ;* ' O my God, my *All* was not here ; Tis
' in Thee. and in Heaven that I have my *All !*
Sirs, Let your *All* be where no *Fire* can
reach !

At the fame time, Do not Sufpect the *Fatherly
Providence* of God concerning you. Do not
*Fear* being well Provided for. Let no *Fear of
want* throw you into any diftreffing Anxiety.
Your *Heavenly Father*, will never caft you off, un-
til you do by your *Diftruft* provoke Him to do
it. You may make a *Living* on thofe Two
Words ; Pfal. XXXVII. 3. *Truft in the Lord, and
Do Good, and Verily thou fhalt be fed.* And, Pfal.
XXXIV. 10. *They that Seek the Lord, fhall not want
any Good Thing.* Children, make the Experiment.
It never yet fail'd fince the World began !

*Laftly.* We that have our Interefts yet *Preferved*, muft have fomething in *our* Behaviour,
that may be Anfwerable.

*Brethren*, our *Houfes* that we ftill Enjoy, with
fo Remarkable a *Prefervation*, Oh ! Let us bring
them under a *Dedication* unto God. [ fee Pfal.
XXX. Tit. ] Put *Sin* from them ; Serve *God* in
them. Let no Pollution cleave to them.
Let

Let us alſo ſhow *Pitty* to them, who have
Loſt their Houſes. To them that are ſo *Afflicted, pitty ſhould be ſhown ;* and will be, if we
have not *caſt off the Fear of the Almighty :*
Them, who cry to us, *Have pitty on us, O our
Friends, Have pitty on us ; for the Hand of the
Lord has touched us !* O Let us Do all we
can for them. What ? A Prophet of God
ſhall inſtruct you : Iſa. LVIII. 7. *Deal thy Bread
to the Hungry ; Bring the poor that are caſt out,
to thy Houſe ; when thou ſeeſt the Naked, cover
him.* And why ſhould not *Creditors* on this
Occaſion exerciſe all due Compaſſions, towards the *Debtors,* whom the *Fire* has diſabled
or Enfeebled ? I know I am ſpeaking among
a very *Merciful* People. The Beginning of
the *Forty firſt Pſalm* is glorioully believed a-
mong them !

And yet, I ſee, I muſt break off in Thunder and Lightning ! Having ſaid thus much,
I am ſorry, that I may not conclude, without ſome Notice of a Thing, which obliges
me to cry out, *An horrible Thing is done in the
Land.*

It is reported, that when a *Conſuming Fire*
is raging, there are *Thieves,* who take that
horrible occaſion to Seiz and Steal, and Keep
the *Goods,* that are Saved out of the *Fire.*
　　　　E 2　　　　　　The

32      *The Voice of GOD,*

The *Vilest Sort of Thieves* that ever were heard of! If any among this People, have been so hideously and so damnably wicked, O *Great God, Wilt thou please to smite their Consciences with Thy flaming Terrors, and so Terrify them that they may feel no Rest in their Guilty Souls, until they do Repent with Restitution!* To *Steal from any Man* at any time, is a *Crying Wickedness.* But, to Steal from the Neighbours, at a Time, when the *Hand of God* is upon them ; to Steal from the midst of the devouring Flames, which the *Hand of God* has kindled ; I tell you truly, 'Tis a Wickedness of a very prodigious Elevation. O Monstrous Wretches ! O Monsters of Wickedness ! What have you done ? You may marvel at the *Long-suffering* of God, that He does not even by *Fire from Heaven,* Lay those Accursed Cottages in Ashes, which have in them, the Goods, that God spared out of the *Fire,* but your Thievish hands would not spare, to the Owners of them. Let me assure you, God will never let you be one farthing the better for the *Stolen Goods ;* You will bring by *them,* a Blast from God, upon all that you have. We read of a *Flying Roll,* that is to say, an *Open Book,* full of *Curses,* that shall *Enter into the House of the Thief.* Wretches, Behold the Open Book ; Jer. XVII. 11. *He that gets Riches, & not by Right, shall leave them in the midst of his Dayes, and at his end shall be a Fool.*

I

*Crying to the City.*

I Charge you in the Name of God, that you make *Reſtitution* immediately; or expect that the Wrath of God will overtake you remarkably. If you have not an Heart willing to make *Reſtitution*, the Holy God will never *Forgive* your Wickedneſs. And, if you *Dy*, not having this Wickedneſs *forgiven* to you, you that *Stole from the Fire*, muſt look to go into a worſe *Fire !* There will *remain* for you, nothing but a *Fiery Indignation to devour you.*

I hope, I have, with the Aſſiſtance of the Glorious Lord, ſomewhat anſwered the preſent Occaſion. What remains, is,

*To beg of thee, O our God, that we may receive Inſtruction, and that thou mayeſt not utterly, or any further depart from us.*

---

# F I N I S.

---

## *Advice from the Watch Tower.*

In a TESTIMONY againſt

# EVIL CUSTOMES.

### A brief ESSAY

To declare the *Danger* & *Miſchief* of all

## Evil Cuſtomes,

### in general ;

And Offer a more particular CATA-
LOGUE of EVIL CUSTOMES growing upon us ;

With certain METHODS for the Pre-
vention and Suppreſſion of them.

Hab. II. 1. *I will ſtand upon my Watch, and
ſet me upon the Tower, and will watch to
ſee what I ſhall anſwer upon my Reproof.*

### Luk. XXI. 13.

*It ſhall turn to you for a* TESTIMONY.

*Vincere Conſuetudinem, dura eſt pugna.* Auguſt.
*Uſitata Culpa obligat mentem, ut nequaquam ſurgere poſſit
ad Reſtitudinem.* Gregor.
*Dominus noſter* CHRISTUS, *Veritatem ſe, non Conſuetudinem, Cognominavit.* Tertul.

*Boſton,* Printed by *J. Allen,* for *N. Boone,*
at the Sign of the *Bible* in *Cornhill.* 1713.

---

# A Faithful Teſtimony

Againſt

# EVIL CUSTOMES.

---

## Jer. XIII. 23.

*Can the Ethiopian change his Skin, or the Leopard his Spots ? Then may ye alſo Do Good, that are* ACCUSTOMED TO DO EVIL.

I Hope, that my Undertaking will not be that of *Waſhing the Ethiopian,* or *Blanching the Leopard!* God forbid, it ſhould be *that!* Indeed, I am Undertaking to Diſſwade, yea. to Reduce, my Neighbours from EVIL CUS-TOMES. 'Tis true, a Recovery from *Evil Cuſtomes,* is as hard as to change the *Skin* of the *Ethiopian,* and the *Spots* of the *Leopard.* We may then cry out, *Who then can be recovered?* But in ſo difficult a Caſe, our Saviour has anſwered, *With God all things are poſſible.* The powerful *Word* of God, is to be Employ'd and apply'd in this Caſe. The *Grace* of God may Set in with His Word, *O Sovereign and*

A 2      *Victorious*

## 4  *Advice from the Watch Tower.*

*Victorious Grace, Do thou set in !* Then, there
is not the blackest *Ethiopian,* there is not the
most Livid *Leopard,* there is not the most *Accuſtomed Sinner,* but what will have a moſt
Glorious *Change* made upon him.

Grievous puniſhments are foretold unto the
Jewiſh Nation.  Hereupon a Queſtion is both
ſuppoſed and propoſed; *If thou ſay in thine
Heart, wherefore come theſe things upon me ?*
When Sad Things come upon people, they
ſhould be Inquiſitive, *Wherefore theſe things do
come ?*  The Anſwer given to that Queſtion, is,
*For the Greatneſs of thine Iniquity.*  Now the
*Greatneſs of the Iniquity* in this people, is
illuſtrated from Two Woful Circumſtances.
Firſt, the *Obſtinacy* of it ; Secondly, the *Variety* of it.   They retained their Iniquity, with
as much *Obſtinacy,* as the *Ethiopian* does his
*Skin.*  And yet, there was as much *Variety* in
their Iniquity as in the *Spots* of the *Leopard.*
Briefly, A *Cuſtome to do Evil,* yea, to do many
ſorts of Evil,  had confirmed them in their I-
niquity.  Being *Accuſtomed to do Evil,* they
were *Incorrigible* in it.  No Corrections would
recover them.   From hence I form this
DOCTRINE, to be now inſiſted on.

EVIL CUSTOMES *are not Eaſily Left off;
and the longer a Sinner is Accuſtomed to
Do Evil, the Leſs Eaſily is that Evil a-
bandoned.*

We are going to Dethrone a mighty *Tyrant*
We

*Advice from the Watch Tower.* 5

We are invading the Kingdom of a Mightier
*Tyrant*, than any one that ever was at *Babylon*. *Cuſtome*, CUSTOME, is that which *Tyran-
nizes* over all the World. It was the Language of Antiquity ; *Nihil tam firmum in rebus
humanis, quam veteris conſuetudinis Tyrannis.*
No *Tyranny* ſo ſtrong, as that of *Cuſtome*. And
I know not, that it has met with any Mo-
dern Confutation.

*I.* We are to begin with a moſt unhappy
Obſervation. 'Tis, That all *Vnregenerate* people, are ACCUSTOMED TO DO EVIL ; are
under the power of *Evil Cuſtome.* We often
read of ſuch a thing as that ; Pſal.I.i. *The way
of Sinners.* All Sinners have their *Way* ; Tis
an *Evil Way* ; Tis a *Way of Wickedneſs* ; they
are *Accuſtomed* unto it. So they continue,
till a Work of *Regeneration* paſs upon them.

Firſt. We are *Born* with an *Habit of Sin* ;
yea, the *Original Sin*, which we are born withal, is a Complication of all *Sinful Habits.*
There is no man but what is born, as *Black* as
an *Ethiopian*, for an Inclination to Sin ; Yea,
with more *Spots* than a *Leopard*, in an Inclination to Sins more than our very *Hairs.* We
read, Gen. VI. 5. *Every Imagination of the
Thoughts of his Heart, is only Evil continually.*
We bring into the World with us, an *Habitual Inclination* to Sin. Our Vitious Inclination is not meerly the Reſult of *Evil Actions.*
*Evil Acts* do indeed ſtrengthen the *Habits of
Sin* in us. But we have the *Habits of Sin,* before

**6**   *Advice from the Watch Tower.*

fore we do any *Evil Acts.* Our *Habits of Sin,* are the fource and fpring of all our *Evil Acts.* Our *Habitual Inclination* to Do Evil, is derived unto us, from our *Firft Parents.* The *Old Serpent* poifoned our Nature. A *Poifoned Nature* is convey'd from our Firft Parent unto us all. In this Corruption of our *Nature,* there is Lodg'd every *Sinful Habit.* There is in it a *Principle* difpofing us to *Every Sin.* There never was any man born into the World, without a Collection of *Sinful Habits* in him ; Except that *One man,* who is *more than a man.* Hence 'tis that we read ; Pfal. XLV. 3. *There is none that doeth Good, no, not One.* The Chriftian Ancients read it fo ; *There is none that doeth Good, Except it be One.* Yea, We will Except *One,* who was *Born of a Virgin* ; *One,* who was *Born an Holy Thing* ; *One,* in whom alone we have the Relief of all our *Evil Habits.* The Bleffed JESUS is that ONE ; *Tis Thou, O Immanuel.*

Secondly. An *Unregenerate man* under the Influence of *Original Sin,* does *nothing but Sin* ; is *Habituated* and *Accuftomed* unto *Nothing but Evil.* Such an *Evil Tree* as an Unregenerate man, brings forth *no Good Fruits.* An Unregenerate man does *no Good Works.* His very *Sacrifices* have *Abominations* in them. His moft Vertuous and Splendid Performances, are attended with *Pollutions,* which degrade them and difgrace them wonderfully. They are all, *Sacrifices* to *Self* ; All, *Idolatry* ; All, *Hypocrifie.* It may be faid, as in Hag. II.

14.

*Advice from the Watch Tower.* 7

14. *This people is unclean before me, faith the Lord, and so is every Work of their Hands.* Ah, poor Unregenerate! How *Low* oughteſt thou to be in thy *own Eyes!* How deſpairing to ſtand before God in thy *own Righteoufneſs!* How confounded for the *Loſs of all thy Time* hitherto! Never, Never didſt thou do *One Good Work* in all thy Life! What is the *Whole Courſe* of an *Unregenerate Man?* The whole Courſe of his Life, is a Courſe of *Sin*; a continual Aberration from that which ought to be the *Rule* and *End* of his Life. *O Enemy of God*; What art thou *always* a doing? *Always* forgetting thy main Errand into the World. *Always* trampling on thy Creator and Redeemer. *Alwayes* Gratifying the Enemies of God, and of thy Soul; and preferring *Temporal* Enjoyments before *Eternal*; Yea, procuring *Eternal* Miſeries for the ſake of *Temporal* Enjoyments. Theſe, Theſe are the Things, to which thou art *Accuſtomed.* Yea, Thou art *Accuſtomed* unto none but ſuch *Evil Things.* Oh! *Abhor thy ſelf, and Repent in Duſt and Aſhes!*

Thirdly: There are ſome EVIL CUS-TOMES, which every *Unregenerate Man,*does follow with ſome *Diſtinction*; they have a *Diſtinction* and *Prædominancy* above others with him. *All* Unregenerate Men agree in thoſe *General Cuſtomes,* which alwayes belong to a Life of Ungodlineſs. It may be ſaid of them, as Tit. III. 3. *They ſerve divers Luſts.* But then, Every Unregenerate Man has his

own

8   *Advice from the Watch Tower.*

own *Evil Cuftomes,* which are Confpicuous in him above the reft. Tho' we are naturally prone to *All Evil,* yet *Natural Temper* carries One man more fenfibly to *One Evil,* and another Man to another. *Education* biaffes One man more Evidently to One Mifcarriage ; and another Man to another. *Company, Employment, Intereft,* Engages one man more notorioufly to one piece of Bafenefs, and another Man to another. One man is more *Accuftomed* unto *Senfualities* ; Another man is more *Accuftomed* unto *Difhonefties* ; A Third is *Accuftomed* unto *Ufurpations,* or to Boifterous *Outrages* ; The *Bull is wont to pufh with his Horn !* Every Unregenerate Man has a CUS-TOME, which above the reft, he may call, Pfal. XVIII. 23. *My own Iniquity.*

Make a paufe. Take a *Sign* of *Unregeneracy.* Would you fee a palpable *Sign* of an Unregenerate State, and of one that *has the Wrath of God abiding on him ?* This is One ; To be wittingly or willingly under the Power of EVIl CUSTOMES. EVIL CUSTOMES, they look *black* ; they are the *Spots* which do not belong to the *Children of God.* Is there a *known Sin* ? And, O man, doft thou know thy felf to be *Accuftomed* unto that Sin? O Lamentable Symptom ! Tis moft certainly a Symptom of one in Ill Terms with Heaven. A *Regenerate* perfon may *fall* into Sin. I cannot fay, how many his *Falls* may be ; tho' I am fure, he will anon get out of them all. But, if a man can make a *Trade,* of a *Plain Sin,* and

if

*Advice from the Watch Tower.* 9
if he be *Accuftomed* unto thofe things, for
which the *Wrath of God comes on the Children
of Difobedience.*-----Oh! Fly out of this Condition. 'Tis a dangerous Thing to *Sleep* in
fuch a Condition. There is Entail'd upon it
a *Damnation that Slumbers not!*

*II.* We will now proceed unto the *Principal Thing,* which we are to Obferve; & unto
the *proof* of it. It is this: Tis not *Eafy* to
Leave off an *Evil Cuftome.* Tis not *Eafy* to
Reform a Sinner of an Evil, to which he is
*Accuftomed.* Is it Eafy, to put a *White Skin*
upon an *Ethiopian?* Is it Eafy to Extinguifh
the *Dapples* of the *Leopard?* Then it may be
Eafy for them that are *Accuftomed to do Evil,*
to Leave off their Evil-doing.
Firft. *Cuftome* fhortly becomes a *Second Nature. In Naturam Convertitur.* We have an
*Evil Nature* before we are actually plunged
into any *Evil Cuftome.* Now *Evil Cuftome*
quickly induces a fort of *Second Nature:* 'tis,
*affabricata Natura,* as *Auftin* calls it. If *Nature* be ftrong, as we know it is; What is the
*Strength of Nature upon Nature?* Verily, No
*Pitchfork* on Earth will fo *Expel* it, but it will
*Return* with *Violence.* We are *Naturally* bent
unto Sin, only unto Sin, and that continually.
When we are *Accuftomed* unto Sin, what was
*Natural* before, becomes much more fo: And
how *violent* will now be our *Bent* unto it?
We *Naturally* Love to Do, what we *Ufe* to
do. Men are *Naturally* wedded unto their
B *Cuftomes.*

10    *Advice from the Watch Tower.*

*Cuſtomes.* Yea, Sometimes *Barbarous* Cuſtomes, *Afflictive* Cuſtomes, *Cuſtomes* that one would think, ſhould have nothing but *Horrors* in them ; yet ſince they are become *Cuſtomes,* people are ſtrangely Reconciled unto them. Yea, people find rather *Pleaſure* than *Trouble* in the moſt horrible Cuſtomes. The Hiſtories of the *Oppreſſive Cuſtomes* in many Nations ; *Cuſtomes* out of which there is yet no perſwading of the Nations ; truly, they would make an aſtoniſhing Entertainment for us. Tis enough to ſay, We all find, that what is become *Cuſtomary* with us, becomes *Natural.* Any thing in our *Eating,* our *Drinking,* our Hours of *Sleeping,* that is become a *Cuſtome* with us ; Tho' it be as very Trifle as, ----( an Indian Weed ; ) if we are *Accuſtomed* unto any thing, we *Naturally Crave* after it. We don't care to *break a Cuſtome* ; Tis a Strain upon our *Nature* to do ſo. One Evangeliſt, ſays ; Matth. XXVII. 15. *The Governour was wont to do* a certain thing. Another Evangeliſt Expreſſes it ſo ; Luk. XXIII. 17. *Of Neceſſity he muſt do the thing.* Truly, that which we are *wont to do,* anon it comes to this, *Of Neceſſity it muſt* be done. This was the Language of Antiquity ; *Conſuetudo eſt jus quoddam, moribus conſtitutum.*

Secondly. *Conſcience* is fearfully Silenced by *Cuſtome.* There is a *Conſcience* in man, and *the Inſpiration of the Almighty has given him an* Underſtanding of much of his *Duty,* and of the *Evil* that will follow on his failing of his *Duty.*

*Advice from the Watch Tower.* 11

*Duty.* At firſt, the *Conſcience* of man rebukes him for doing *Evil.* It makes that Cry in his Ears; Jer. XLIV. 4. *Oh, do not this Abominable thing!* But the oftener a man does refuſe to hear his *Conſcience,* and *Rebel againſt the Light,* the more *Silent* his Conſcience grows. He that is *Accuſtomed to do Evil,* goes often againſt the Charges and Rebukes of his *Conſcience.* To *Sin often againſt the Conſcience,* is, to give a Deadly Check unto the Operations of it. We read of ſuch a thing as that; 1 *Tim.* IV. 2. *A Conſcience ſeared with an hot Iron.* A *Sinful Cuſtome* is that which iſſues in a *Seared Conſcience.* Many a man has made the woful Experiment. At firſt, when he did an *Evil Thing,* his *Conſcience* made him very uneaſy at it; his *Conſcience* reproved him, reproached him, Chaſtiſed him. He *Repeats* the Evil; the *Remorſe* of his *Conſcience* abates upon every Repetition. At Laſt, he is *Accuſtomed to do Evil.* Then he does it without any *Remorſe* at all. The *Hardened* Sinner gets the upper-hand of *Conſcience. Conſcience* is kept under. The Vigour of *Conſcience* never is reſumed, until God raiſe it, as an Inſtrument of His Everlaſting Vengeance upon the Sinner in another World. But if the Reſtraints of *Conſcience* be gone, how ſhall a Sinner be Reclaimed! A Sinner *Accuſtomed to do Evil,* eſcapes from under the Reſtraints of Conſcience. *Unbridled Sinner,* What is there to bring thee back?

Thirdly *Cuſtome* will beget *Courage. Impunity*

12    *Advice from the Watch Tower.*

*nity* in Sin, does *Embolden* and *Encourage* thofe
that are accuftomed unto it.  We read, Eccl.
VIII. 2. *Becaufe Sentence againft an Evil Work
is not Executed fpeedily, therefore the heart of
the fons of men is fully fet in them to do Evil.*
Men that are *Accuftomed to do Evil*, find that
the *Sentence againft an Evil Work*, is *not Executed fpeedily.*  They Sin, and Sin, and Sin,
and there is no *punifhment* Executed upon them
for their Sin.  *Cuftome* in Sin, begets in men
an Opinion of *Safety* in Sin.  We read of, *A
Sinner, doing Evil an hundred times, and yet his
Dayes prolonged.*  A Sinner *Accuftomed to do
Evil*, finds he may *do Evil an hundred times*,
and yet no Damage come of it.  This makes
him Grow *Bold* in Sin:  He becomes Head-
ftrong, and there is no ftopping of him.  So
does the Almighty thunder upon the *Accuftomed* Sinner.  *I keep Silence, and thou thinkeft,
I am fuch an one as thy felf!*  The Forbearance
of God, with a Sinner *Accuftomed to do Evil*
makes him dream, that God *forgets him.*  So
he *forgets God*, until he be *torn to pieces*, and
there be *none to deliver him!*

Fourthly.  *Satan* gets poffeffion by *Cuftome.*
When people *do Evil*, they obey the *Devil*,
who is the *Evil One.*  By their *Obedience* to
the *Devil*, People Refign themfelves up to the
*Poffeffion* of that *Evil One.*  When people are
*Accuftomed to do Evil*, the *Poffeffion* that *Satan*
has of them, improves into a fort of *præfcripti-
on.*  *Satan* was difpoffeffed once, with a more
than ordinary Difficulty ;  and we read the
Occafion,

*Advice from the Watch Tower.* 13
Occafion, Mar. IX. 21. *How long is it ago fince
this came unto him ? He faid, Of a Child.* E-
very New *Compliance* of any man with the
*Devil*, ftrengthens the *Intereft* of the *Devil*
in him. The oftner the *Devil* fubdues any
man, the *Fafter Hold* he has of that man.
The *Strong Armed One* has the Stronger
Hold in any man, the longer he has held
him, and the oftner he has gain'd upon him.
One that is *Accuftomed to do Evil*, has given himfelf to *Satan*, fo often, fo freely, fo
fully, you may be fure, it will be no little
matter to caft him out. It is with furprize,
that we hear the Language of thofe Mon-
fters, who wifh *the Devil to take them.* Ah,
Fool-hardy Sinner ; As often as thou Sin-
neft, thou doft monftroufly Refign thy felf
to the *Wicked One*, and bid him to *take thee.*
*Satans Commiffion* to have and to hold the
Sinner, is *Renowed* as often as there is a *New
Sin* deliberately ventured on ? Sinner, Doft
thou know what thou doft ?

Fifthly. By *Cuftome in Sin*, a *Withdraw of
Grace* is provoked. We read of fuch a dreadful thing as that ; Pfal. LXXXI. 11, 12. *They
would not hearken to my voice ; fo I gave them
up unto their own Hearts Luft.* People *Accuftomed to do Evil*, often, *often* provoke the
God of Heaven ; often, *often* refufe the Offers of His *Grace.* The Spirit of God, with
His Word, often moves the Sinner to *Forfake his Wicked Wayes*, and his *Unjuft Tho'ts.*
He that Sins, does reject the Motions of
God,

14 *Advice from the Watch Tower.*

God, and His Good Spirit. He that makes a *Cuſtome of Sinning*, does often, *often*, *often* Reject the Good Motions. The Holy God withdraws, and with-holds His *Grace* on ſuch a provocation. But, *Wo unto them, if I depart from them, ſaith the Lord !* There will be no bringing of the Sinner to *Do Good*, if the Divine Grace be with-held from them O Child of *Evil Cuſtome* ; Tis a Dangerous Thing by *Cuſtomary Sinning* to Diſoblige the Grace of God !

Laſtly. Tis what we *See every Day.* Tis a Rare Thing to ſee an *Old Sinner* Converted unto God, and Serious Piety. One of the Pagan Poets, I find reflecting on the Difficulty of Tranſplanting an *Old Tree.* Yea, *Diogenes* could ſay, *Senem admonere et mortuo mederi idem eſt* ; As good talk to a *Dead man*, as to an *Old man.* It is a doleful Account, about a *Cuſtome* of *Doing Evil* ; Prov. II. 19. *None return again, neither take they hold of the paths of Life.* O Sinner, What a miracle of Mercy would it be, if thou mayſt be *One* ! There was an *Old Sinner*, that became a Subject of a notable Converſion, in the Primitive Times. At firſt, no body would believe it. When they did come to the Belief of it, they ſo wondred at it ; as to make their Hymns, their Shouts in the Church, upon it ; *Victorius is become a Chriſtian !* How rare a thing is it, for an *Old Muckworm* to become a *Spiritual-minded* man ; One of a *Converſation in Heaven* ! How rare a thing, for an *Old Swearer*, One
that

*Advice from the Watch Tower.*　15

that hath a *Tongue set on Fire of Hell,* *Accuftomed* unto the Language of *Fiends,* to put on the *Golden Curb,* and *keep his mouth from Evil?* How rare a thing, for an *Old Drunkard,* One that has *Lien among the pots,* till *Gray Hairs are here and there* upon him, *accuftomed* unto Befotments, to become Sober, and make the Flights of Goodnefs, to be made by the *Silver Wings of a Dove!* The Sins of *Unchaftity,* the Wretches *accuftomed* unto them, how rarely are the footy *Ethiopians* purified, how rarely the fpotted *Libbards* brought unto better manners? It was a Remark made a great while a-go; Eccl. VII. 28. *One man among a thoufand have I found, but a Woman among all thofe have I not found;* that is to fay Reclaimed from the Sins of *Unchaftity.* Firft, Of *Men,* there is *but one of a Thoufand accuftomed* unto Sins of Unchaftity, but what goes on until his *Eftate* is wafted, and until his *Body* is wafted, and when he is an *Old Fool,* and one would have fuppofed him to have Out-lived his Impurities, yet even *then* he will have the Tokens of an Impure, Filthy, Rotten Soul upon him. And then, Of *Women,* there is *not one of a Thoufand.* Tho' the moft Solemn Warnings are given to her; tho' fhe fees the awful Judgments of God on thofe that have gone before her; tho' fhe has alfo brought her felf under infinite Scandal; yet fhe will go on till *Rottennefs* enter into her Bones, and the *Curfes* from the Left Hand of God the Eternal Judge do fall upon her. But the Subject is now ripe for

APPLI-

16    *Advice from the Watch Tower.*

## APPLICATION.

*I.* PARENTS, You ought *Betimes* to break your Children of *Evil Cuſtomes.* We read ; Prov. XXII. 6. *Train up a Child, in the way he ſhould go ; and when he is Old, he will not depart from it.* But then, What if you ſee the Child running in the *Way wherein he ſhould not go ?* Oh ! Draw, or Drive the Child out of that Way ; elſe, *When he is Old he will not depart from it.* The *Veſſel will keep long the Tincture,* that while it is young, it is firſt of all imbued withal.    Tis a common *Theme* given to our Little Sons at School.    And they will bring their *Teſtimonies* for it, from the Poets they Learn there ; *Adeo a teneris aſſueſcere multum eſt.*    And, *Nil conſuetudine majus.* Beware, Leſt in the worſt ſenſe of it, the *Sons* themſelves prove the *Example* of the *Theme.* We ſhould be careful of our Children that they do not fall into a *Cuſtome* of any *Indecency* ; A *Cuſtome* of Indecent *Speaking,* Indecent *Reading,* Indecent *Walking* ; Any thing that will render them unacceptable.    But, Oh ! What a watchful and careful eye ought we to keep on our Children, leſt they fall into a *Cuſtome* of any *Iniquity !* Leſt they *Deny God,* and it become their *Cuſtome* to do ſo ! Parents, Enquire after the *Cuſtomes* of your Children.    And be not *Angry* at ; No, be very *Thankful* to, thoſe who will faithfully Inform you, what the *Cuſtomes* of your Children are.
When

*Advice from the Watch Tower.* **17**

When Parents are so Foolish, that they will not bear to be faithfully told, of the Hazards which there may be, Lest their Children take the *Paths of the Destroyer*, but will by Raging and Raving against such Friends, and by Clamorous Demands for sending and proving, dishearten them from the Exercise of that Faithfulness, they make the *Sins* of those *Children* become *Their own.* Ah! House of *Eli*, What, what will the Scourges of Heaven do unto thee? Such Parents will certainly see, that which will be an *Heaviness* unto them. No, Parents, 'Twill be your Wisdom, to *Cherish Informations.* And, Can you find, That the poor Child is *Accustomed to do Evil?* Is it a *Child that will Lye*, One *Accustomed unto Lying?* A Child *Accustomed* unto *Stealing*; A Child *Accustomed* unto the Speaking of *Wicked Words*; A Child *Accustomed* unto *Sabbath-breaking?* A Child *Accustomed* unto *Playing of Truant?* A Child *Accustomed* unto the keeping of *Wicked Company!* Oh! Contrive Early Methods, and Exquisite Ones, to *Save* the Child from such *Untoward Customes.* The Happiness of the Child in *Both Worlds*, will turn upon its being Saved from these *Customes.* Reclaim the Child, or else, alas, thou hast *bro't it forth for the Murderer!* Thou art thy self its *Murderer!* It was a cutting word, which the Lord spoke about the Children of Degenerate *Israelites*; *They are to me, the Children of Ethiopians.* Truly, the *Children of Ethiopians*, that cannot *Change their Skin*, [I may add, the

C                                              Whelps

18   *Advice from the Watch Tower.*

Whelps of *Leopards,* ] are not fo Vile, as the
Children that are *Accuftomed to do Evil.* Convince the Child of the Follies in the *Evil Cuf-*
*tomes.* Make the *Cuftomes* painful to the Child.
Reward the Child, if it Abftain from the *Cuf-*
*tomes.* And, Oh, pour out your *Prayers* unto
the Glorious Lord, That He would *Change the*
*Heart* of the Child ; Give a *New Heart,* a
foft one, and a pure one, to the Child. A *New*
*Heart,* That, That would put a period unto
all *Evil Cuftomes.*

*II.* You may now fee the Madnefs of every
*Delay* to Turn to God.   Verily, till you
Turn to God, you Lead a Life of *Evil Cuftomes.*
You are *Accuftomed to do Evil,* until you are
Converted unto God.   The Holy God may
fay to every Sinner, that is not yet *Converted*
*from the Error of his Way* ; Jer. XXII. 21. *This*
*has been thy manner from thy Youth, that thou*
*obeyedft not my Voice.* The Longer you put
off your Converfion, the more you are *Accufto-*
*med to do Evil.* By being *Accuftomed to do Evil,*
you render it very *Uneafy* to Turn to God ;
very *Hazardous* whether you ever fhall Turn
to God. *Souls, in the Bond of Iniquity,* Had
you not better hearken to the Calls of the
Gofpel, without any more Delay ? We read,
Heb. III. 7. *To Day if you will hear His Voice,*
*harden not your Hearts.* Ah, Children of Un-
perfwadeablenefs ; Your Hearts are growing
Harder and Harder every Day.   Your *Cuftome*
of Sinning is growing *Inveterate.* The more
*Invete-*

*Advice from the Watch Tower.* 19

*Inveterate*, the more *Incurable !* It is an *Eafy thing* for the *Almighty* One to Convert you, tho' you have *gone on ſtill in your Trefpaſſes*, and in your *Evil Cuſtomes* never ſo far. But yet you will not be *Eaſily Converted.* It will coſt you the *more Contrition*, the more Bitterneſs, the more Agony, the *Longer* tis before you come unto it. Yea, you make it a *Peradventure* little ſhort of Deſperate, whether you ever ſhall come unto it. Procraſtinating Souls, The beſt Advice that can be given you, is this ; *Immediately* Give up your ſelves to God in His Covenant. *Immediately* put your ſelves under the Conduct of your Great Saviour. *Immediately* ſay, *Lord, I am Thine, Save me !* Yea, O Young People, May That be your Attainment ; Pſal. CXIX. 147. *I prevented the Dawning of the Morning, and I cried ; I hoped in thy Word.* Child, Thou canſt not make too much Haſte, in Leaving off thy *Evil Cuſtomes !*

*III.* You may take it for granted, That to be *Accuſtomed to do Good*, is a very Good Thing. There are ſome that are *Accuſtomed to do Good.* I recommend it as a way to *Facilitate* your *Doing of Good.* We have a Saviour, whoſe *Converſation* was all full of *Good Cuſtomes.* We expreſly read concerning one of them ; Luk. IV. 16. *As His Cuſtom was, He went into the Synagogue, on the Sabbath-day.* Oh ! that we were more Like to our Lovely Saviour ! Indeed this is one thing, which we ſhall do excellently well, to make our *Cuſtome* ;

20 *Advice from the Watch Tower.*

I cannot propound a Better. Let it be our *Cuſtome* often to Think on the *Example* of our Holy JESUS. Often, often ſet the Exemplary JESUS before our Eyes. Think, What He *did* ; Think, How He *Walk'd* ; Conform to Him ; Study all poſſible *Conformity* to Him. I will then ſay ; Syrs, Tis not enough to do a Good Thing Once or Twice or ſo ; you muſt make a *Cuſtome* of it. Let it be your *Cuſtome*, to maintain Communion with God in Secret, more than once every Day. Let it be your *Cuſtome*, to Worſhip God with your Families Morning and Evening. Let it be your *Cuſtome* to Sanctify the Lords-Day, and fill it with Religious Exerciſes. Let it be your *Cuſtome*, to keep your Speech under a Good Government ; under the Law of Prudence, and of Kindneſs. Let it be your *Cuſtome* to Relieve the Miſerable, with all poſſible Alacrity and Liberality. Let it be your *Cuſtome*, to conſider what Improvements you ſhall make of the Calamitous or the Comfortable Things diſpenſed unto you in the Providence of God. Let it be your *Cuſtome*, often to think, *What Good ſhall I do ? How ſhall I be a Bleſſing to all about me ?* Such *Good Cuſtomes*, how ſweetly, my Brethren, how nobly, will they *Habituate* you, to the Doing of Good ? I may tell you, That the Good GOD has His *Cuſtome* to ; And *you* that are thus *Accuſtomed unto Well-doing*, ſhall have a Bleſſed Experience of it. So it was petitioned ; Pſal. CXIX. 132. *Look thou upon me, and be merciful unto me, according to*
*the*

*Advice from the Watch Tower.* 21

the *Cuſtome* towards *thoſe that Love thy Name.*

I have only this Counſil to add. Beware of meer *Cuſtomarineſs* in the Doing of *Good.* Whatever *Good* you do, Let it not be done *meerly out of Cuſtome.* That will ſpoil All ! Alas ! A Great part of the *Religion* in the World, is a *Cuſtomary Religion* ; Tis nothing in the world but *Cuſtome.* Higher Things are Expeſted from *you,* O Chriſtians ; To do Good upon an Higher Principle ; And a *Reaſonable Service.*

IV. But the *Concluſion* of my Diſcourſe muſt yet more nearly anſwer the main *Intention* of it. A Faithful TESTIMONY againſt the E-VIL CUSTOMES getting in amongſt us, is now to be born and brought unto us. Let not our ſtanding here, be, AT THE LABOUR IN VAIN, I urgently require it of you ! The Great GOD expreſſed a Concern for His people of Old, Lev. XVIII. 30. That they might *not be Defiled with any* ABOMINABLE CUS-TOMES. I know not any one thing, which they that have at Heart the Welfare of this People, have cauſe to be more concerned for, than this ; That ABOMINABLE CUSTOMES may not get head among us. It was a *Cuſtome* among the *Cretians,* That when they would wiſh the *worſt thing* imaginable to an Enemy, their wiſh would be, *Let ſome Evil Cuſtome come upon them :* And as *Valerius Maximus* makes his Remark upon it, *Modeſto Voti genere Efficaciſſimum ultionis Genus reperiunt.*

The

22    *Advice from the Watch Tower.*

The Expreſſion ſeem'd as if it had a little *Mo-deſty* in it; but it was impoſſible to breathe out a *Revenge* with more *Efficacy*, with more *Malignity.* On the other ſide, I am upon de-ſiring ſome very *Good Thing* for the Nighbour-hood; And I cannot eaſily think of a Better than this; Oh! May no *Evil Cuſtomes* prevail upon us. Oh! May a due Horror of all *Evil Cuſtomes* be awakened in us! Oh! That if we are falling into any *Evil Cuſtomes,* we may be quickly Reſcued from them. It were to be deſired, That we may none of us be Led aſide unto any *Cuſtome,* whereof the Beſt of men may diſpenſe that Rebuke unto us; 1 Cor. XI. 16. *We have no ſuch Cuſtome.*

I ſhall do the part of a *Watchman,* as one that muſt anon give up an Account unto God, by moving for ſome very Important Things, which may be reduced into the Enſuing Arti-cles.

*I.* If any one perſon among you, be Conſci-ous to any one *Evil Cuſtome* indulged with him; Oh! Let the *Wicked forſake his way, and Return unto the Lord*; Return, with wonder, that there is yet Room and Hope, to be *Abun-dantly pardoned.* Yea, Tis poſſible, that a *Godly perſon* may be unawares overtaken with an *Evil Cuſtome.* And unto ſuch alſo will the Advice be very pertinent. My Friend, Be aware, Be aware of thy Condition; and, Oh! do not continue in it!

Hearken to the propoſals of Piety.

Firſt

Firſt. It would be richly worth the while, for us every one to Examine himſelf, upon that point; *Is there no Evil Cuſtome that I am us'd unto?* My Hearers, I earneſtly preſs it upon you, to *Commune with your own Hearts* in ſuch a *Self-Examination.* Be able to ſay; Pſal. LXXVII. 6. *I commune with my own Heart, and my Spirit makes diligent ſearch.* Enquire, Is there no *Paſſion,* or *Exceſs,* which it is my *Cuſtome* to be eaſily overtaken withal? Enquire, Is there no *Way of miſpending my time,* which it is my *Cuſtome* to abandon my ſelf unto? Enquire, Is there no *Wrong Step,* which it is my *Cuſtome* to hurt my ſelf withal? If but this *One Thing* were obtained of our People, Oh! what a world of Good might be thereby introduced among us. I beſeech you, Syrs, Deny not ſuch a *Service,* and ſuch a *Juſtice,* unto your own Souls this Day: To Retire and Ponder, *What Evil Cuſtome am I prone unto?*

Secondly. Having found out an *Evil Cuſtome,* Oh! Be ſenſible of the *Evil* that is in it. Confeſs it, Bewayl it, Bitterly mourn for it before the Lord. It is no ſmall Aggravation of an *Evil,* when it may be ſaid, Pſalm XXXVI. 4. *It is a Way that is not Good*; It is the mans *Way* to do ſo. Argue thus; *Had I done ſuch a thing but once, my Sin had been great; But, Oh! for me to make a Cuſtome of doing ſuch a thing! Lord, How Sinful am I!* You muſt not imagine a *Cuſtome* to be an *Excuſe* for a Sin. Tis brought as a plea for ſome,

who

24  *Advice from the Watch Tower.*

who have a Licentious Way of Talking, *Why, Tis his Way.* His *Way!* So much the *Worfe* for *That.* Some feem to Extenuate a Crime, fuppofe it *Swearing,* or *Drinking,* or *Gaming,* with faying, *I have got a Cuftome of it.* Alas, my Friend, The more *Criminal* becaufe tis a *Cuftome.* It feems, tis a Crime, that you have *often, often,* been guilty of. But has not the Great GOD a *Cuftome* too; Even to deftroy them *who go on ftill in their Trefpaffes?* Oh, Ly in the Duft with a Diftreffed and a Pænitent Soul before the Lord.

Thirdly. *A Pardon, A Pardon,* A Pardon muft be fought for. But is it poffible, for not only a *Sin,* but alfo a *Cuftome in Sin,* to find an Expiation? Yes, Tis poffible. O Sinner, Be aftonifhed at the Tidings. Tis poffible; yea, it is *Provided,* and it is *Proffered.* But Remember, That with a *Pardon* there will always come a *Power* to break off, and refrain an *Evil Cuftome.* Nothing but a *New Nature* will thoroughly Cure an *Old Cuftome* of doing Evil. The *Pardon* of an *Evil Cuftome,* will alwayes bring with it, the Grace to Abhor the *Cuftome,* to Forfake the *Cuftome.* You muft ardently ask for *both* of thefe together; Ask for *both* of them with an equal Ardour. But now, what is there to obtain fuch a *Purification* for us? My Brethren, That which will turn *Scarlet* and *Crimfon* into *White,* will take away the *Skin* of the *Ethiopian,* and the *Spots* of the *Leopard.* Now, the *Blood* of our Great Saviour applied unto us, will do that for us. Oh!

What

*Advice from the Watch Tower.* 25

What a sweet Word is that! Isa. I. 18. *Come now, and let us reason together, saith the Lord; Tho' your Sins be as Scarlet, they shall be as white as Snow, tho' they be Red like Crimson, they shall be as Wool.* This then is to be the Strain of our Cries unto Heaven. ' O my Saviour, Thy ' *Blood* has been my *Sacrifice* . For the sake of ' that *Blood*, Let my Sinful *Customes*, which ' have bound me over to suffer the Venge- ' ance of God, be all Forgiven to me; And ' for the sake of that *Blood*, let my *Bonds of* ' *Iniquity* be taken off; Let no *Evil Customes* ' Ly as the *Chains of Death* upon me; *Let no* ' *Iniquity have no Dominion over me!* When you are *Effectually Called* out of this World, by a *Work* of *Grace* upon you, Then, Then you will be Sav'd from the *Customes* of it; For the *Customes of the People are Vain.*

Having arrived thus far, you, may *now* proceed, Lastly, to *Special Resolutions. Resolve* now to Reform your *Evil Customes*; *Resolve* to take up *Good Customes* contrary to your *Evil* Ones. *Resolve* to *Do Good* just contrary unto that *Evil*, unto which you have been *Accustomed.* Yea, Resolve to be and to do something that shall be *Exemplary*, in direct Opposition to what was once an *Evil Custome* with you. That Good Woman *Monica*, the Mother of *Austin*, had unawares fallen into a *Custome* of Drinking somewhat more freely than became one of her Profession; One Reproached her for it : God sanctified the Reproach; Upon it she became as bright a Pattern of

D                                        *Tempe-*

26    *Advice from the Watch Tower.*

*Temperance* as ever was in the World. *Repentance* ufes to take fuch *Revenges* as this! But,
O Refolve nothing in your *own Strength*. By
his *own ftrength ſhall no man prevail*, againſt
thoſe worſt of Enemies, *Evil Cuſtomes.* Let
that Clauſe be more than a *Parentheſis* in
every Refolution; Let it be the main Stroke
and Force of the Refolution, Phil. IV. 13.
*THROUGH CHRIST WHO STRENGTH-
ENS ME.* Keep then a *Memorandum* of
what you Refolve. And be able to ſay, *E-
go non ſum Ego.* Yea, Let all your Obſer-
vers, have cauſe to ſay, *This is not the man
that once he was!* It was Ancient, but wholeſome Advice, *Abſcindatur ferro accutæ Com-
punctionis, Ulcus inveteratæ Conſuetudinis; ſi
eſt acerbus Dolor, Leniatur Unguento Devo-
tionis.*

*II.* If we are apprehenſive of any *Evil
Cuſtome,* that is more *Generally* getting head
among us, moſt certainly we ſhall do well
to *Nip it in the Bud.* I fear, I fear, we
ſhall find many ſuch; I ſay, *Many ſuch.*
And perhaps, My Whole Country, could
not be addreſs'd with a more wholeſome
Counſil than this; *Let Serpents be cruſh'd in
the Egg;* and *Bad Cuſtomes* be diſcouraged,
before the Torrent be grown ſo ſtrong, as
to carry all before it.

I will not pretend at this time to bring
in a compleat CATALOGUE OF EVIL
CUSTOMES, that are breaking in upon us.
                                        But

*Advice from the Watch Tower.* 27

But I have a fufficient Commiffion to Lay before you a few Neceffary Advertifements.

Firft. I am to advertife you, That very many of the *Evil Cuftomes*, which debauch other parts of the World, are getting into this place as faft as they can. The *Cuftomes* which have turned Reafon and Vertue *Upfide-down*, and have gotten the Upper-hand of it, are *Coming hither alfo!* If *Religion* once paffed into this *American Strand*, famous *Herberts* Prophecy is fulfilled ; SIN, *Sin has traced and dogged it inftantly.* Good Men are grieved at what they fee, and cry out, *Lord, We are afraid of thy Judgments!*

Secondly. I am to advertife you, That fome of our *Evil Cuftomes* call for a very *Speedy* Animadverfion, a very *Speedy* Reformation. I will fay more particularly. The *Cuftome* of reforting to the *Liquor of Death* in the Bottel ; This is apace, drowning the *Senfes* of men ; drowning all our *Interefts.* *Men of Ifrael, Help!* ---And as eafily the *Ethiopian* or *Leopard* changed, as the *Slaves of the Bottel* recovered. Encroachments on the *Religion of the Sabbath* alfo grow into a *Cuftome* among us. And, I am fure, The *Cuftome* of *Mifpending the Lords-Day Evening* is an in-let unto many Abominations.

Thirdly. I am to advertife you, That when *Foreign Cuftomes* would be Entertained with us, all *Prudent Cautions* are to be ufed about them. There may be *Innocent Cuftomes,* yea, *Laudable Cuftomes,* brought in ; Some that

D 2       might

28    *Advice from the Watch Tower.*

might befriend our Sobriety ; polifh our Converfation ; defend and improve our *Morals.*
But then, there are the *Cuftomes,* which our
Nation may call, *The Vain Converfation received by Tradition from our Fathers.* I am freely
to tell you ; One Main End of our Predeceffors Coming hither, was to keep their Children unacquainted with fuch *Foolifh Cuftomes.*
To introduce them, can be no *Kindnefs* to us.

Laftly ; I make the MOTION : Let every
*Wife man,* have his *Eyes in his head.* Let every Good man, take a due Notice of *Evil Cuftomes* breaking in ; And let no man be afraid
of making *Remarks* upon them, *Complaints* a-
bout them, *Oppofitions* unto them. Efpecially, O you MINISTERS of God, You muft
not be *Dumb* Things ; and, *Sleeping, Lying
down, Loving to Slumber.* Syrs, Be Awake :
*Fight,* O ye *Stars* in your *Courfes* ; Fight a-
gainft all *Evil Cuftomes,* and *Evil Courfes,* that
you may fee coming in like a *Sweeping Flood*
upon us. *Cry aloud, Spare not, Lift up your
voice like a Trumpet, fhow the People,* what *E-
vil Cuftomes* they are in danger of. If any
Cenfure you, as not *Keeping your Poft,* fhow
them the III Chapter of *Ezekiel,* and Silence
them.

*III.* I have One word more to fay. My
Text mentions, the *Ethiopian,* I have fome
thing to fay about the *Ethiopian.* This Land
has of late years, yea, divers times of late
Months, had fome Tragical Things, wherein
*Ethiopi-*

*Advice from the Watch Tower.* 29

*Ethiopians* have been deeply concerned; Thefts, Rapes, Murders, and fome Capital Executions. I am verily perfwaded, God calls us to Confider, Whether we have no *Evil Cuftomes* among us, relating to *Ethiopians.* The Trade relating to their *Importation,* I doubt, has *Evil Cuftomes* enough. And have we none about their *Education?* Oh! That more pains were taken, to fhow the *Ethiopians*, their *Sin,* which renders them fo much *Blacker* than their *Skin!* And to Lead them unto the Saviour, who will beftow upon them a *Change* of *Soul,* which is much better than a *Change* of *Skin!* Oh! For more pains, that they may not be *Ethiopians Accuftomed to do Evil;* but that they may themfelves look on all *Evil Cuftomes* as worfe than any part of their *Slavery!* Oh! That more were done, to accomplifh that word; Pfal.LXVIII. 31. *Ethiopia fhall foon ftretch out her hands unto God!* I take this to be the Voice of God unto us, in fome *Ethiopian* Occurrences. Let the Voice of GOD be hearkened to!

But at this time you Expect, and allow, no more than a Short W I N T E R S E R-M O N. I have no Time Left me now to proceed any further, or to fpeak any more on a Subject, that can hardly be too much fpoken to.

*Cuftome*

## Cuſtome in Sin.

Conſidered in an Hymn of Mr.

# ISAAC WATTS,

AS well might *Ethiopian* Slaves
Waſh out the Darkneſs of their *Skin* ;
The Dead as well may leave their Graves,
As Old Tranſgreſſors ceaſe to Sin.

Let the Wild *Leopards* of the Wood
Put off the SPOTS that Nature gives ;
Then may the Wicked turn to God
And change their Temper and their Lives.

When Vice has held its Empire long
'Twill not Endure the leaſt Controul ;
None but a Power Divinely Strong
Can turn the Current of the Soul.

Great GOD I own thy Power Divine,
That works to Change this Heart of mine ;
I would be form'd a-new, and bleſs
The Wonders of Creating Grace.

A

# A Black Lift

Of fome

# EVIL CUSTOMES.

Which begin to appear among us ; And a
Propofal of P R O P E R  M E T H O D S
to difcourage them.

I. THo' *fome* of our Towns are fo happy, that
there is hardly known fo much as one
*Prayerlefs Family* in them, yet *all* have not this Happinefs. In fome, the *Families that call not upon God,*
or that are not conftant in their *Morning* & *Evening*
Sacrifices, grow too numerous.

*Rem :* Let the *Paftors* be informed, who the *Prayerlefs Houfholders* are ; and upon fuch information,
Lovingly vifit them, and fervently perfwade them,
and leave little Books of *Houfhold-Piety* in their
hands, and give not over, till their Neighbours
promife them to leave off their *Paganizing.*

II. It is to be fear'd, that *becaufe of Swearing, the
Land may mourn* ; and *Oaths* may be too *fuddenly* ad-
miniftred, and too *eafily* multiplied, in cafes brought
before the *Place* of *Judgment*, by People paffionate-
ly engaged againft one another.

*R.* It were to be wifh'd, that they whofe Office
it is, to give the *Oath*, would with all due folem-
nity inculcate the *Fear of an Oath*, upon thofe who
are going to take it ; Explain to them the *Nature*
of a *True Oath*, and the *Danger* of a *Falfe* one ; and
upon a Juft Sufpicion of their being like to Per-
*jure*

32    *Advice from the Watch Tower.*

jure themfelves. delay and prevent their Folly.

III. The *Lords-Day-Evenings*, are by many People, with much vanity, proftituted unto purpofes very difagreeable to the præceding Day, and fuch as have a tendency to defeat all the Good of the Day. It is indeed complained, That fuch a Divertive way of fpending thofe *Evenings*, has gained upon us, as greatly to annoy the Intereft of Religion, and corrupt the Manners of the People.

*R.* Tis to be defired, That *Houfholders* would more generally Reftrain their Families from unfuitable Excurfions, on thefe Evenings ; and employ this *Golden fpot of Time*, in Inftructing of their Families, and in all Exercifes of Piety, fuitable to the State of them, who know not how near they may be to the *End of their Time* ; but know they muft give an Account how they have *fpent their Time*.

IV. In many of our Towns, the *Morning & Evening* Sacrifices of the *Lords-Day*, have no very Long Intermiffion. Many People have their Habitations at fuch a Diftance from the Place of Publick Worfhip, that they cannot repair home in this Intermiffion. Sometimes this proves an occafion for *Difcourfes* and *Actions*, not very fuitable to the *Religion of the Sabbath*, among the People who now ftay at the *Taverns*, or in other Places.

*R.* Tis to be defired, That the *Paftors*, with the affiftance of the Wife and Grave Men in their Neighbourhood, would bring into practice among the People thus detained near the Meeting-Houfe, as Religious and Profitable ways of fpending the *Lords-Day noon*, as they can think upon. *Wifdom* would foon *find out ingenious Inventions !*

V. The *Games of Hazard*, fuch as *Cards* and *Dice*, grow too frequent among our Children. And very particularly in Places where their Hazardous Condition lays them under peculiar Obligations to all Sobriety ; fuch as our *Garrifons*.

*Advice from the Watch Tower.* 33

much inculcate on all that are under their Influence, the fentiments of the Minifters formerly
more than once or twice publifhed among us;
They were Expreffed in fuch terms as thefe.

'There is at leaft a great fufpicion brought on
'the *Lawfulnefs* of thefe *Games*, by the *Lottery* which
'they turn upon. *Lotts* being mentioned in the
'Sacred Oracles of the Scripture, as ufed only in
'*Weighty cafes*, and as an Acknowledgment of *God*
'*fitting in Judgment*, with a defire of His Power and
'Providence to be manifefted, and not without an
'*Invocation of God*, for the *End of Strife* therein im-
'plied ; They cannot be made the*Tools* and *Parts* of
'our *Common Sports*, without at leaft fuch *Appearance*
'*of Evil*, as is forbidden in the Word of God.

'The *Ill Character* given to thefe Ufages, not on-
'ly by *Chriftians* of all Sorts and Ranks, and in all
'*Ages*, whofe juft Invectives againft them would
'fill Volumns, but by the Sober and Moral *Pagans*
'alfo, has brought them among the things of *Evil*
'*Report*, which by *Chriftians* are to be avoided,
'That Mans Heart is inordinately fet upon *Play*,
'who had rather do things under fuch an *Univerfal*
'*Condemnation*, than forbear a little *Play*, which may
'certainly be forborn without any Damage.

VI. At many *Weddings* the Diverfions are im-
proved into fuch *Revels*, as are not well confiftent,
with the *Sobriety* of *Chriftianity*.

*R.* Tis to be defired, That the *Parents*, or other
*Superiours*, who have the ordering of matters on
thefe occafions, would Over-rule the rafh & Lewd
Inclinations of Younger Perfons ; and with a
Watchful Eye forbid all *Diforders* ; Left the *Lord*
*Judge their Houfe*, for the *Iniquity*, for which they
will become Refponfible, when the *Children make*
*themfelves Vile;* and they *Reftrain them not* : But rather have their *Weddings* ennobled with fuch Ac-

E                                  know-

## 34 *Advice from the Watch Tower.*

knowledgments of GOD, as may invite the pre-
fence of the Holy JESUS at them.

VII. To *Drink Healths*, growes a very common
Ufage ; Even among fuch Profeffors of our Holy
Religion, as ought leaft of all to Learn the Wayes
and Works of the *Heathen,* or keep the *vain Converfation received by Tradition from their Fathers,*

R. It were to be defired, That Chriftians would
ferioufly confider, what this *Relick of Paganifm* was
in its firft Original ; and what *Idolatrous* and *Super-
ftitious* Intentions they were that gave the Frft Rife
unto it.

And the Advice offered by an Affembly of Worthy Men, who were no *Fanaticks,* deferves a Room
in the Thoughts of them that have the Regards of
Piety in them.

' Not only the Numberlefs and prodigious Exor-
' bitancies of *Health-drinking,* are to be avoided by
' every Chriftian, but the very propofing of *Cups to*
' *the Profperity* of what is therein Remembred. 'Tis
' a vain Plea, That we drink no more than a *Civil*
' *Remembrance* of the Perfons or Affairs mentioned
' in our Cups. Why is the Action of *Drinking*
' fingled out, rather than any other, for the *Token*
' of the Remembrance ! And why is there fuch a
' ftrefs Laid upon a concurrence in the Action ? It
' is but a Continuation of the *Old Paganifm,* which
' had better be utterly abolifhed, than thus refined
' and preferved. Every thing that ferves, either to
' Revive, or to maintain the Old *Pagan Follies,* and
' hardenMen in them,fhould be declaimed by them
' that would *Adorn the Doctrine of God their Saviour.*

VIII. *Chriftmas-Revels* begin to be taken up, a-
mong fome vainer Young People here and there in
fome of our Towns.

R.

*Advice from the Watch Tower.* 35

R. It were to be defired, That Chriftians *aboun-ding* in *Wifdom and Prudence,* would Weigh in Equal Ballances, what is to be faid, againft their keeping any *Stated Holidays,* which our Glorious Lord him-felf has not inftituted; and what more is to be faid, about affigning a *Wrong-Day* to Commemorate a great Work of God, as *thereon* accomplifhed; and moft of all, how offenfive it cannot but be un-to the *Holy Son of God,* for Men to pretend his Ho-nour in Committing Impieties, which the Confcience of every Man cannot but affure him, that they are Abominable Things, and hateful to the God, who has not pleafure in Wickednefs.

IX. The *Riots* that have too often accuftomed our *Huskings,* have carried in them, fearful Ingra-titude and Provocation unto the Glorious God. R. It is reported, That thefe are *Abated.* May the *Joy of Harveft* no longer be proftituted unto vi-cious purpofes. *Hufbandmen and Houfholders*: Let the *Night of your Pleafure* be turned into *Fear,*; a Jealous *Fear,* Leaft your Children take their Leave of God, and of Piety.

X. It is to be hoped, The *Shroves-Tuefday Vani-ties,* of making *Cakes to the Queen of Heaven,* and Sacrificing of *Cocks* to the Pagan Idol *Tuifco*; and other Superftitions Condemned in the *Reformed Churches*; will find very few Abetters, in a Coun-trey declaring for our Degree of *Reformation,* Should fuch things become ufual among us, the great God would foon fay with Indignation, *How art thou turned unto the Degenerate Plant of a Strange Vine unto me !*

XI. In the *Building* and *Sailing* of our Ships, it is Complained, That fome *Ill Things* are grown too *Cuftomary.*

Among thefe, that Imitation of a *Baptifm,* in giv-ing a Name to a Veffel, with breaking a Bottle up-

E 2                                            on

36    *Advice from the Watch Tower.*

on her, at her Launching, is a moſt horrid and
Shocking Profanity.

*R.* It is to be hoped, That the Conſiderate
Chriſtians, who have at any time the Ordering of
Matters at a Launching, will take Effectual Care,
that *none ſhall do any more ſo Wickedly.*

And it is to be Wiſhed, That the *Commanders of
Ships,* would be ſo ſenſible of their Obligations to
keep in good Terms with Heaven, as to diſcoun-
tenance all thoſe *Wicked Cuſtomes* Aboard, which
are contrary to the Glorious Rules of our Saviour,
and of all Goodneſs.

XII. To *Sleep in the Publick Worſhip of God,* is a
thing too frequently and eaſily Practiſed, by very
many People ; and even by ſome noted Profeſſors
of Religion, who ought, of all Men, to give a Better Example. It may even be wondred at, how
ſuch Perſons can enjoy themſelves, in a *Reflection*
on their conduct in the Houſe of God ; or, whether they do at all *Reflect* upon it. The *Name* of
the Glorious GOD is greatly profaned ; and the
Benefit of His Inſtitution greatly defeated by this
Inadvertency.

*R.* It is to be deſired, That the Awe of the
THIRD COMMANDMENT were more *Awak-
ened* in the People of God. And that it might grow
more faſhionable for People of all Ranks, to do the
Charitable Action of *Waking one another,* where they
ſee *Drowſineſs* prevailing, and not ſay, *Am I my Bro-
thers Keeper :*

XIII. It is too frequent a thing for Perſons not only
to *Run into Debt* when they have no Rational proſpect of
getting out but alſo to *Lye in Debt,* without any concern on their minds, whether they ever get out or not
As a Branch of this Evil practice , There are ſome, who
trade upon other Mens Eſtates, and Live higher in
their Domeſtick Expences of Table and Habit than
they ought to do, and go on from year to year in the
Dark, without ſettling their *Accounts,* to ſee how much
they

## *Advice from the Watch Tower.* 37

they may be fallen behind hand. Anon they
break ; and their Creditors have *a plain Theft* Committed on them.

R. A Gentleman when he Lent any Books, ( things
oftener *Borrowed*, than honeſtly Reſtored ; Another *Evil
Cuſtome* !) he wrote on a Blank leaf at the Beginning, The
*Wicked borrowes, and payes not again.* His Books were alwayes Returned ! It were to be wiſhed, That *this Word*
of God were more thought upon. It were to be wiſhed,
that People would more ſtudy the meaning and the
extent of the EIGHTH COMMANDMENT. It were
to be wiſhed That Creditors, would be ſo wiſe for themſelves, as to Compel thoſe People to look ſeaſonably into the State of their Buſineſs, who they may ſear are too
Negligent.

XIV. Tho' the *Law* of the Province, about the *Chuſing
and S tt ing of a Miniſter* in a Town ( which has had the
Royal Sanction ) be a very wholeſome Law, and have
much of the Goſpel in it ; yet there growes upon the
Inhabitants, who are not yet come into the Communion of the Churches, a Diſpoſition to Superſede it, and
Over-rule it. The *Churches* themſelves recede from the
Rigour of the Law, with ſo much Condeſcention, as to
make a *Nomination of more than one,* for the reſt of the
Inhabitants to join with them in their Votes, to determine, which of theſe thus Nominated, ſhall be their
Miniſter. And yet the Inhabitants will not accept
their *Nomination,* but refuſe to act upon it, and will not
allow the *Church* any way to go before them.

R. Should this Iniquity proceed, there might eaſily
and uſually be *choſen* to Adminiſter *all ſpecial Ordinances*
unto a Gathered *Church* of our Lord, a *Paſtor,* whom not
One man in the ſaid *Church* has Voted for ; A *Paſtor* Entirely Choſen, by thoſe who do not at preſent attend
the *Special Ordinances,* nor perhaps intend quickly to do
it. The Conſequences would be fatal to the *Church-
State* of the Countrey ; and may bring on an *Impoſition* of
Miniſters, without any Election of the People at all.

The Churches ought with all poſſible Tenderneſs,
to conſult the Edification and Satiſfaction of the Chriſtian Inhabitants who are to joyn with them in ſupporting their Miniſter. But yet they muſt not Betray, and
Give up, the *Right of Chuſing their Paſtor,* and put it into
in-

## 38 *Advice from the Watch Tower.*

incompetent Hands. If the Inhabitants are fo *Unreafonable,* as to demand it, they fhould be powerfully advifed and exhorted to defift from fuch a Diforder. If
fome Eminent Perfons of a Publick & Excellent Character be prevailed withal, to come unto the *Town-
Meeting,* and there difpenfe to the Inhabitants the
needful Admonitions, it may be they'll be hearken'd
to. If ever they will not hearken, Let the Churches
*go on with the Steps of the Law.* It may be, God will
blefs the Means ufed by the Council that comes together, on fuch an Occafion.

XV. The *Members* of our Churches removing from
one place to another, are not Expreffive enough in
having the *Removal of their Relation* from One Church
to another Signified. The Exercife of Difcipline is
incommoded by this Neglect; and the ferviceablenefs
of the Chriftians to the Churches, with which they
refide, has Encumbrances upon it.

R. It is to be defired, That *Church-Members* would not
be Long in a *New Place,* without having it in fome con-
venient Way Certified and Recognized, that they have
their more *Immediate Relation transferred* unto the Church
there. And that, if they too long delay it, the Churches whereto they belong, do of themfelves take a proper
care, that the thing be in an orderly manner accomplifhed.

XVI. It is too common a thing, for perfons on their
*Perfonal Prejudices* againft this or that particular Com-
municant, at whom they have taken offence, to *Withdraw from the Communion* at the Table of the Lord.

R. It is to be defired, That Chriftians may be made
more fenfible of the *Evil* and *Folly,* which there is in
their omitting their own *Duty,* and renouncing their own
*Comfort,* becaufe *Another man* has not done what he ought
to do; and in their *Separating* from the Church ( and as
it were. *Excommunicating* of it, ) while the *Church* has as
yet no Mifcarriage to be charg'd upon it. If fuch Perfons are Obftinate in their *Schifm,* they ought themfelves
to be Ecclefiaftically dealt withal.

XVII. The *Support* of the *Evangelical Miniftry* in feveral parts of the Country, is difcouraged with divers
*Bad Cuftomes* attending of it.

R. An Excellent Remedy for fome of them, would be,

## *Advice from the Watch Tower.* 39

if what is already the practice of some Towns, were more generally practised ; That is, for *all the Town Charges*, to be Levied, in *One Undistinguishing Collection* ; that so the Minister, and the School-Master, and other Officers that have *Salaries*, may have nothing to do, but receive them out of the *Town-Treasury*. Many grievous *Temptations* would be in this way avoided.

XVIII. To Elude the Law about *Schools*, is too Customary. It argues, that a due sense of that Grand Concern, the *Education of Children,* is too much laid aside among us.

Tis *Wonderful !* Tis *Wonderful !* That a People of our Profession should seem so unconcerned, Left the next Generation be miserably Uncultivated, and have hideous *Barbarity* grow upon it !

XIX. It should be Enquired, Whether many of our *Solemnities*, as our *Funerals*, our *Trainings*, our *Lectures*, &c some of our *Anniversary Occurrences*, may not insensibly have needless *Expences* of *Money*, and of *Time*, ( which with Wise men, is of more account than *Money*, ) and also *Divers Vanities*, growing upon them. Such things ought seasonably to be regarded and rectified,

It is more particularly complained, That there are Places where *Horse-races* are too much practised, and *rash Wagers* are laid on those Occasions ; which introduce very many more Disorders.

R. Good men should not only withold their *Presence* from these *Riotous Actions*, but also in all other proper ways express their Dislike of them. They should make people sensible of many just Exceptions against the *Exercise* it self in regard of Mischief both to the *Horse and his Rider*. They should show them the Iniquity of throwing away their Money so impertinently as in *Wagering* on those Contingencies. And show them, to how much better purpose, and with how much better Account they may spend their *Time*, than in such *Impertinencies*.

XX. But of all our EVIL CUSTOMES, there is none more fatal, to us, than the Use of the BOTTEL growing upon many parts of the Countrey. The *Rumbottel*. Ah, Thou Destroyer ; How many have been *cast down wounded* by thee ? How many *Strong Ones have been Slain*, by thee ? When once the *Spirit of the Bottel* has *bewitched* men, alas, their *Estates* are melted away ; their

*Fami-*

## 40 *Advice from the Watch Tower.*

*Families* are foon brought into a Wretched Condition their *Faculties* are fo wounded, that they become incapable of any notable Improvements ; Men that were once thought fhining Patterns of Godlinefs, have their *Lamps* going out in obfcure Darknefs. All Good Order is likely to be drowned,, where *Strong Drink is Raging* !

R. Good men muft be Awakened out of their Lethargy, & be apprehenfive of our Danger. Infamous RUM fhould no longer be the ufual Entertainment of a Friend at our Houfes : Men muft be thought *Unqualified* for *Preferments* and *Employments* ( as they really are ) if they be much given to it. Finally ; The pitty of Heaven, to a People in a *Wildernefs*, whom the *Dragon* would *Swallow up in a Flood* of Strong Drink, is to be implored, with a general and unceafing Importunity.

¶ Tho' there is now brought in fo large a *Flying Roll* of the *Evil Cuftomes* that are getting in among us, yet it is to be feared, that fome, yea, much *Addition* may be made unto a *Catalogue* already fo full of *Lamentation and Mourning and Wo.* It is therefore now to be further moved, That Confiderate Men would make this a Great Article, of *Obfervation* with themfelves, and of *Converfation* with one another, [ And why not *Affociate* for that purpofe too ? ) *To Confider, what Evil Cuftomes are growing upon us*; *And, What fhall be done to cure them* ? And apply this Confideration in a very particular manner ; to the *Unjuft Methods, of Trade*, which people too eafily fall into.

Oh ! That we may be *Led into a Land of Rectitude* !

---

## Liberavi Animam Meam.

# The *SAVIOUR* with his RAINBOW.

---

A

# DISCOURSE

Concerning the

# COVENANT

WHICH

G O D will remember, in the Times of Danger paſſing over his Church.

---

*By* COTTON MATHER, *D.D.*

---

---

*LONDON*:
Printed by *J. D.* and ſold by *T. Harriſon* at the *Exchange*. 1714.

---

# T O

# *Mr.* Thomas Vennor
## *of* Warwick.

*S I R,*

I Do, at your *Request*, *furnish you with a Copy of a Sermon which my Bro-ther preach'd and publish'd in* New-England. *Your Design of* Re-printing *it, is, in my Opinion, worthy to be encourag'd. I do hope the great Ends of God's Glory, the Honour of Jesus Christ, and the Good of his Church, will be promoted hereby.*

*I am, Sir,*

*Your Servant,*

*Nov.* 10. 1713.

S A M. M A T H E R.

( 5 )

---

# The SAVIOUR with his *Rainbow.*

---

## REVEL. X. 1.

### *A Rainbow was upon his Head.*

IT is the *Head* of your admirable Saviour, which, O diftreffed People of God, now appears before you. Oh! behold it, with fweet Encouragements; with juft Aftonifhments! The *Head* about which we now fee the comfortable *Rainbow,* is *thy Head,* O thou Church of the Living God; it is he, whom God has placed as *thy Head,* and thou thy felf haft chofen him, haft owned him.

When you fee what it is that this *Mighty Angel* comes down from Heaven to do; that he comes with a loud Voice to proclaim the End of the *Time* for the Reign of Sin and Satan in the World, and make a Demand of this Lower World, for the Kingdom of the Great Redeemer; how, how, can you forbear a loud Voice of Supplications ; *Great God, fend this mighty Angel down among us !*

The Servant of God had feen the Fate of the *Roman Empire,* down as low as the conclufion of the *Saracen* Oppreffions, and the *Turkifh* Hoftilities ; the very Period unto which we are now certainly arriv'd. Then there appears unto him a *mighty Angel,* in fo

ftately

( 6 )

ſtately and ſo ſplendid a Pomp, that many Interpreters can hardly allow him to be any leſs a Perſon than our great *Saviour* himſelf. He appears to exhibit a *new Scene* of things Marvellous and very Amazing. And if this be the Period for the Appearance of ſuch an Angel, I do a very *ſeaſonable* thing this Day, in ſhowing him among you. I diſpute not, whether this *Angel* be our *Saviour* himſelf, becauſe he deſcends with a Glory too big and bright for any Creature ; or, whether he be a *cıeated* Angel: for, if he be *ſo*, yet he comes in the *name* of our *Saviour* ; and he comes with a Repreſentation of that *Glory*, which belongs to none but our *Saviour*.

The Deſign of the Deſcent made by this *Mighty Angel*, is, to foretel, and bring on, a wonderful *Reformation* of the World. If he appears in a *Cloud*, this muſt not be wondred at. There is a Super-celeſtial *Cloud*, which from the Beginning has been employ'd as a *Symbol*, and a *Cover* for the Majeſty of our God, in his Appearance. Not only the *Iſraelites*, who were favour'd ſometimes with an actual view of ſomething that belong'd unto that vaſt *Cloud*; but even the *Pagans* alſo, and their *Poets*, had ſome Tradition of it.

There is an Intimation in it, that there will be *unſearchable* Circumſtances, *unſearchable* Diſpenſations in his Appearances. And if thou wilt come unto us in *cloudy Times*, O glorious Lord, Thy Will be done : yea, *Even ſo come unto us !*

The only thing that we now ſingle out for conſideration, is that *particular Glory* of our Appearing Saviour ; *A Rainbow was upon his Head.* The *Rainbow* is a well known *Meteor*, often beheld, but not with Eyes devout enough among us, in the *Day of Rain*. Perhaps, there is nothing in all the *meteorous Kingdom* ſo very Beautiful. Such is the *Beauty* of the *Meteor*, that while the Heathen *Mythology* made it *The Daughter of Wonderment*, *Cicero* makes it a matter of Wonderment that it was not lifted in the number of their Gods. Let thoſe declaim on this *Beauty*, who can fetch a Text from the Son of *Sirach*, that ſays, *Look on the Rainbow, and Praiſe him that made it ; very Beautiful it is in the Brightneſs thereof.* That which it becomes us moſt of all to ponder, is, That the Sovereign Creator of the World has, in his Wiſdom

‡ ſtamp'd

( 7 )

ftamp'd a *Sacramental Character* on the *Rainbow*; he has Inftituted the *Rainbow* for a *Sign*, and *Seal* of his *Covenant* with the World. All Chriftians are appris'd of the Signification which the *ninth Chapter of Genefis* has left upon the *Rainbow*, for our perpetual Confolation ; and as our Affurance, that the World fhall no more be *drowned* as it was in the Days of *Noah*. Wherefore our Saviour appearing to us, *with a Rainbow* about his *Head*, propofes to preach this joyful Doctrine unto us :

*Our glorious LORD will remember his Covenant with his People, even in the moft cloudy Times that are paffing over them.*

And this is the *Doctrine* which I am now to infift upon ; I wifh you had a more able *Barnabas* to infift upon it. My *Doctrine*, may it *drop as the Rain*; as the fweet and fmall Rain from a *Cloud*, that has a *Rainbow* brightning of it. We may fee *Cloudy Times* ; yea, we may apprehend fuch a *Flood* of Calamity, as will carry all before it: yet now, O People of God, you are a People in *Covenant* with him ; a Reliance on your *facrific'd Saviour*, fecures your Title to his *Covenant.* O now look up to your dear Saviour ! fee, he appears to you in your *Cloudy Times*, with a *Rainbow about his Head*. He declares unto you, that he will *remember his Covenant*; he has not *forgotten to be gracious :* you fhall not be *overwhelm'd* ; the evil things, which threaten you, fhall not be too hard for you: you fhall, you fhall be glorioufly deliver'd.

I. In the firft place, I will fhow the *Rainbow about the Head of a Saviour*, unto every *particular Believer* on that faithful Saviour. My Friend, apply the glorious *Rainbow* to thy own *particular Condition* ; thy Saviour invites thee to do fo. I will venture to lay this down, as a *Rule* of Application ; " The *Promifes* which belong " to the whole Church of God, are the Portion of " every *particular Believer*, and he is welcome to make " ufe of them, as far as ever he can find his own *cafe* " adapted in them." According to this *Golden Rule* of Faith, and of Fellowfhip, I now fay ; Believer, Doft

thou

( 8 )

thou not fee *Cloudy Times* ? I know, thou doft: There is no Believer, but what has his Times of *Darkneſs*; no *Child of Light*, but what ſometimes *walks in Darkneſs*, and ſees no Light. 'Tis often, often the Cafe of every Believer: *Lament.* 3. 1, 2. *I am the Man that hath ſeen Aſfliction ; he hath brought me into Darkneſs.* He cannot underſtand the meaning of the Divine Dealings with him; he cannot fee the Face of God favourably ſhining on him; he cannot but fear a ſad Iſſue of the things which are breaking of him. His Temptations make it the *Hour* and *Power of Darkneſs* with him. He knows not what to do, nor what God intends to do : perhaps it comes to that Extremity ; *Lord, thou haſt covered thy ſelf with a Cloud, that my Prayer ſhould not paſs through.* In ſo *dark* a time, the afflicted Believer is afraid of a *Flood* that will totally over-power him, that he ſhall *periſh in his Aſfliction.*

But now, *Comfort ye, Comfort ye* my Children, faith the Lord. Show my *Rainbow* unto them; tell them, that I will be *ever mindful of my Covenant.* The Children of God may be ſure, that in Remembrance of his Covenant with them, he will ſave them from the *Floods* which threaten Deſtruction to them : only, my Brethren, be ſure that you remember one Direction ; *Pſal.* 32. 6. *For this ſhall every one that is godly, pray unto thee, in a time when thou mayſt be found : ſurely in the Floods of great Waters, they ſhall not come nigh unto him.* [One has thus given us the true ſenſe of it : *For this ſhall every good Man pray, when thou art to be found ; and ſhall be ſafe in mighty Floods, when other Men are drown'd.*] I will firſt of all ſhow you what the *Comforts* are, that may delight and ſupport your Souls, and keep you from *ſinking* in the *multitude of your Thoughts within you :* The Comforts to be read in this *Rainbow* on the Head of your lovely Saviour.

Firſt, Have you a *Flood* of *Adverſity* beating on you ? Perhaps you may ſuffer a vaſt weight of *Adverſity,* troubleſome Occurrences, innumerable, irreſiſtible. The roaring Billows of *Adverſity* rolling in upon you, may make you cry out, *Save me, O God, for the Waters are come in unto my Soul, I am come into deep Waters, where the Floods overflow me.* Hear the Anſwer from the *Rainbow* : Ah, thou *afflicted and toſs'd with Tempeſt* ; be thou comforted ; thy Lord will ſtep in and ſave thee. He will fulfil that

Promiſe

( 9 )

Promife of his *Covenant* unto thee, Ifa. 43. 2. *When thou paffeft thro the Waters, I will be with thee, they fhall not over-flow thee.*

Again; Does a *Flood* of *Corruption* rife in your Souls? Perhaps, the Power of *Corruption* in you may be fuch, that you may think, *I fhall one Day perifh by the Hand of fuch or fuch a Sin!* *Luft* may fo prevail againft *Grace*, that you can fee no hope of *Grace* ever getting the upper-hand. O Soul, *mourning* becaufe of the *Oppreffion* of an *Adverfary that provoketh thee fore*; mourn on, mourn on; and then know, that the Spirit of God will *dry up thofe curfed Waters.* Tho thy *Grace* be but a *Spark*, yet *many Waters fhall not quench it, neither the Floods drown it.* Thy Saviour will fulfil unto thee that Promife of his Covenant; *Rom.* 6. 14. *Sin fhall not have Dominicn over you.*

Furthermore, in the *Affaults of Hell* upon your Souls; does the *Enemy come in like a Flood* upon you? It may be, the *Powers of Darknefs* are pouring in upon you. Your tempted Souls are exceedingly born down, diforder'd with hideous *Injections*, terrify'd at the *Noife of the Water-fpouts:* yet, O molefted Chriftian, that Saviour hath *fet Bars* to the Tempter, and faid, *Hitherto fhalt thou come, but no further, and here fhall thy proud Waves be ftaid.* That Promife of his *Covenant* fhall be fulfill'd unto thee, 1 *Cor.* 10. 13. *God is faithful, who will not fuffer you to be tempted above what you are able.*

Once more, we read concerning *the Floods of the Un-godly.* Sometimes the Servants of God are uneafy at the *Power*, the *Number*, the *Malice* of Men that are difaffected unto them If they are engag'd in more notable *Servi-ces* for God, they may be expos'd unto the Rage of wicked and reftlefs Men; which may make them afraid, left their *Serviceablenefs* be utterly extinguifh'd. There may be Times wherein *Hell* may be evidently and furi-oufly broke loofe upon them. The foaming Waves of *Hell* may dafh, and beat againft them, and make a noife that reaches up to Heaven: Times when the *Workers of Iniquity* do, as it were, make an *Infurrection*, and *bend their Bows to fhoot their Arrows*, even *bitter Words.* How accommodated a *Rainbow* for fuch Times! What is the *way, which, O Lord, thou knoweft thy Servants ufe to take*, in fuch Storms as thefe! They repair humbly, with Repen-

B

tance,

tance, with Prayers, and with Tears, to their compaffio-nate *Saviour.* All their *Opportunities* to *do Good,* they put into his gracious Hands. Lo then, *then!* they fee the *Rainbow* about the Head of their ftrong Friend in the Heavens concerned for them. He fends this Advice unto them, and the Promife is fulfill'd unto the Sur-prize of all wife obfervers; *Ifa.* 41. 10, 11. *Fear thou not, for I am with thee; Behold all they that were incenfed againft thee, fhall be afhamed and confounded.* This, this was the antient Experience: *The Floods of ungodly Men made me afraid. In my Diftrefs I called upon the Lord, and cried unto my God. He drew me out of many Waters; he deliver'd me from them which hated me!*

Finally; The Fate of *Mankind,* under the *Law of Mortality,* is thus defcrib'd unto us; *Pfal.* 90. 5. *Thou carriest them away as with a Flood.* Believer, thou alfo muft, in thy Father's time for it, be *carried away. Death,* Death is unavoidable. But thy *Head* is always above *Water;* thou fhalt not always lie among *the Dead.* The quickning Spirit of that *Head* will fetch out of the Grave, all that belong unto him. When the *black Waters* of *Death* have *compafs'd* thee *about,* and the Depth *has clos'd* thee *round about,* and thou art gone down *to the bottom of the Mountains;* thou fhalt not have caufe to com-plain, *The Earth with its Bars is about me for ever!* No, thou wilt *bring up our Life from Corruption;* we know it, we know it, O Lord our God. Ah, dying Believer; thy Saviour who was once dead, is rifen from the Dead. On the *Rainbow* about his Head, O read what is writ-ten; *Behold, I am alive, and I live for evermore. Becaufe I live, thou fhalt alfo live. Heaven,* that high Seat of the *Rainbow,* yea, an higher Heaven fhall be the Seat of the *rais'd Believer* too. The *rifen Saviour* will infallibly raife the Believer Child of God, thy *Sin* has wafh'd thee o-ver-board. O *cruel Wave!* it lays thee in the *Deeps.* But the Hand of thy kind Saviour will take thee up; — will pull thee up, and *fhow Wonders to the Dead;* — thou fhalt *Rife,* and *Praife* him! *

[

---

* Quickly after the Preaching of this Sermon, there died a Perfon of fhining Piety, a Chriftian of uncommon Holinefs, Devotion, Pa-tience,

I will go on, and ſhow you, *Secondly*, Some ſpecial *Seſſons*, wherein you will do exceeding well, to make uſe of theſe Comforts. And there are eſpecially *two* ſuch *Seaſons*, that I will commend unto you. I ſhall ſenſibly ſerve the Cauſe of Piety, by commending of them.

First, On the ſight of the *natural Rainbow*, theſe comfortable Meditations on the *Covenant* of God, and of Grace, will be very ſeaſonable. It is a real *Fault* in the People of God, that they can be Spectators of the *Rainbow*, with no more proper, holy, heavenly Thoughts, produc'd in their Souls; a very faulty *Unthankfulneſs* to our Great Saviour, who has plac'd it as his *Bow* in the *Clouds*, and ſaid unto us, *O my dear People, Do you look upon that, as a Memorial of my Covenant!* The *Goſpel of the Rainbow*, is truly one of the *Deſiderata*, among the Subjects that ſhould be cultivated in the Church of God. At preſent, I will only ſay; the *Covenant* with our Father *Noah*, whereof we have the *Rainbow* for an Obſignation, had ſuch an Aſpect upon the *Meſſiah*, that we may fairly be led by the *Rainbow*, to remember the whole *Covenant of Grace*, in all the *very great and precious Promiſes* of it. Concerning the *Covenant* which God has made with our Saviour, for the Redemption of his People, we read, *Pſal.* 89. 37. *It ſhall be eſtabliſh'd, as the faithful Witneſs in Heaven.* By the *faithful Witneſs in Heaven*, is meant the *Rainbow*. Well then; when we have that *comely Work* of God before our Eyes, let us entertain ſuch Thoughts as theſe: " May a glorious CHRIST " be my *Saviour*, and my *Surety*; how Happy, how Hap-" py am I! My Sins will be caſt into the *Depths of the* " *Sea*; I ſhall not my ſelf be caſt thither for them. O " my Soul! be not thou *caſt down.* Be not *afraid of all* " *thy Sorrows*; thy Lord will not leave thee to *ſink* in any " of thy Sorrows. Tho the *Grave* do ſwallow me up, Oh!

---

tience, and Humility, Mrs. *Abigail Whippo*; gloriouſly triumphing over Death. God marvelouſly bleſs'd this Sermon, to produce and aſſiſt the Triumphs of her Soul. With Rapture ſhe gave Thanks to Heaven for theſe Conſolations; ſaying, *O the dear Saviour, that I am now to ſee with a* RAINBOW *about his Head! I am ſure he will remember the Covenant, which he has help'd me a thouſand times to lay hold upon! I am ſure he will do me Good, according to his Covenant!* I do with Pleaſure anſwer the Deſire of ſome, to preſerve the Memory of ſuch a Chriſtian.

" let

( 12 )

" let me not *fear to go down* into the Grave; my Lord
" will *bring me up again!* I fee a *faithful Witnefs in Heaven*,
" that puts me in mind of an *Eftablifh'd Covenant* for
" fuch Bleffings of Goodnefs."

Secondly, When we fee the *Baptifm* of the Lord ad-
miniftred, thefe Meditations may be very feafonably a-
waken'd. It is no fmall Advantage to be minded of
the *Covenant*, which our God has made with our JESUS
for us, and with us, in our JESUS. We are minded
of this *Covenant* after an excellent manner, by the Adminiftration of *Baptifm* in our Congregations. God fanc-
tifies the fight of this Adminiftration, as well as the o-
ther *Ordinances* in the Affemblies of *Zion*; and it is a profane Folly to make light of a thing which God ufes for
an *Inftrument* of fo much Good unto the Souls of Men.
As in any *fprinkled Water*, the *Light* eafily caufes a fort
of a *Rainbow*, fo in the *Baptifmal Water*, we fee the *Rainbow* about our Saviour; he there and thence calls to the
Beholders, *O my People, I will be ever mindful of my Covenant!* Let our glad Souls be fenfible of this. I mention it
the rather, becaufe I find, 1 *Pet.* 3.19. *Baptifm* is made the
Antitype of the *Flood*, unto which the *Rainbow* has relation. The *old Man* in us, is like the *old World*; under a
Curfe. The *Blood* of our Saviour wafhing away the
Guilt of our Sin; and the *Spirit* of our Saviour taking
away the Life of our Sin; are both of 'em compar'd
unto *Waters*. By thefe *Waters*, the *Old Man* is deftroy'd
in our Souls, as the *Old World* was by the Flood. The
*New Man*, like *Noah* in the *Ark*, is by thefe Waters *rais'd
up*, and brought nearer to God. In this way 'tis, that the
Bleffings of the *Covenant* become our Portion. Sirs, when
you fee a Perfon *baptiz'd* in our Congregations, then
think! " O that bleffed *Covenant!* according to that
" only my *Sin* fhall be drowned; but I my felf fhall be
" *rais'd* unto the neareft Communion with Heaven. Yea,
" a *Refurrection from the Dead* will be beftow'd upon me!"

But thus I leave every *particular Believer* to his own
Meditations, on his own fhare in the *Covenant* of God.

II. I am now to tell you, what a *Meffenger* [excufe
and indulge me if I make Reprifals of the Term, a
*Meffenger*] of happy Tidings, the *Rainbow about the Head*
of

( 13 )

of the Saviour, is unto the *Church in general*, unto the whole *Church of the Living God* upon Earth.

The *Covenant* of God, for the *Continuance of his Church in this World*, and its Fruition of Blessedness in a *New World*; this was included in the *Covenant* made with our Patriarch after the *Flood*. Our holy God never gave the *Rainbow* for a Token, that he would preserve a World, only to be a Rendezvouz of *Traitors* and *Rebels*: a Field for none but *wicked People* to graze upon. The preservation of the World is, that so our Saviour may have an *Elect People* here prepared for him, and that anon there may come on a Resolution, wherein the *whole Earth* shall be fill'd with that People, and his Kingdom. You should read this glorious thing written on the *Rainbow* with Capitals! And hence this *Covenant* of God is engross'd in those Terms ; *Isa.* 54. 9, 10. *This is as the Waters of* Noah *unto me: for as I have sworn, that the Waters of* Noah *should no more go over the Earth, so — my Kindness shall not depart from thee, neither shall the Covenant of my Peace be remov'd, saith the Lord, that hath Mercy on thee.* We are fallen into *Cloudy Times*; and, *the Floods have lifted up, O Lord, the Floods have lifted up their Voice, the Floods lift up their Waves:* But we have a Lord with a *Rainbow* about his Head ; and this our Lord is *mightier than the mighty Waves of the Sea.*

O People of God, and you that have *Jerusalem* coming into your Minds; look up, look up, see a *Rainbow* about the Head of your Saviour; and hear that ravishing Voice come out of his Mouth, *I will take a sufficient Care of my Church in the World. My Covenant for my Church, there shall be no breaking, no failing of it !*

And is not this the meaning of that Exhibition ? *Rev.* 4. 3. *There was a* Rainbow *round about the Throne.* Our JESUS is *enthroned* in the Heavens; the Scepter of God is in his Hands; but he will so manage every thing, that his *Covenant* for the Preservation of his Church in the World, shall be most punctually accomplish'd.

First, I will give you some *Reasons* why the *Rainbow* about the Head of our Saviour, will not prove an *empty Show* ; but he will fulfil to his Church, the *Covenant* of his Mercy. 'Tis for such Reasons as these.

1. The

( 14 )

1. The Blessed God, is a most *Faithful God,* the *God of Truth.* Oh! let our God *be true,* in our Praises of him, and *every Man a Lyar,* that has the least Murmur of his being any other. In the midst of our deepest *Lamentations,* we must own that thing ; *Lament.* 3. 23. *Great is thy Faithfulness.* He is the *Unchangeable* one. He makes a *Covenant,* and he *changes not* ; therefore the Church to be preserv'd, according to his Covenant, shall *not be consum'd.* His Nature, and his Glory, is that, *Psal.* 3. 4, 5. *The Lord is Gracious and full of Compassion ; he will ever be mindful of his Covenant.*

Again ; Our Saviour with the *Rainbow about his Head,* appears before his *Father,* as well as unto his *People.* The Eternal Father is the *God of our JESUS,* he is in *Covenant* with him. Our JESUS is the *Head* of the *Covenant* which is made for the People of God ; it is made with him. Our Saviour presents himself before God, as the *Mediator* of the *Covenant.* He pleads the *Cause* of his Church ; he pleads for its Preservation. We are sure of that ; *Heb.* 9. 24. *He is gone into Heaven it self, now to appear in the Presence of God for us.* This *Angel with the* Rainbow, if he who *took not on him the Nature of Angels,* and he who is *above all Angels,* may be ever call'd *an Angel* ; he is the *Angel of the Covenant* ; and I will add, he is the *Angel of his Presence.* In the *Presence* of the Eternal Father, he makes this Demand ; " O " my Father, my Father ; the Church which I have dy'd for, " it must not be lost ; Oh! let it live Eternally !"

Lastly, The *People* of God, they mind him of his *Covenant* ; they point him to his own *Rainbow.* They are a *Praying* People. Because they see a *Rainbow about the Throne* of Heaven, this emboldens them to approach the *Throne* ; they come with Boldness unto it, as a *Throne of Grace.* They lay hold on all the *Promises.* The Cry of their incessant *Prayer* to God is that, *Jer.* 14. 21. *O remember, break not thy Covenant with us.* They are a People that also wait upon God in the *Sacraments* of his *Covenant.* By attending on the *Sacraments,* they celebrate the *Covenant* of God ; they sollicit for the performance of it. Yea, when they see those *Commemorations of the Covenant* in the Churches of the Lord, they lift up their Hearts unto him ; *O thou Great God, who keepest Covenant and Mercy, remember thy Covenant of Mercy to thy People !*

And,

( 15 )

And, I hope, the View of the *Rainbow* will now more than ever, have the like Improvement with them. The glorious *Hearer of Prayer* will take notice of it.

I will proceed, Secondly, to set before you some *Articles* in the *Covenant of Mercy* to the Church, which are declar'd and confirm'd unto us, by the *Rainbow about the Head* of our merciful Saviour. Be the *Times* never so *Cloudy*, and the *Floods* never so boisterous, never so mountainous, the Church of God has the *Expectations of the Rainbow* to live upon.

They are such as these.

First, The *Church cannot be drown'd.* The Church of God may read that Motto on the *Rainbow*; Jer. 46. 28. *I will not make a full end of thee.* Our Saviour will always have a Church, yea, a *Visible Church* in the World. Tho it may fly, for some Ages, into the *Valleys* of *Piemont*, yet even there it shall be *Visible.* No *Flood* shall utterly swallow it up. A number of People visibly embracing the *Truths*, and obeying the *Laws* of the only Saviour, will be always upon the Face of the Earth. We read, *Psal.* 125. 1. of a *Mount* Zion, *which cannot be remov'd, but abideth for ever.* I will not say, this was a Covenant for the literal *Mount Zion*; for this has been remov'd ; the *Hill* was dug down with a vast Labour of three Years, in the Days of the *Maccabæan Simeon.* The *Jews* on certain accounts of Policy, dug down their *Zion* with their own Hands. But, O *Church* of our blessed JESUS, thou art that *Mount Zion*, the most *antient* of all the Mountains, the most *lasting* of all the Hills, eternally Impregnable ! No *Flood* can roll over the Top of the *Holy Hill of* Zion. There is a word in the BIBLE, which has been as an *Ark* for the Church of God, in the most *Cloudy* and Stormy Ages of it; that word, *Mat.* 16. 18. *I will build my Church, and the Gates of Hell shall not prevail against it.* I incline to think, that our Saviour alludes to what occur'd in the *Flood*, which once *overthrew the Foundations of the Wicked.* In that *Flood*, we read, *The Fountains of the Great Deep were broken up* ; and, *The Waters prevail'd exceedingly upon the Earth*; *they prevail'd, and the Mountains were covered.* Yet the *Family* of the Just One perish'd not. Sirs, it will be so! tho the Bars of the Bottomless Pit should be *broken up*, and should pour out a *Flood* of Mischiefs on the Church, yet there shall not issue out

such

such a *Flood* from thence, as to drown the *Family* of our Saviour. The *Flood* shall not *prevail* so far, as to *drown* the *Church* in the World. Our Lord *sits King on the Floods*, and sets Bounds to them; they shall not *prevail* to carry all before them. *Had it not been for this Word*, the Church had been *drown'd* in the Days of *Dioclesian*, when he set up his Pillars with this Inscription on them, *Christiana Superstitione Deleta*. Wretch, the Inscription on the *Rainbow about the Head* of our Saviour, confounded thine! *Had it not been for this Word*, the Church had been drown'd by the *Flood*, which the *Dragon cast out* of his Mouth in the *Arian* Heresies; when, *the World sigh'd, that it saw it self become almost entirely* Arian. *Had it not been for this Word*, the Church had been drown'd in the *Flood* of the *Romish Apostacy*, at the latter end of the *Fifteenth Century*; when there were left One Little Flock of *Taborites* in their *Caves*: and these poor *Speculani* sent four Agents to the several Points of the Compass, to find, if it were possible, any pure Church in the World; and they all return'd with a sorrowful Report, That there was none to be met withal. Were it not for *this Word*, the Grand *Assyrian* of this Day would be Master of *Europe*, and the Religion of Christ be every where little better of it, than it is in his own Bloody Dominions. But, O thou *Monster of Baseness*, the *Daughter of* Zion despises thee! And, O thou *Troubler of the Nations*, a few Months more shall bring thee down to the *Sides of the Pit*, and it shall be said by them that consider thee, *Is this the Man that shook the Kingdoms of the Earth?*

In short, the Church of our Saviour must *out-live* all the Attempts of Earth and Hell against it. The *Story* of the Church surviving all the Attempts of its Adversaries in the former Ages, is a wonderful Story. The *Thred* of the Story shall never be broken off! our JESUS will have *Subjects*, his *Bible* will have *Students*, his *Spirit* will have *Temples*, let all the Devils in Hell do what they can to defeat such Intentions of Heaven. The Saviour with the *Rainbow about his Head*, will tread on the *Head* of the *Old Serpent*; all the Plots in that *bruised Head*, shall come to nothing!

Secondly, The most *Cloudy Times* that pass over the Church of God, have their *Mixtures* of Mercy, and of Moderation in them. There's a *Rainbow*; the *Clouds* of

Wrath

( 17 )

Wrath are not fo thick, not fo fpread, but there is a
*Sun-fhine* of Mercy with them. If the *Floods* rife high ;
yet not fo high, that *all* fhall be cover'd, *all* overcome.
It was a thing propos'd, *Hab.* 3. 2. *O Lord, revive thy*
*Work in the midft of the Tears, in Wrath remember Mercy.*
His *Church* is his *Work.* In the midft of the Seventy Years
affign'd for the Captivity of the *Jews*, they found a remarkable Favour from the Court of *Babylon*, in what
was done to one who reprefented them there. This
*reviv'd them in the midft of the Tears :* this was *Mercy*
*in the midft of Wrath.* Indeed things may go very
bad with the Church, yet never fo *bad*, but they
might be *worfe.* O the amazing *Supplies of Grace*, which
are fent in unto the Church, under its greateft Lan-
guifhments! There will be at leaft a *little Reviving :*
what *Ezra* of old call'd, *A little Reviving to fet up the*
*Houfe of our God.* The Church will find that thing, *Pfal.*
78. 38. *He does not ftir up all his Wrath.* The Church
will find the *Saviour* with his *Rainbow*, dealing according to that Word ; *I am with thee, I will correct thee in*
*meafure :* That Word, *He ftays his rough Wind, in the Day*
*of the Eaft Wind.* The Calamities of the Church have
glorious *Mitigations.*

Thirdly, The *Church* can't be totally *drown'd* ; the
*World is :* but the *Flood of Wickednefs*, which overfpreads
the *whole World*, is going off. We have a fad Account
of this wretched World, 1 *John* 5. 19. *The whole World*
*lies in Wickednefs.* Alas, the *whole World* is under that
*Flood*, which we find before the *Old Flood*, and the Caufe
of it ; we ought with unutterable Anguifh, to make the
Complaint, *Behold, the Earth is corrupt before God, and all*
*Flefh has corrupted his way upon the Earth.* A Flood of
Wickednefs, has laid Mankind *groaning under the Waters.*
The *Exceptions* to the Epidemical, the Univerfal Wickednefs of Mankind, are fo very few, that we may ftill
complain, *They are all gone afide ; they are together become*
*filthy !* But, my Brethren, it fhall *not always be fo.* The
Saviour of Mankind fhows himfelf unto us with a *Rain-*
*bow about his Head.* It is to inform us, that the *Flood of*
*Wickednefs*, in which the World is at this Day buried, fhall
one Day be roll'd off. Of the *Angel* coming down from
Heaven with a *Rainbow on his Head*, we read, *He fets his*
*right Foot on the Sea, and his left Foot on the Earth.* Our

C

Saviour

Saviour will come to take poffeffion both of the *Sea*, and of the *Earth*. He will poffefs himfelf of Mankind, both on the *Sea*, and on the *Earth*. He will affert his Dominion both on the *Sea* and the *Earth*. He will chain up the *Deceiver* of the Nations. But, *howlong, O Lord, holy and true, how long e'er thou fo come down unto us!* There is a Day a coming, in which, according to the antient Prophecies, *Pfal.* 22. 27. *All the Ends of the World fhall turn unto the Lord.* And, *Pfal.* 86. 9. *All Nations whom thou haft made, fhall come and worfhip before thee, O Lord, and fhall glorify thy Name.* Moft certainly, there will come a Day when there fhall be more *godly People*, than there are now *wicked People* in the World. I am certain, God will one Day *deftroy them that corrupt the Earth*; we fhall fee an *Earth* wherein fhall *dwell Righteoufnefs*; it fhall be fill'd with *righteous* ones. The very firft time that an *Hallelujah* occurs in the facred Scriptures, it is on this occafion, Pfal. 104. 35. *Let the Sinners be confum'd out of the Earth, and let the Wicked be no more. Hallelujah.* There will come a time, when that *great Hallelujah* fhall be heard in the World!

Fourthly, Our great Saviour, the *Ruler* of the World, aims at the *Good of his Church*, in all the *Changes* which he brings upon the World. This is a very turnable World, very changeable. Others befides that King of *Egypt*, the great *Sejoftris*, whom our *Bible* calls by the name of *Shifhak*, have feen a *Wheel turning about*. 'Tis a moft elegant and expreffive *Hieroglyphick*, which our Prophet *Ezekiel* had of it, in his *Vifion* of the *Wheels*. There is a Tradition, that *Pythagoras* invented his from his Acquaintance with *Ezekiel's*, who was his Contemporary. He faw *four Wheels*. Will you give me leave to fay, that here is a *Wheel* for each of the *four great Monarchies?* The laft of them is now turning apace. Our immortal *King* is *bringing the Wheel over that wicked Empire*. Will you give me leave alfo to fay, that here is a *Wheel* for each of the *Four Quarters* of the World? Then be fure *America* muft be concern'd in the turning of the laft *Wheel*; and verily, we find it fo to our Wonderment. Well, but who has the management of all thefe *Wheels?* Truly, our Saviour with a *Rainbow* about him. All the *Angels* in Heaven, who have their uncontroulable Influences on human Affairs, are but the

*Officers*

*Officers* of our Saviour ; they execute his Orders ; they are the *Minifters which do his Pleafure*. We read how the *Wheels* are manag'd, *Ezek.* 1. 26, 28. *On the Throne, there was the appearance of a MAN above upon it :* [That MAN, 'tis our JESUS, 'tis our JESUS! we know 'tis he!] It follows ; *As the Appearance of the Bow that is in the Cloud in the Day of Rain* ; [The RAINBOW!] *fo was the Appearance of the Brightnefs round about.* From our JE-SUS on the Throne, we are now fo advertis'd ; " *I re-* " *member my Covenant for you*; *and in all the Turns which I* " *bring upon the World, I am fulfilling of it !* "

This is he, whom the *Difciple that Jefus loved*, had his Allowance to look upon !

But may we alfo at this Day, be allow'd and advanc'd unto a View of that glorious One ! Yea, O People highly favour'd of the Lord, unto *you* does the Saviour with a *Rainbow about his Head*, give that glorious Call : " *Behold me, behold me, O my People* ; *behold, and believe* " *my Remembrance of my Covenant, in all the Cloudy Times* " *that are pafling over you.*"

We are fallen into a Day, whereof we may fay, what we read, *Zech.* 1. 15. *It is a Day of Trouble, and of Diftrefs, a Day of Clouds and of thick Darknefs.* Yea, 'tis a Day wherein the People of God have their Fears, *Left the Waters overwhelm us, left the proud Waters go over our Soul.* In the midft of thefe *Clouds* our Saviour appears to us, with a *Rainbow about his Head.*

And the *firft* thing with which I would animate my Brethren, is, That he is *our Head*, and we may fafely truft him with our *All.* On that Paffage, *Ecclef.* 2. 14. *A wife Man's Eyes are in his Head*; I remember two of the antient *Gregories*, both a *Greek* one and a *Latin* one, have a devout Glofs; which is rather an Allufion than an Expofition: our glorious *Chrift* is our *Head*; and fay they, in *him* we have our *Eyes.* This I may very reafonably fay, O *Church* of the Lord, thy *Eyes* are in thy *Head*, even in that *Head* which has the *Rainbow* about it. His *Eyes* will be on the *Look-out* for thy Welfare ; he will *fee* to the fulfilling of all that his *Covenant* has engag'd for thee.

What tho there be difmal *Clouds !* the *Clouds* gather, look very difmally, 'tis true : But, of thy Saviour, thou haft been told, *Behold, he cometh with Clouds !*

( 20 )

I will go on to fay; 'tis a dreadful thing unto good Men, to fee fuch a *Death* upon all that is *good* in the World. Every thing lies *Dead*; *Zeal*, 'tis Dead; *Love*, 'tis Cold and Dead; the *Life of Religion* is gone. A *publick Spirit*, 'tis Dead; the *Succefs of the Gofpel* feems Dead. *Churches*, oh! how *Cadaverous* are they? What Putrefactions in them! O ye *Witneffes* of the Lord, you alfo are either *Dead*, or at leaft have not got off your *Grave-Clothes*. And yet, *this* may the rather be *the time* for a fpeedy Appearance of our Saviour. It was a Prediction, *Mat.* 24. 28. *Wherefoever the Carcafe is, there will the Eagles be gather'd together*. I take it for a Prediction of our Lord's coming with his Gofpel, as the *Lightning*, to ruin *Antichrift*, and reform his People. The Church at this time is to be like a *dead Carcafe*; partly fo by *Sufferings*; much more fo, by *Corruptions*. Our Saviour will now come as a glorious *Eagle*; fo he did, when he brought his *dead People* from *Egypt* of old. And, becaufe he will ufe his *mighty Angels* in what he is to do, marvel not, that you hear of *Eagles*, in the Plural Number, for it.

And, yet, I judg it not amifs to acquaint you, that there is of late, within thefe few Years, a moft furprizing *Revival of good things* in the World. Should I fpeak of but one *Country*, there are fome ftrict Obfervers of the Signs of the Times, who have lately publifh'd a *Collection* of obfervable things; wherein the Kingdom of God has been more fenfibly opening it felf in the heart of *Germany*; things of an holy and hopeful Tendency, to bring on a more ample Reign of *Piety:* the Collection contains no fewer than *Fourfcore and Four Articles*. In many other Places, there are fome excellent things a doing. *Effays to do Good*, begin to be in requeft: They grow more fafhionable and reputable. *North-Britain* will become a peculiar Seat, and Example of them. Among the reft, there is this to be obferv'd; A *Spirit of Affociation* for noble and pious purpofes, has of late begun ftrangely to vifit the World; it begins to do wondroufly. Some *Societies* perhaps, are yet only laying *Foundations*, for purpofes of a more exact Regulation hereafter to be built upon. But as far off as in *Switzerland* they prognofticate upon them; " *They annunciate a more illuftrious* " *State of the Church of God, that is expected in the Conver-* " *fion*

( 21 )

" *fion of* Jews *and* Gentiles." Thefe things are the *Rainbows of the Day.*

In the next place, I will freely confefs to you, that there is not any one thing at this Day a doing, which I have my Eye more upon, than the *Fate,* and I hope, the approaching *Fall* of the *Ottoman Empire.* There is a Coincidence of more than as many things, to perfuade us, that the *three hundred and ninety odd Years* allotted for the *Turks* to be the Plagues of the *Roman Empire,* expir'd at the late Peace of *Carlowitz.* If that Empire fhould once fall, what a *Jubilee* would arrive to the poor *Greek Churches!* Oh! let us pray more for them! Yea, the *Jews* as well as the *Greeks* would feel a quickning Energy upon it. Now, a mighty fhake feems to be giving unto the *Ottoman Empire.* There are Millions of opprefs'd Chriftians, who begin to fee a *Rainbow* in that thing, if God will pleafe to give the Word. If it fhould be fo, that the *Ottoman Empire* be falling, then, then, that *great Trumpet is going to be blown,* which brings on the Kingdoms of this World, to be the *Kingdoms of the Lord.*

I have one thing more to fay. The Grandeur of *Antichrift* is plainly on a decline: yea, the *Clouds* of this Day, are big with defolating *Thunderbolts,* to be difcharg'd upon him. The *twelve hundred and fixty Years* of the Papacy, could not commence much later than the year Four Hundred and Fifty, or Sixty. All rational Computations confpire to proclaim this, *A great and notable Day of the Lord is at hand*; the Day is *near, it is near, and it hafteth greatly!* The *Papal Authority* now fuffers a marvellous Diminution; it is irrecoverably diminifh'd. Its *Bulls* roar very infignificately. Let it *fulminate* what it will, People do but *fquib* at it. The *Spirit of Perfecution,* which wherever 'tis found, is the *Spirit of Antichrift,* it is wondrous to fee how 'tis going out of the World; Men grow afham'd of it : they that would fain be at it, yet *they* alfo *occafionally* acknowledg, that it is *contrary to the Spirit of Chriftianity.* Some that have been moft notorious for it, labour mightily to fhift off the Charge.

I greatly fufpect, that we are fallen into the Period, for the Effufion of the *Vials,* which brings the *laft Plagues* on the *Papal Empire :* It looks as if the *firft* of them were newly difpens'd, *A Bile on the Earth* ; a *Peftilence* on the *Inland Parts* of that Empire. I tremble at the *Second —.*

But

( 22 )

But they will all be *Rainbows of Hope*, for the pure Worshippers and Followers of the Holy JESUS.

Finally, But muſt *NEW-ENGLAND* have no part
in the *Rainbow*, about him that has hitherto been the
*Hope of NEW-ENGLAND*, and the *Saviour thereof in
the time of Trouble !* Yea, and tho there is no *particular
Church* but what may be *drowned*, yet, I ſuppoſe, 'tis not
until it negleſt the *Rainbow*, and by overgrown Impiety
and Impenitency forget the *Everlaſling Covenant.* I confeſs, we are very Criminal, and all our Crimes have peculiar Aggravations. Yea, there are ſome very *baſe People*
among us, People who do things that *Pagans* would abhor
to do ; People who bring a Blemiſh on all the Country.
But yet, firſt, the Body of the People, are a *ſober, honeſt,
well-inſtruſted* People. All *Civil Travellers* who do them
Juſtice, give them this Teſtimony. Then, there is alſo
ſcatter'd all over the Country, a Generation of Serious,
Prayerful, Watchful *Chriſtians* ; many that make no Noiſe,
are the humble Favourites of Heaven, the *Chariots and
Horſemen of the Land*, and yet by their Modeſty almoſt *In-
viſible.* The *Charities* of theſe Chriſtians, eſpecially in
this Town, they are going up as *Memorials before God* continually. There is likewiſe a Set of *young Miniſters*, and
Candidates for the Miniſtry, who are full of Goodneſs ;
lovely young Men ; *Sons of* Zion, *comparable to fine Gold* ;
Nazarites, *purer than Snow, brighter* than Pearl ; *their Pol-
liſhing, that of Sapphire.* God grant the *Rainbows* may
multiply ! O multiply our *Tokens for good.*

I will conclude with ſaying this thing. Methinks, a
*Saviour with a Rainbow about his Head*, ſhould moſt mo-
vingly invite every Sinner to come in unto him. I have
read ſomewhere, a ſorrowful Relation of a Man who
was a *drowning*, at the very Inſtant when he ſaw a
*Rainbow* in the Sky before him ; whereat he cry'd out,
*Hæc Iris, quid mihi proderit, ſi Ego peream ?* " What Ad-
" vantage to me the *Rainbow* which ſecures the World
" from *Drowning*, if now I my ſelf be *Drowned ?* " This
I will ſay, O poor Sinner, what Advantage canſt thou
expeſt from a *Saviour with a* Rainbow *about his Head*, if
thou deſpiſe that Saviour, and provoke him to caſt thee
off ? Wherefore, Oh ! hearken to the Voice from the
*Cloud* about the *Glorious High Throne* of our Saviour ; *Ah,*
*repenting,*

*repenting Soul*, *I remember my Covenant of Mercy*; *I am ready to receive thee!* Behold his *Bow*, there are no *Arrows* in it. But if any of you will *go on still in your Trespasses*, think on that word, *Psal.* 7. 11, 12, 13. *God is angry with the Wicked every Day*; *if he turn not*, *be has bent his Bow*, *and made it ready*; *he ordains his Arrows against him*. Verily, the *Clouds* about him, will *pour down* terrible *Thunderbolts!*

---

*F I N I S.*

# *A Voice from Heaven.*

## AN
# ACCOUNT
### Of a Late
## 𝕌ncommon 𝔄ppearance
### IN THE
# HEAVENS.

## With REMARKS upon it.

Written for the Satisfaction of One that was defirous to know the meaning of it.

By ONE of the Many who obferved it.

---

—*Rumpe Moras, Meteoraque fufpice cæli;*
*Illa aliquod Semper quo Monearis habent.*
                                                *Frytfchius.*

---

*BOSTON:* in *N. E.*
Printed for *Samuel Kneeland,* at his Shop in King-Street. 1719.

# A brief Account of a Late Uncommon Appearance in the 𝕳𝖊𝖆𝖛𝖊𝖓𝖘.

### With REMARKS upon it.

E are fensible, that of *Later Times*, there has been much *Difcourfe*, and fome *Wonder*, about a *Meteor*, which the Learned agree to call, *The Northern Twilight*. The *Pyramidal Glade of Light*, obferved by *Childrey* and *Caffim* and others in the Northern Hæmifphere of the *Fixed Stars*, has gone by the Name of *Aurora Borealis* ; And an Appearance of Light under various Forms in our *Meteorous Regions* has had the Name applied unto it. It fhould feem, that the Appearance of it, grows a little more frequent in the *Later Times* than it was in the Former; the caufe whereof, if the *matter of Fact* be really fo, may be worth Enquiring. Be that as it will, this *Aurora Borealis*, has been accounted a Subject worthy to be Regiftred in the Writings that are to be tranfmitted unto Pofterity, and pondered by the moft confummate Philofophers of the Age.

Our

[ 3 ]

Our *Stow* has in the Reign of Q. *Elizabeth*, more than once counted it an Article worthy of a *Chronicle*, That there were Nights wherein the *Heavens did seem to burn.* And I make no doubt, That some of the *Terrible Blazing Stars* Recorded by our *Hollinshead*, in the Reign of K. *Henry* IV. were no other than the *Meteor*, we are now taking into our Contemplation. The *Miscellanea Berolinensia*, have given us ample Relations, of the *Radiations* in the Heavens, which were seen extending from the *North-West* to the *North-East*, in several parts of *Europe*, since the Beginning of the present Century. But *Gassendous*, has thought it worth his while, to give us a larger Description of such an Appearance; which was not long after the Beginning of the former, seen all over *France*; and *Cambden* says, it was also seen in *England.*

IT was very much Resembled, by what was lately a matter of some Observation, (and unto some, of *Consternation*) all over *New-England*; whereof an Account shall presently be given you.

THE Large Accounts, that have been given of the *Phænomena* in the irradiated Sky of the Night, which have lately found work for the *Wise Men of Enquiry* in *Britain*, and over good part of *Europe*, you can be no stranger to. The Ingenious Pen of my worthy Neighbour and Brother, who

A 2                     was

[ 4 ]

was an Eye-witnefs to fome of them, has oblig'd us with a punctual Relation of what *he* faw, when the Heavens look d as if He that is to be *Revealed from thence in flaming Fire*, had been making His Defcent unto us.

THE Story of what we have juft now feen, may then hope to come in among the reft, without any indecency,

OF *Our* late *Aurora Borealis*, I muft obferve what *Gaßendous* does of *His* ; That fuch a Vapour muft needs be of a *Vaft Altitude*, above the Earth ; fince the Convexity of the Earth was no hindrance to its being Vifible, and in the fame Scituation, to Places remotely diftant from one another.

BUT the Account of *Ours*, which I now haften to give you, is ; That on the Eleventh of this *December*, (1719.) In the Evening, we were here at *Bofton*, pretty much furprized, with a Luminous Appearance in the *Northern part* of the Heavens, which extended in the Form of an Arch, from the *North-Weft* unto the *North-Eaft*; a confiderable way. It was a fort of a *Cloud*, but fo thin, that the *Stars* could be feen through it ; and firft of a *Lighter*, but anon of a *Redder*, and a more *Bloody* Afpect. The Region of it, was much higher than the ordinary Clouds, which were plainly feen moving below it. Of this, we were foon more fully fatisfyed, when we received Accounts from our Friends, Fifty

Fifty Miles to the Northward, and twice
Fifty to the Southward of us ; That (as One
Letter informs us) at this time the Hæmif-
phære being very clear, (which it was not
at *Bofton*,) and not a Cloud in the Sky, they
faw a *Glade of Light*, grow from a fmaller
Bulk, firft into paler Flames, and then into
Redder, and fo into the colour of Blood.
And, That (as Another) the *Red* was darker
at the *Weftern* End of it, and Brighter at the
*Eaftern*. It feemed fomething to *Expire*, and
then to *Revive* again. As midnight came
on, it Renewed with what was commonly
thought a *more Terrible Afpett*, than in the
former part of the Evening. Yea, fome Hours
after *That*, it fo Revived, that People at Work
about their Saw-Mills, perceived their *Trees*
to look *Red* with the refleftion of it ; and
they could fee to manage their work by it,
as if the Light of the Moon, (which was
now fet) had favoured them.

IT is Remarkable to fee, how much we
are left in the *Dark*, and how much our *Philofophy*, is at a lofs, about the *Lights*, that are
ever now and then enkindled in the Heavens
that are fo near unto us. We may talk fome
fine Things, about the *Sulphur* and the *Nitre*,
and the *Je ne fcay quoy*, in the compofition
of them, and make our felves be admired
for our Learned *Jargon*, among them that
have not learned the Language. We may
alfo

[ 6 ]

alſo propound unto Conſideration, how far
the Origin of ſuch a *Northern Twilight*, as
*Gaſſendou's*, and *Our* late One, may be found,
in that conſtant *Milky way of the Sun*, or,
*Glade of Light* which every Year ſtrikes from
that part of the Horizon where the Sun ſets,
up towards and almoſt unto the *Pleiades*, in
the latter End of *February*, and the Beginning of *March*, whereof there is in the Poſt-
humous Works of Dr. *Hook*, an Account Endeavoured. But ſtill the Old Philoſophers
ingenuous cry of, *Darkneſs, Darkneſs!* will
return upon us.

I Don't ſee, That the *Extent* of our *Atmoſphere* is hitherto well determined. For
tho' 'tis pretended, That our *Baroſcope* has
fixed it, for leſs than Fifty Miles; yet *Hart-
ſoeker* will perſwade you that the Reports
of that *Mercury* in this matter are not ſo
to be relied upon, but that our *Atmoſphere*
may extend ſome Hundreds of Leagues;
And, I confeſs, that for ſome Reaſons, which
at preſent I don't care to mention, I incline
to that Opinion.

BUT how poorly Qualify'd are we then
to form a Judgment on many Things that
are doing it may be up towards the *Selvidge*
of this *Atmoſphere*.

THE known Principles of *Mechaniſm* failing
us in ſome occurences of *Nature*, ſome that
are little enough tinged with *Enthuſiaſm* or
*Fanaticiſm,*

[ 7 ]

*Fanaticifm*,own themfelves compelled here‑
unto, to confider the Operations of *Angels*
Good & Bad ; *Intellectual* &*Voluntary*Agents.

'TIS true, There can be nothing fo Ridi‑
culous, as the *Mahometan Philofophy*, which
makes the *Angels*, to be the doers of all
that is continually done in the works of*Na‑
ture* ; and particularly,makes thofe *Meteors*
which we call,*Falling Stars*, to be the *Fire‑
brands* with which the Good *Angels* chafe
away the Bad, when they come too near the
Heavens, to Eves-drop the Secrets there.
But yet we have all poffible Affurance,that
there are *Angels* both Good and Bad ; Our
own Country affords Teftimonies enough to
overwhelm all the *Sadducees* in the World.
And fo inconteftible it is, That all Ages have
believed our*Atmofphere* to have fome of the
*AngelicalTribes* replenifhing it. OurSacred
Scriptures do fufficiently affure us, That the
*Angels* both Good and Bad, are fometimes
particularly concerned about the *Meteors*
in this *Atmofphere*; the *Tempefts*, and the
*Thunders* raifed there : yea, That the *Hea‑
vens do Rule*, and the *Invifible World*, has an
aftonifhing fhare in theGovernment of*Ours*.
As *Unphilofophical* as it may feem, to talk
at this rate ; the further our Improvements
in Philofophy are carried on, the lefs will
it be found *Unreafonable*.

THE*UncommonOccurrences* in the*Heaven‑*
A 4 *ly*

[ 8 ]

*ly Places* of our *Atmosphære*, have doubtlefs their *Natural Caufes*. And yet they may Rationally enough fet the admiring and a•mazed Spectator a thinking, *What unknown Things may be doing among the Rational Inhabitants of thofe Regions ?* This we do know, That *there fhall be fearful Sights, and Great Signs from Heaven,* and *there fhall be Signs where we fee the Sun and Moon and Stars,* and the *Powers of Heaven fhall be in Commotions,* (and it is poffible, be at work in producing fome of the *Fearful Sights)* among the *Fore-runners* of a *Day* that all Sober Men do look for.

INDEED, it is a Weaknefs, to be too Ap-prehenfive of *Prodigies,* in all *Uncommon Oc-currences.* Yea, fome things may be thought *Prodigies,* which may really be *Kindneffes* to the World ; among which things we may particularly reckon *Exploded Meteors.* Be fure, People are never more fanciful and whimfical, their Imaginations are never more fertil, than when they have *Uncommon Oc-currences* in the *Clouds* to work upon. And it becomes not Serious Chriftians to be *Dif-mayed at the Signs of Heaven, as the Heathen are difmayed at them.* Not only the *Prodi-gies* which the celebrated Roman *Livy,* fo fills his Pages withal, but alfo thofe which *Lycofthenes* and other later Hiftorians have given us, were very many of them doubt-lefs

[ 9 ]

less meer *Fancies* or *Fables*. Nevertheless, a total contempt of all *Prodigies* is an Extreme on the other hand, which is to be avoided by them that would *walk wisely*, and *neither turn aside unto the Right Hand, nor unto the Left*. Nor have *some* of the *Prodigies* related by *Josephus*, as foregoing & foreboding the Destruction of *Jerusalem*, found a general Disdain among the most Judicious of his Readers.

THE Learned and Famous Dr. *John Spencer*, Entertained the World, with a Treatise full of Erudition, on a Design to sink the Opinion of *Prodigies*. But the Venerable Dr. *Increase Mather*, visiting of him, on 27d. IVm. 1689. at *Bennet*-College in *Cambridge*, took the Opportunity to Enquire of him, whether he still continued of the *same Opinion* concerning *Prodigies*? To which he made a modest Answer; ' That he was a ' very Young Man, when he wrote his Book ' on that Subject; and had not since much ' considered it; But that he believed the *Demons* had *prænotions* of many things, and ' might give strange *præmonitions* of them ' in the way of *Prodigies*. And, that he did ' not know, whether he might not err in ' something of an Extreme, on one side, as ' others did on the other. Wherefore, tho' I will not say,

*Nunquam futilibus resplenduit Ignibus æther,*

Yet

[ 10 ]

Yet I will not utterly deny, but that something may be *Read* sometimes by the *Light* of those *Fires*. There is *not* always *Nothing* in them.

IN Men of a Superiour Wisdom & Goodness, it cannot but move a compassion for a miserable World, when One sees the *Terrors of Death* so generally seizing and frightning People, upon any *Uncommon Occurrences* ; and especially upon any *Blazes* in the Heavens over them. *Certainly*, it may be thought, *Certainly the poor Children of Men, are generally conscious to this, that they are in IllTerms with Heaven ! Upon every fiery Eruption seen above, they take it for granted, that the Wrath of GOD is going to be Revealed from Heaven, against all the Ungodliness and Unrighteousness of Men, which the Earth is filled withal.* People that know themselves Reconciled unto GOD, would never be so Terrified, as most People are, when they see any *Fires* kindling in the Welkin over them.

IN the mean time, it would Vex One to see how ready, & (in their own conceit) skilful, People are to *Prognosticate* upon the Things, which they take for *Prodigies*, where the *Rules of Prognostication* are so Uncertain, Ambignous & Precarious ; But how little Notice they take of those things which are much more *horribly Prodigious*, and on which they may found a *Prognostication* with a much more infallible certainty.    THIS

[ 11 ]

THIS is very fure; Prodigious*Impieties*,& Prodigious *Divisions*, raging in a Place, are much more *certainOmens* of *Evil to come*,than any *Sights in the Air*,which appear never fo formidable. But at thofe Things, how few can fay, LORD, *Horror with a Tempeftuous Force has taken hold on me, on the account of Wicked Men who do forfake thy Law.*

THE Gentlemen,who had not arrived unto the Skill,(which according to *Seneca's* Prediction) fome of our lateft Aftronomers have now attain'd unto,of Calculating the *Motions* and *Returns* of *Comets*,have reckon d up (as I remember *Lubienietzki* does) about Four Hundred & Fifteen *Comets*,of whofe Appearing fince the Beginning of this World, we find fome Footfteps in Hiftory. But were fo many *Comets* all feen Blazing at once,I muft freely fay, That tho' fuch *Worlds in a ftate of Punifhment*,would be a very awful Spectacle,yet I fhould not be apprehenfive of fuch *horridPrefages* in them, unto a *Baptized Nation*,as I fhould, if I faw, in fuch a Nation, a *Kingdom Divided*; or an Epidemical corruption of Manners in Inftances, hardly known among Infidels ; or the Inftitutions of our SAVIOUR proftituted unto very unrighteous purpofes ; or Impious Attempts to degrade the Infinite &Eternal Son of God,into the Clafs of *Creatures*, & render Him in all things Different from, & Inferiour to His

Glorious

[ 12 ]

GloriousFather; and the higheftProfeffors
of theChriftian Religion fall into fuch a *La-*
*odecean* Temper,as to be fhye of appearing to
affert the moft Vital Point in the Faith of
Chriftianity.

FOR my part, fhould I *Really* fee, (what
many under the prepoffeffions of a ftrong
Imagination, have *fuppofed*, when the *Clouds*
have anInfolitAfpeĉt upon them; I fay,fhould
I *Really* fee) theSky covered with*Phantafms*
of *Swords* & *Spears*, and *Rivers of Blood*,and
*Armies* or *Navies* Engaging one another,and
the *Canon* with a roaring mouth vomitting
out *Fire* upon one another ; I don't know,
that I fhould look on thefe things as more
*Ominous*,or be more affeĉted with them,than
if I fhould be fo unhappy as to fee, the*Spirit*
*of Piety* generally loft, & what fhall be quite
the *Reverfe* of it,prevailing among a People
that have made an high Profeffion of it ; Or,
See a *Spirit of Extortion* generally difpofe a
People to nothing fo much as *Preying* upon
one another ; Or, See the Bleffings of a *Good*
*Education* generally defpifed&negleĉted; Or,
See aPeople confeffing that fuch &fuch*Need-*
*lefs Expences* ruin them,& yet generally refolving to Retrench none of them ; Or, See
a People that have but *Few Friends* in the
World,madly fet upon theDifobliging& the
Difcouraging of them ; Or, See a People E-
vidently near a dreadful *Convulfion*,& yet no
Men

[ 13 ]

*Men of Senfe Uniting* to find out Methods for the Relief of the Publick Diftrefles, but all generally Alienated from one another, broken into Factions, & Sacrificing all to *Curfed Animofities* : Or, Finally to fee a *Faithful Man* torn to pieces, if he tell a People of the Perils he fees them expos'd unto.   If our Country have yet the Happinefs, to have no fuch *Symtoms* in any Degree upon it, I fhould think, we may defy all the *Prodigies* in the World, for any *Prædictions* of *Evil*, which they may give unto us. I hope therefore we fhall Unanimoufly deprecate 'em ! A Reign of *Piety*, & *Honefty*, & *Charity*, among us, would be fuch a *Token for Good*, that the *People in the Wildernefs* could fee no *Tokens*, that they fhould have any caufe to be *Afraid* of.

BUT yet, that I may more fully Explain my felf, and give you my plain Sentiments on this Point ; *What Interpretation is to be made of the* Aurora Borealis, *that Heaven has lately fhown unto us ?* I will fay, That tho' I can do very little by way of *Prognoftic*; And I would not fay that like the People of *Gibeah*, when we fee a *Pillar of Smoke and a Flame afcending in Heaven*, we muft conclude, That *Evil is coming upon us* ; Nor would I think the *Meteor* to be a *Signal Forerunner* of whatever happens to *Follow* after it , Like the Honeft Old Man upon *Tenderton* Steeple : Neverthelefs, No doubt the
other

[ 14 ]

other *Meteors* of theHeavens,as well as the *Rainbow*, are defigned for *Inftructive* ones. The Glorious GOD, who is their and our Creator, (even HE, who is alfo our SAVI-OUR,) fays of us, whom He calls to be the Spectators of them, *Surely they will Receive Inftruction*.

Well Sang the Poet,

*Qui Meteora videt liquido radiantia Cælo,
Hic videt Æterni facta ftupenda Dei.*

Who fees brightMeteors in theLiquidSkies,
The wondrousWorks of the Eternal Spies.

A ReligiousMind may even with fome*Elegancy* of Devotion, confider fome Intimations from Heaven, which our *Aurora Borealis* may, at leaft, by way of *Occafional Reflection* lead one to think upon. Whether the *Aurora Borealis* were a *Prodigy* or no, the *Man* is *One*, who fhall ridicule fuch an Improvement of it.

THE Sieur *le Peyrere*, has given a moft wonderful Account, That in *Greenland*, where the Night in the Winter is exceffively long, when they don't enjoy the *Moon*, there arifes a *Light* in the *North*, (called therefore the *Northern Light*,) that fhines over all the Country, as if the *Moon* were at the Full; The Darker the Night is, the Clearer the Light; It looks like a Flying Fire; it mounts up like a huge Pole; it
passes

paſſes from one Place to another; it continues the whole Night; and it is of incredible uſe to them in the Buſineſs of their Lives.

WE may alſo render our *Northern Light* of ſome uſe unto us, in the Greateſt Buſineſs of our Lives, if it awaken in us the *Right Thoughts of the Righteous.*

MAY not the *Fiery Appearance,* make us Inquiſitive, Whether we have no *Fires* among us nere below, that ſhould be lovingly Extinguiſhed? Or, whether no Raſh Doings may threaten to raiſe *Fires* in our Churches, that will not be eaſy to be Extinguiſhed! Sollicitous, therewithal to *Put far from our Tabernacles,* thoſe *Iniquities,* that may be puniſhed by *Fires* without a Metaphor laying our Houſes in Aſhes?

MAY not the *Bloody Appearance,* admoniſh us, to beware of that *Wringing,* which we have been told, what it will *bring,* if it be perſiſted in! And to quicken our Cares and Prayers for our *Eaſtern Plantations!*

MAY not *Rare Sights* calling us to look more than without them we ſhould have done unto the *Heavens,* very well put us upon thinking, whether we are not ſo *Buried* in the Buſineſs of the *Earth,* as to need ſomething that may call us off, to converſe in a more Divine way, with more *Heavenly Objects?*

IT is an Ancient Prophecy, *I will ſhew wonders in Heaven above, Blood & Fire & Vapour of Smoke,* before the *Great and Notable Day of the Lord come.* Why ſhould not this *Fiery* & *Bloody* Appearance, in the *Vapour of Smoke* lately before us, put us in mind of that *Great & Notable Day?* A Day, when the *Great GOD our SAVIOUR* ſhall be *Revealed from Heaven in flaming Fire,* with *His mighty Angels;* A Day, that ſhall *Come as a Thief in the Night, and the Elements ſhall melt with fervent Heat;* A Day, which, O Secure

[ 16 ]

Secure and Sleeping World, *it is near, it is near, and it hasteth greatly!* 'Tis well for us if we *are*, and no little part of our Business to *be*, *Ready* for it. The *Pagans* themselves had a Tradition,

———*affore Tempus*
*Quo Mare, quo Tellus, Correptaque Regia cæli Ardeat, et Mundi moles operosa Laboret.*

WE *Christians* have a *more sure word of Prophecy*, which has given us the Warning of a tremendous *Conflagration*, and being *Warned of GOD*, we do in these *Oracles* find the Methods prescribed, wherein we are to make *Preparation* for it. The whole Work of Christianity! *Fires* in the Heavens, how properly do they for this purpose become our *Monitors!*

Finally; WHAT *Extraordinary Spectacles* may be Exhibited in the *Heavens*, before that Grand REVOLUTION, which the *Multitude of the Heavenly Host* making a Descent from thence, is to bring upon the World, I know not. But I am certain of This, That whether any foregoing *Signs* be given of it in the Heavens or no, the Day must be very Near, when the *Stone cut out of the Mountains*, will *break in Pieces and Consume all the Ten Kingdoms*, which it is to fall upon, and the *Kingdom of GOD* shall come on, wherein we shall see *Glory to GOD in the Highest*, and *Good-will among Men*: What cannot be Accomplished, but by Dispensations to be *trembled* at, as well as *longed* for!

BUT *so much* —— [if this may be thought *Enough!*] to satisfy on the present occasion. I am very much of *Avicens* mind; *Quicquid sufficientia additur superfluitati ascribitur.* And if the Thoughts to which I have devoted one little piece of a Day prove so *Acceptable* to you, that you may judge, that they may prove also *Serviceable* unto any others, you have my consent unto any Communication, you may think proper for them.


*Written, 24d. Xm.*
1719.        *F I N I S.*

# A
# SERMON
### Preached at the Time
### Of the Late
# STORM,
#### February 24. 1722,3.

# The Voice of GOD
## in a TEMPEST

# A
# SERMON

Preached in the Time of the

# STORM;

Wherein many and heavy and unknown Losses were Suffered at BOSTON, ( and Parts Adjacent,) Febr. 24. 1722-3.

By One of the MINISTERS in *Boston*.

Micah VI. 9.
*The Voice of the LORD crieth to the City.*

BOSTON: N. E.
Printed by S. KNEELAND. MDCCXXIII.

# The Occaſion.

ON *February* 24.1722·3. *A Violent* STORM *coming up in the* Night, *One of the Miniſters in* Boſton, *choſe in the Morning to Entertain his Auditory with a Diſcourſe, which in the Time & the Heighth of ſuch a* Storm, *would not be unſeaſonable : And which as far·as could be Recovered, and very near to what it was Delivered, is here again Exhibited.* When ſuch as could hear the Sermon *went home at* Noon, *they found that* GOD *had in an uncommon and ſurprizing manner,* poured *the* Waters *of the* Sea *upon the* Earth ; *and the Tide having riſen conſiderably higher than was ever known in our Memory, the Damage which the* City *ſuffers was incredible :* How *many Thouſands of Pounds, it cannot eaſily be computed !* The Damage alſo done in many other Places *of the* Country *is incomputable !*

But ſhall nothing be done, that we may on the beſt Accounts *Gain ſomething by our Loßes ?* PIETY *requires, that the* Voice of GOD *in ſuch Things have a due Notice taken of it : And the* Maxims *and* Leſſons *of* Piety *agreeable to ſuch an Occaſion, are here Publiſhed, that they may be Lodged in ſome few Hands, where they will not be unacceptable or unprofitable.*

# The Way of the Glorious GOD in a STORM.

February 24. 1722-3. Forenoon.

### Nahum I. 3.

*The LORD hath His Way in the STORM.*

WHEN the *Word of Truth,* which is the *Gospel of our Salvation,* arrives unto us, under the Advantage of Lively Colours cast upon it, in *sensible Occurrences* which we meet withal, the *Word* becomes very Observable ; the *Gospel* is Reasonably like to have the more Notice taken of it ; there are lively *strokes* given to the *Nails* that are driven by the *Masters of the Assemblies.* Good & Great Things are spoken about, *A Word in Season.* Certainly, When we *feel* the *signatures* of the *Word* in the *Characters* of the *Time* when it comes unto us, and if there be something in

A 3                                    the

## 2 *The Voice of* GOD *in a* TEMTEST.

the *Season*, to make a *Right Word* become *Forcible*, we shall have, *A Word in Season !* Such a *Word* is this Morning to be endeavoured. A mighty *Storm* is the Last Night begun, which this Morning we find so growing upon us, that I have thought it *seasonable*, to make someEssay with a *stillVoice*, of which yet, I hope, theNoise about us will not hinder our hearing, that what there is of GOD speaking to us in the *Whirlwind* may have a due Regard paid unto it.

THERE were *Terrible Things* a coming upon the Greatest City then in the World. The Fate of *Ninive* is here foretold, which was in a most astonishing manner fulfilled, in the days of King *Josiah*, by *Nabopollasar* & *Astyages* unitingtheirForces, that utterly destroyed that Renowned City. It was once called, A *City of GOD*; it may be for the special *Care* that GOD had of it. It was a City, which had vast & thick Walls, extending Sixty Miles, as *Diodorus Siculus* tells us, in the Circuit of it. But according to the Prophecy, GOD *has made an utter End of the place* thereof, and, *The place is not known* where it stood. The most profane Man of all the Pagans confirms this Prophecy, and says, *No Footstep is left of it, neither can any Man living tell where it was.* The Old Geographers, express a Desultory Levity, and strangely contradict themselves as well as one another, in assigning the *Place* of it. My incomparable & inquisitive *Bochart* himself,

himfelf, owns 'tis in vain to look for it. We
are fure, that *Mofal,* which at this day they
fhow for it, is net fo much as on the fame
fide of the River with the celebrated *Ninive.*

THE *TerribleThings,*which were to produce
this Deftruction, are in the Claufe now before
us, compared unto a STORM. And the *Way*
of the ETERNAL GOD in the *Storm,* is particularly propofed unto our Confideration.

THIS therefore is theDOCTRINE of GOD
that fhall *diftil* as the gentle *Rain* upon you,
while the *ftormy Wind & Tempeft,* with the
*Great Rain of His ftrength,*is doing the Execution, which anon you will find perhaps done
in the Neighbourhood.

*WHEN a Stormy Time comes upon us, the*
*WAY of GOD in the STORM, is to be*
*Confidered with us.*

THE *Way of the* LORD ! That is to fay,
Firft, The *Work* which is done by GOD in the
*Storm.* For a *Storm* is the *Work* of that GOD,
who *flies upon the wings of the Wind.* If a
*Storm* rife, we are to confider,That it is GOD
who raifes it. We read ; Pfal. 107. 5. *He*
*commandeth and raifeth the ftormy wind ; which*
*lifteth up the waves of the fea.* The *Winds* and
the *Seas* are the Creatures of GOD. *In Him*
*they move !*— as well as *have their Being.* All
their *Motions* are under His command. And
becaufe our SAVIOUR is the *Moft High*GOD,
therefore

#### 4. *The Voice of* GOD *in a* TEMPEST.

therefore we find the *Winds* & the *Seas*, even *Miraculously* under the Command of our Blessed JESUS. No *Storm* comes, without *His* commanding of it.

THE *Way of the* LORD *!* That may mean, Secondly, The *Work* which GOD would have us to do in the *Storm*. For in a *Storm*, there is a *Work*, wherein GOD enjoins us to pay our *Homage* unto Him, who is now giving a Shock unto us. When a *Storm* comes, we are to consider, that there are *Good Things*, which the Lord our *GOD now requires of us*. And in these Things, we do what we read, Psal. XXXVII. 37. *Wait on the Lord, and keep his way.* It may be, we are out of our *Way*, and a *Storm* comes upon us, as upon *Jonah*, to drive us into the *Way of the Lord* ; Or, 'tis to prevent our diverting from the *Way*, wherein we should keep *undefiled*, and seek for the *Rest of our Souls*.

Furnished with such Præliminary Thoughts, Let us now hearken to the Admonitions of GOD.

*I.* WHEN we are visited with *Natural* STORMS, [ *As we are at this Moment !* ] the *Way* of the Glorious GOD, is to be considered in them.

First, THE Glorious GOD is to be Adored, as the *Author* of the *Storms* that beat upon us ; Even that Glorious GOD who has *gathered the Wind in his Fist*, and who has *bound the Waters as in a Garment*. We read, Psal. CXLVIII. 8. *Praise*

*The Voice of* GOD *in a* TEMPEST. 5

8. *Praife the Lord, O ftormy Wind.* He is to be *praifed,* as the *Maker* and *fender* of the *Stormy Wind.* Whatever may be the eneigy of *Evil fpirits,* in any of our *Storms,* as well as in *Jobs,* and whatever the *Prince of the power of the Air,* may be able to do in Violent *Agitations* of the *Air,* 'tis all, *By the Divine Permiffion.* He holds all his Power, *By the Divine Permiffion.* GOD *Limits* it, as well as *Permits* it. Yea, GOD employs the *Evil Angels* as His Inftruments. And it is His *Indignation* which by them does inflict fuch *Trouble* upon us. The *Wrath* of Hell does *Praife* and ferve Him, and the *Remainder of that Wrath does he reftrain.* My Friends, I befeech you, to fee the Glorious GOD at work in fuch *Storms* as are battering of us. There is a *Flood* breaking in upon us, but GOD *fits upon the Flood, GOD fitteth King forever :* Oh! Let us thus in His *Temple* now *fpeak of His Glory!* Of them that were to undergo a Storm, we read ; Pfal. LXXXIII. 16. *Lord, make them afraid of thy Storm.* Truly, Lord, *It is Thy Storm that is now upon us !*

BUT then, Secondly ; The Glorious GOD is to be Revered in the *Way of Duty,* which by fuch *Storms* we are loudly call'd unto, ftrongly chas'd unto.

Firft ; A *Contemplation* of the *Perfections* in the Infinite GOD, which are *difcovered* in the *Storms,* wherein the World is *Rebuked, O Lord, at the blaft of the Breath of thy Noftrils ;* Methinks, This

## 6  *The Voice of* GOD *in a* TEMPEST.

This is what we muſt be compell'd unto. Our
GOD is *Fearful in Praiſes* ; His *Praiſes* are
diſplay'd, are beſpoke, in the *Fearful Storms*
that we tremble at.

HOW Conſpicuous the *Power* of our GOD!
when it had been ſaid, *The Lord hath His Way
in the Storm,* it ſoon follows, *Who can ſtand
before His Indignation ! And who can abide in
the Fierceneſs of His Anger ? The Rocks are
thrown down by Him.* How agreeably may we
now Entertain ſuch Thoughts as theſe ? ' How
' Irreſiſtible is the *Power* of the Glorious GOD,
' who can break down whatever ſtands before
' Him, and at his Pleaſure bring in a Roaring
• Ocean to overwhelm whatever He ſhall be
' diſpleaſed at ! Oh ! Let me not *harden* my
' ſelf againſt a GOD, who can *tear* me, and all
' about me *to pieces,* and there *ſhall be none to
deliver us !*

HIS *Juſtice* is at the ſame to be confeſſed,
in all the *Hurt,* that the *Storm* ſhall do unto
us.    LORD, our Sins have raiſed thy *Storms.*
' In all the ſad Things that are done unto us,
' when the *Winds* and the *Seas* are made *ſpoilers*
' unto us, 'tis the *Lord againſt whom we have
' ſinned,* that gives us and our Subſtance up
' unto them.   Thou art *Holy in all thy Ways,
' and Righteous in all thy Works* ;  yea, Thou
' doſt *puniſh us leſs than our Iniquities have
' deſerved·*

FOR, Oh ! how Illuſtrious the *Mercy* of our
GOD ! ſhould He let out but a very little more
of

of the Wrath, whereof there are such *Trea-sures* with Him, *Lord, what would become of us!* Did not our Merciful GOD *stay* His *Rough Wind* in the *Day* of His *East Wind,* LORD, *what would become of us?* Verily, 'Tis from the *Compassion* of our GOD, that we are *not consumed.*

I mind, that this Clause, *The Lord hath His Way in the Storm,* is introduced with such an Acknowledgment as this, *The* LORD *is slow to Anger, and great in Power.* If the Great GOD be *slow to Anger,* we must know, 'tis not for want of *Great Power* to Revenge Himself upon the Wicked. The *Assyrians* were not presently destroyed upon the Prædiction of what was to come upon them. No, *Ninive* continued a Hundred Years after this. Experience at length told the Jews, who might be discouraged at the *Assyrian Grandeur,* that the *Great Mercy* of GOD unto them, was not from any Defect of *Great Power* in Him. Syrs, 'Tis from the *Great Mercy* of our GOD, this His *Great Power* does not bring upon us, a *Storm* that shall make us very *Desolate !* The Memorable and Unparallel'd *November-*Storm which fill'd the English World, with Horror near Twenty Years ago, was but a very little to what the Omnipotent GOD *can do,* if He shall *come,* and it shall *be very tempestuous round about Him.*

Secondly, *Resignation* to the *Will* of the Sovereign GOD, in all the *Harms* that our *Storms* may do unto us ; This is what the *Storms* of our *Foul Weather* may very *fairly* lead

lead us to.  When the *Perfect & Upright Man*
of the East, had his House blown down by a
*Storm*, we find him with wondrous patience
only saying, *The LORD gave, and the LORD
has taken ; Blessed be the Name of the LORD.*
*Storms* will bring *Losses* upon us.    I know
not what *Losses* you may see, when the Tide
is at its Heighth an Hour or two hence.  But
this I know ; It will become us to say, ' *Lord,*
' *Thou takest* nothing from me, but what thou
' first *gavest* to me ;  And, *Thy Will be done !*
' If my GOD will enable me to glorify Him,
' with a *sweet submission to His Will* in all that
' befalls me : and bestow more of His CHRIST
' and His *Grace* upon me, *The Lord gives me*
' *much more than all this !*    A Servant of GOD,
meeting with Disasters could say, Psal. XXXIX.
9. *Thou didst it.*   Behold, The *Epitaph* which
is to be written on the *Ship*, the *Wharff*, the
*Goods* that are lost in the *Storm !* LORD, *Thou
didst it !* Methinks, O *Pious Loser*, [Gaining
in *Piety !*] This will be enough to quiet thee.
      Thirdly. *Brotherly-kindness and Charity* for
those who may be most in danger of perishing
by the *Storms* ; This now belongs to the *Godly
Man,* who is *a Tree bringing forth Fruit in the
Season* thereof.  It is extremely probable, that
in such an Hour as this, we may have some
of our *Sea-faring Brethren* on the Coast, whose
Hazard may be much greater than ours. Very
probably there may be some in that Condition;
Matth. VIII. 24. *Behold, There arose a great*
                                  *Tempest*

*The Voice of* GOD *in a* TEMPEST. 9

Tempeſt *in the ſea, inſomuch that the ſhip was covered with theWaves* ; and either Foundring, or in hazard of being Stranded, and all to be loſt. I pray, let us be ſollicitous for theſe our *Sea faring Brethren* ; Full of Concernment, Full of Sympathy. Lift up a Prayer for them. *Charitable Soul,* Thy GOD may hear thee on the behalf of them, who may never know how muoh they fare the better for thee. Or, However *thy Prayer will return into thine own Boſom !*

Fourthly, SINCE I have ſpoken a Good Word *for* the *Sea faring* People, I hope, they will hear me ſpeaking *to* them. *To* them I ſay, My Brethren, Oh ! That you would ſo behave your ſelves at all *other Times,*that you may with *Courage* look up to Heaven when *Storms* do oblige you to it. The *Diſtreſſed Mariners,* however unmindful they have been before their *Diſtreſſes* come upon them, yet now they come to that, Pſal.CVII.28.*They cry unto the* LORD *in their Trouble.* You won't be worſe than *Jonah's* Mariners ! But Ah ! with what Confuſion muſt theDevotions of *PrayerleſsVeſſels* be performed, when *Storms* are diſtreſſing of them ! If in *Fair Weather* there is nothing to be heard aboard, but the Language of Fiends, nothing but *Swearing,* and *Curſing,* and *Obſcene Talk,* and Reviling and Slandering of *Good Men,* in *Bad Weather* only you betake your ſelves to your *Prayers :* what cauſe will you have to ſay as he in Ezr.

B                    IX. 6.

**ɪo** *The Voice of* GOD *in a* T E M P E S T.

ɪX. 6. *O my GOD, I am aſhamed, and bluſh to lift my Face unto thee!* We read, *The ſtormy Wind fulfills the Word* of GOD. How juſtly may He employ the *ſtormy Wind* now to deſtroy them, who never did *Fulfill His Word,* but always *Rebel* againſt Him *!* Had I a *Speaking Trumpet,* that would make my *Voice* reach to all the Tribe of our *Zebulon,* I would ſpeak this unto them; O our poor *Brethren,* Our Wiſhes for you are, That you may *Fear the Lord Exceedingly,* and get into ſuch Terms with Heaven, and lead ſuch *Lives* in the ſight of GOD, as you may in the Times of the greateſt *Perils by Sea,* with Comfort look back upon.

*II.* I may now properly Enough go on to ſay ; When we are conflicting with *Figura-⁺ive Storms,* there is the *Way* of the Glorious GOD ſtill to be conſidered in them. We have *Storms* befalling of us, in all that brings us into *Diſturbing* & *Uneaſy* Circumſtances. And when do we find, *this preſent EvilWorld* without them ! Now,

Firſt. THE Glorious GOD is to be acknowledged as the *Orderer* of all the *Storms* that incommode us. We are ſo taught of GOD, Job. V. 6. *Affliction comes not forth of the Duſt, neither doth trouble ſpring out of the Ground.* All our *Storms* are of an Higher Original. O *Magian,* O *Manichee* ; Dream not of an *Evil God,* who in ſpite of the *Good*
One,

*The Voice of* GOD *in a* TEMPEST. 11

One, may bring the*Storms* upon thee. With an Eye doubtlefs to fuch Fools once abounding in *Perfia*, our *Good* GOD fays, Ifai. XLV. 7. *I create Darknefs, I create Evil, I the Lord do all thefe things.* Chriftians, In every thing that proves an Exercife unto thee, think ; *I have to do with the Glorious* GOD *in what now befalls me. There is no Evil in the City, which that Good One is not the Doer of !*

BUT then, Secondly. The Glorious GOD is to be acknowledged in the *Way of Duty* which by fuch *Storms* we are put upon. When we are *tried* with *Storms*, there is a *Way of Duty*, wherein we are to *meet our God*, and be able with glad Hearts to fay, Job. XXIII. 10. *He knows the way that I take, and when he hath tried me I fhall come forth as Gold.*

More particularly,

Firft, THE *Storms* of *Afflictions*, which difcompofe our Affairs, and which diforder our Spirits ; Thefe are *Storms* that muft have the *Way of the Lord* confidered in them. The Afflictions, which we *know* will *abide* us, have that Refemblance; Amos I. 14. *A Tempeft in the Day of the Whirlwind.* We meet with Humbling Things, wherein we *go down the Wind.* We meet with Articles of *Adverfity*, wherein it may be faid, *The Winds are contrary*, and whereof we too fuddenly fay, *All thefe things are againft me.* We fhall anon find, That we have this day met with *Hum-*

*bling*

32    *The Voice of* GOD *in a* TEMPEST.

*bling things,* which the laſt Night we dreamt not of. And *we ſhall ſhortly find more a coming.*

BUT what is, *The Way of the* LORD, that is to be taken in the Storm ?

Firſt. LET the *Hand* of the Glorious GOD in the *Adverſity,* be diſcerned. It is demanded; Job XXXIV. 29. *When he giveth quietneſs, who then can make trouble ?* And who can *diſquiet* thee, or, *Tempeſtuate* thee, O Man, with any *Adverſity,* if GOD will have no *Trouble* ſent upon thee ? Be not ſuch a *Philiſtine* as to ſay, *It was a Chance that happened unto me !*

Secondly. LET the *End* of the Glorious GOD in the *Adverſity,* be anſwered. It comes upon ſome *Errand,* which muſt be complied withal, ſome *Intent* which muſt be attended unto. Be thoughtful on that point ; Job. X. 2. *Shew me wherefore thou contendeſt with me.* There is a *Repentance,* which *knoweſt thou not, O Man,* that thy *Tempeſtuous Adverſity* ſhould ſcourge thee to ? Find out what is to be *Reformed,* and let it be amended ; Find out what is to be *performed,* and let it be practiſed.

Thirdly. *Supplications* are now to be a-bounded in. It was preſcribed of old, Jam. V. 13. *Is any among you afflicted, let him pray.* GOD allows it ; *Call on me in the day of Trouble* ; Expects it, *They will pour out a Prayer when my Chaſtning it upon them.* The *Adverſity* that ſets us a *Praying,* the *Storm* that brings us down on our knees, verily, 'tis a *Kindneſs of* GOD unto us.                Fourthly,

Fourthly. DON't indulge Frightful Apprehenſions, That you *ſhall be Tempted beyond
what you ſhall be able to bear.* A Diſconſolate
Perſon under the Advance of *ſtormy Adverſity*
may be ready to ſay, *I am afraid of all my
ſorrows ;* yea, to ſay, *I ſhall periſh, by what is
coming upon me.* But ſay not ſo ! Particularly ;
If any of you feel riſing in you, a Suſpicion,
That you ſhall *come to want* before you dye ;
lay aſide that Evil Surmiſe. Rely on the
*Providence* of your Heavenly Father, and be
aſſured, that you ſhall be *provided* for. Take
the *Sixth Chapter of Matthew,* and make a
*Living* upon it. *Live* upon ſuch Words as
thoſe ; Pſal. XXXIV. 10. *They that ſeek the
Lord, ſhall not want any good thing.*

Secondly. THE *Storms* of *Paſſions* Enraged
from the *Provocations* which in the boiſterous
*Elements* here below, we may meet withal ;
theſe are *Storms* that muſt have the *Way of
the Lord* conſidered in them. We are liable
to *Storms* of *Grief,* in that *ſorrow of this World*
which *works Death.* We are liable to *Storms*
of *Wrath,* when we are, as we often are, Mal-
treated by our Neighbours. Alas, the *Storms*
render us too often like thoſe, of whom we
read, Iſai. LVII. 20. *They are like the troubled
ſea which cannot reſt.*

BUT what is, *The Way of the Lord,* that is
to be taken in the *Storm ?*

Firſt. BEHOLD a *Juſt,* and a *Wiſe,* and a
*Faithful* GOD, Operating in all that is done
unto

unto you. Stop not at *Second Caufes.* Let the *Faith of the Operation of God,* lun the *Storm.* Take that courfe to filence all the uproar within ; Pfal. XXXIX. 9. *I was dumb, I opened not my mouth, becaufe thou didft it.* Tho' it be a *Chaldæan* that preys on you, fay, *The Lord hath taken away.* Tho' it be a *Shimei* that rails at you, fay, *The Lord has bidden him.*

Secondly. BELIEVE *Gracious Defigns* cf GOD, in all that is done unto you. Will it not quell the *Storm,* to hear a Kind GOD faying to you in the midft of it, *I will do you no Hurt!* Tho' you may be fomewhat *Sea-fick* with what you are fo royl'd withal, yet be confident of this ; Gen. L. 20. *God has meant it unto Good.* Child of GOD, Thy *Humiliations* are only to *Do thee Good in the Latter End!*

Thirdly, THE *Storms* of the *Fears* which a *Guilty Confcience* raifes in a Soul, that GOD *is not well pleafed* withal ; Thefe are *Storms* that muft have, *The Way of the Lord,* confidered in them. In the Portion of the Ungodly we find, Pfal. XI. 6. *An horrible Tempeft* ; or, *A fpirit full of ftorm.* A Soul *felf-condemned* for vile Impieties and Impurities ; A Soul vexed with the Reflections of a Mind filled with the *Fury of the Lord* ; A Soul that fees GOD Angry with it, Hell gaping for it, the Devils ready to feize upon it ; and a Devouring Fire and Everlafting Burnings affign'd unto it ; furely fuch a Soul is in an *Horrible Tempeft!* Unpardoned Soul, If a *Dead fleep* worfe

worſe than *Jonahs* were not on thee, we ſhould
hear thy Outcries of the Horrible Tempeſt.
They would be, *Lord, Thy wrath lies
hard upon me, thou haſt afflicted me with all thy
waves !* They would be, *Save me, O God, for
the waters come into my ſoul; the floods over-
flow me.*

BUT, What is, *The Way of the* LORD, that
is to be taken in the *Storm ?*

Firſt. BE ſuitably affected with the *En-
couraging Invitations* of a JESUS, who *ſaves us
from our ſins*; a JESUS who threw himſelf
into the formidable Ocean, when the Wrath
of GOD, with ſwelling and roaring Billows,
was ready to ſwallow us up ; and ſo appeaſed
the *Storm* : A SAVIOUR, who came into the
World, that He might *ſave the Chief of Sinners.* That there is a JESUS, who is Able to
*ſave unto the uttermoſt all that come unto God
by Him,* and who *will caſt out none that Come
unto Him*; This is *Goſpel.* And of this *Goſpel,*
there is that *Order* given, Mar. 16. 15. That
it ſhould be *preached unto every Creature.*
Polluted Soul, Be thy Sins never ſo many,
there is a *Blood* which *cleanſes from all ſin* ;
And this *Blood* is a *Fountain ſet open* for thee.
GOD invites thee to it. Thy SAVIOUR invites thee, Look *unto me, and be ye ſaved* ;
tho' thou art *at the Ends of the Earth,* and tho'
thy Sins have carried thee to never ſo great a
Diſtance from Him. With ſuch a Word thy
SAVIOUR now ſtretches out His Hand unto
thee

thee as unto *Peter*, when he was ready to
fink.   After this, Vile Defpair, *Be ftill !*

Secondly,   DON't   imagine your felves
*Utterly Forfaken* of GOD, when there is no
real Ground for any fuch Imagination. *Zion*
was miftaken, when fhe faid, *The Lord has
forfaken me.*   And fo are her Children too.
Say not, *I have committed the Unpardonable Sin.*
'Tis a *Sin* for any of *you* to fay fo ! Say not,
*The Spirit of GOD will make no more Impreffions
on me.*  Thou art *now* under His *Impreffions.* It
was pleaded, Pfal. CXIX. 8. *I will keep thy
Statutes* ; *O Forfake me not utterly.*   Soul, if
thou art *Willing* to be helped in *keeping the
Statutes* of GOD, and *forry* that thou haft
*kept* them no more, GOD has *not utterly forfaken* thee ;  No, and He never will do fo.

Fourthly, THE *Storms* which threaten the
*Church* of GOD in the World, with a total
Defolation, and a woful Extirpation ; In thefe
alfo, Let the *Way of the Lord* be taken with
us.   The State of the Church, may procure
that Compellation for it ; Ifai. LIV. **11.** *O
thou afflicted, and toffed with Tempeft.*   Yea,
*The Floods have lifted up, O Lord, the Floods
have lifted up their Voice ;  the Floods lift up
their waves*, at fuch a rate, that the *Church*
of all that People whom GOD has *Redeemed
from the Earth*, would be utterly fwallowed
up, if we had not a *ftrong Redeemer*, and a
SAVIOUR, who is *Mightier than the Mighty
waves of the fea.*   Yet let not the *Floods of*
                                                    *the*

*The Voice of* GOD *in a* TEMPEST. **17**

*the* Ungodly make us *afraid.* But let our *Cry*
come to our GOD in His Temple. *The Way
of the Lord,* now to be taken, is, by our *Cry*
to call upon a Lord, who *waits that He may be
Gracious,* ( waits to hear our *Cry !* ) That He
would *Awake* for the Help of His *Church* and
*Cauſe* in the World. The Diſciples in the
ſinking *Bark* did ſo! But in doing ſo, Let us
cheerfully depend on the Promiſe of our SA-
VIOUR concerning His *Church* ; That tho' as
in the *Flood* of old, the *Fountains of the Great
Deep were broken up, and the waters prevailed
exceedingly upon the Earth,* yet the *Gates of
Hell pouring out a Flood*(be it of Perſecutions,or
of Corruptions, or of Contentions) upon His
*Church, They ſhall not prevail againſt it.* A
Glorious CHRIST is aboard His *Church* ; And
therefore,—*Fluctuat, at nunquam mergitur illa
Ratis.*

THE Great GOD has begun a *Storm* upon
upon the Nations ; and a Storm that will not
go over, till ſome ſpacious and ſpeciousBuild-
ings, (founded on the *ſand of Humane Inventions,*) will fall, and *Great will be the Fall thereof!* There are *Fooliſh Buildings* which GOD
is going to *Rend with a ſtormy wind in His
Fury !* Our Safety in ſuch a *ſtormy time* will
be to have as much of a Glorious CHRIST
with us as may be ; and keep cloſe to Him,
and His Inſtitutions ; and as for the *Fooliſh
Children,* whom their *Mothers* here with
*heavy Hearts* behold bringing in a *Lifeleſs Religion*

18　*The Voice of* GOD *in a* TEMTEST.

*ligion* and an *Irreligious Life* among us,—*From such turn away!*

Fifthly and Finally, THERE is a STORM near unto us all ; Yea, *It is near, it is near, and it haftens greatly upon us!* A Storm, which will blow down our *Clay-Tabernacle ;* The Storm of DEATH ; which there will be no ftanding before: A Storm that carries with it the *Terrors of Death.*

AND, Oh! What is *The Way of the Lord,* which is to be taken, that we may Enjoy a *Calm* within when that *Storm* fhall teardown all before it ? O Man ready to *Dye,* Get a Soul full of a CHRIST ; Lay hold on Him in His Offers ; and let the *precious Thoughts* of Him keep continually filling of thy Soul. Yea, get a CHRIST formed in thy Soul, with a Principle of PIETY there conforming thee to Him, and Quickening thee to Live unto GOD. In the Shipwreck which the *Storm* of *Death* will bring upon thee, *now* thou art fafe : Thy Soul will get fafe in the *Fair Haven* of the *Reft that remains for the People of God.*

¶ IN the mean time, Let the *Voice of the Lord* this Day *Crying to the City,* have all due Refpect paid unto it.

LET it be Enquired, What Mifchiefs in *Storm* of Contentious Outrages, and a *Flood* of Intemperate Exceffes, may do unto us ; and, Let us *have no more of them!*

LET

277

*The Voice of* GOD *in a* TEMPEST 19

LET the *Diſtraction* which this Day makes the LORD'S DAY a Day of ſo little *Reſt* unto us, cauſe us to Examine how poorly we have Sabbatized at other times.

LET the *Uncertain Riches*, on which we ſee *One Element* this Day make ſuch Depredations, and, GOD *knows how ſoon Another may do more!*—have no more ſo large a Room in our Hearts, but let our *Affections* be more *ſet upon the things that are Above* ; where *Tides* can't *break thro' & ſpoil* ; and where we have a *Better & a Laſtiug ſubſtance.*

*F I N I S.*

# Dr. *Mather's*

# REMARKS

## ON THE

# EARTHQUAKE

That ſhook NEW-ENGLAND,

In the NIGHT,

Between the 29 and the 30 of *October.* 1727.

The Terror of the LORD.

## Some ACCOUNT of the

# Earthquake

That shook NEW-ENGLAND,

In the NIGHT,

Between the 29 and the 30 of *October*. 1727.

## With a SPEECH,

Made unto the Inhabitants of BOSTON,

Who Assembled the Next Morning, for the proper

## Exercises of Religion,

On so Uncommon, and so Tremendous an Occasion.

2 Cor. V. 11.
*Knowing the Terror of the LORD, we persuade Men.*

*B O S T O N*:
Printed by *T. Fleet*, for *S. Kneeland*, and Sold at his Shop in *King Street.* 1727.

# REMARKS
## UPON THE
## Earthquake.

THE *Night* that followed the Twenty ninth of *October* [1727.] was a *Night* whereto NEW-ENGLAND had never in the Memory of Man, feen the like before. The *Air* never more *Calm*, the *Sky* never more *Fair* ; every thing in all imaginable Tranquillity : But about a quarter of an Hour before Eleven, there was heard in BOSTON, paffing from one end of the Town to the other, an horrid rumbling like the Noife of many Coaches together, driving on the paved Stones with the utmoft Rapidity. But it was attended with a moft awful *Trembling of the Earth*, which did heave and fhake fo as to Rocque the Houfes, and caufe here and there the falling of fome fmaller Things, both within Doors and without. It cannot be imagined, but that it gave an uncommon Concern unto all the Inhabitants, and even a degree of Confternation, unto very many

ny

2    *Remarks upon the Earthquake.*

ny of them. This *firſt Shock,* which was the moſt Violent, was followed with ſeveral others, and ſome Repetition of the Noiſe, at ſundry times, pretty diſtant from one another. The Number of them is not entirely agreed; but at leaſt Four or Five are allow'd for; The laſt of which was between Five and Six of the Clock in the Morning.

How far this *Earthquake* extended thro' the Countrey, we are not yet informed; But that it extended Scores of Miles, we have already a certain Information. And what added unto the Terrors of it, were the terrible Flames and Lights, in the Atmoſphere, which accompanied it. The Veſſels on the Coaſt, were alſo made ſenſible of it, by a ſhivering that ſiezed on them.

When the greatly affected People, had a little Opportunity to look about them in the Morning, the Paſtors of the *Old North Church,* directed the *Bells* to be rung, that ſuch of the People as could and would, might aſſemble immediately unto ſome ſeaſonable Exerciſes of Religion. The Paſtors of the *New* joined with them in ſending up unto Heaven, the Supplications which the ſolemn Occaſion called for. And the Paſtors in the other part of the Town, made a ſpeedy and hearty Appearance, and moſt affectionately united in a Concurrence with them. The Aſſembly that came together, did more than croud and fill the moſt capacious of our Meetinghouſes; And as there was a multitude of ſerious Chriſtians, who are acquainted with

*Real*

## *Remarks upon the Earthquake.* 3

*Real* and *Vital* PIETY, fo the whole Auditory expreffed a Devotion which was truly Extraordinary.

When thefe Exercifes were finifhed about Two in the Afternoon, after fome fhort Intermiffion of an Hour or Two, feveral Churches in the other part of the Town, followed the Exemple, and with vaft Congregations, continued the proper Exercifes of Religion, until about Eight a Clock in the Evening. For the Animation thereof, there was not only the joint Inclination of the *Paftors* and the *People*, but likewife a Recommendation from His Honour the L. GOVERNOUR; Whofe *Piety*, ever difcovered on every other, as well as this, Occafion, difpofed him, to Direct alfo the keeping of the *Thurfday* following (which is the Day of the ufual weekly Lecture,) as a Day of SUPPLICATIONS in all the Churches of the City.

In the Year 1580. *England* felt an *Earthquake*, which tho' no confiderable Damage was done by it, awakened the Government of the Nation, to call upon all the Subjects throughout the Kingdom, to be fervent and inftant in Prayer, that the Wrath of GOD whereof the *Earthquake* was a *Token*, might be averted from the Land. Such a Difpofition poffeffes our *Commander in Chief*, and his People moft readily come into it.

One of the MINISTERS, who did their part, in the Great Affembly of the Morning, judg'd it Expedient, yea, Neceffary, that PRAYER
fhould

4

should have the WORD accompanying of it. He thought, that if ever he did *preach the Word IN SEASON*, he should now do so. by taking the Present SEASON to render the *Voice* of the Glorious GOD, in the EARTHQUAKE, while it was yet scarce over, Articulate and Intelligible unto the Hearers: 'Twould be Emphatically, A WORD IN SEASON. And he hop'd, that *Hearts made soft* by the ALMIGHTY *Troubling* of them with the Occurrences of the Night before, would be more likely than ever, to receive Good Impressions, and be moulded into durable Resolutions of Godliness; Yea, that as the primitive *Outpouring* of the Holy SPIRIT, was attended with an *Earthquake*, so the EARTHQUAKE would now be attended with such an *Out-pouring* of the Holy SPIRIT as would make an Holy, and so an Happy People. Accordingly, with the Divine Assistance, he made a SPEECH, [or, if you please, A SERMON,] which was no sooner offered in the Assembly of *Zion* there convened. but it was desired, that it might be further offered in the way of the Press, for the Service of PIETY, not only here, but in other parts of the Land, which *GOD makes to Tremble.* He durst not reject the Desire. Tis true, There can be expected none but a mean Preparation. from a few Minutes of a Morning filled with Disturbances; which may be an Apology for the Deficiencies which a curious Reader may soon discover in it.

But

But our Gracious GOD is pleafed fometimes to make ufe of *fuch*, to do Good in the World ; that fo, *Man* may be Nothing, and HE may be *All in All.* Tis not poffible for him to give Word for Word, a Difcourfe which he could have no Time to Write, before it was delivered. But it is here without many material *Additions*, & perhaps, with fome Forgetful *Subftraction*, Exhibited as very near as can well be asked for, to what was delivered.

O ! May the Holy SPIRIT of our GOD, make it come with *Efficacy* !

We find, the *Hill* on the North fide whereof *Jofhua* was buried, had [Jofh. XXIV. 30.] the Name of, *Har-Gayafh*; which Name fignifies, *The Mountain of Trembling.* The Jews have a Tradition, That at the Time of his Burial, the *Mountain Trembled* with an *Earthquake*, to teftify the Difpleafure of GOD againft the People. My Friends, We approach as to an *Har-Gayafh*, in what is now to be fet before us.

A

B

---

# A

# SPEECH,

## Made by One of the Minifters, to the Inhabitants of BOSTON;

### Affembled the Morning after the EARTH-QUAKE. *Octo.* 30. 1727.

THE Glorious GOD has *Roared out of Zion.* We have the laft Night heard the terrible *Roaring* ; with general and uncommon Terror, heard the awful Repetition of it. Who is here of you, among them who felt the *Earth trembling* under them, that faid not upon it, *When I heard, my Lips quivered at the Voice, and I trembled in my felf, that I might find Reft in the Day of Trouble!* Who is there that faid not, *Lord, my Flefh trembles for fear of Thee, and I am afraid of thy Judgments!* The *Lion hath roared ; Who will not fear?* We are worfe than *Beafts*, if we *tremble* not.

Never did the City of BOSTON, in the Ninety feven Years that have rolled over it, fee
such

ſuch a *Night*, as what we ſaw a few Hours ago.
A MIDNIGHT CRY was heard; The Conſternation whereof is not this Morning over
with us; An *Anguiſh* like that on a *Travailing
Woman*, ſiezed upon *Men* as well as *Women*. What
*Fear*, from the Apprehenſion of going to the *Pit*,
by a ſtroke like a *ſnare* upon us !

We have had the repeted, more than three
times repeted *Shocks*, of a Formidable EARTH-
QUAKE· And GOD knows, whether there
are any more to come, or what Execution they
may do, when they come.

When the never-to-be-forgotten *Sicilian*
EARTHQUAKE in our Days, had given ſome
*Shocks* which only terrified the People, after an
Intermiſſion of Two Days, there came on thoſe,
which horribly deſtroy'd them; A *Beſom of Deſtruction* that ſwept away near one hundred and
fifty Thouſand of them.

The Ancient Cry of the *Prophets*, is now moſt
certainly the Cry of our *Earthquakes*; Hoſ. X.
12· *It is Time to ſeek the Lord.* The poor Popiſh
*Idolaters*, in their *Earthquakes*, make their Procef-
ſions & their Addreſſes to, *Lying Vanities*, & ſilly
gods that *cannot ſave* them ; *They cry, but there is
none to ſave them !* We will *walk in the Name of*
JEHOVA-JESUS, *who is our* only GOD, as
thoſe unhappy Creatures *walk in the Name* of
Theirs. *Their Rock is not as our Rock;* We have
a SAVIOUR, in whom we find a ſufficient *Refuge,* for us, and a *very preſent Help in Trouble,*
when

8 *Remarks upon the Earthquake.*

when the *Earth is moved* under us, and the *Mountains are shaking* about us. We will invert the
Order of the *Eighteenth Psalm* ; The Psalmist
said, *In my Distress I called on the Lord, and cried
unto my GOD. Then the Earth shook and trembled.*
We will say, *Since the Earth shakes and trembles ;
Now in our Distress we will call on the Lord, and cry
unto our GOD.* It is with pleasure that I read in
*Eusebius,* a Letter of *Antoninus,* who was a stranger to the True GOD, but yet complains, That
the *Pagans* urged him to persecute the *Christians* ;
‘ Whereas (he says) I understand, that they are
‘ a good People, and whenever there happens
‘ an *Earthquake,* their Course is to go and pray
‘ unto their GOD, that His Wrath may be
‘ turned away from us ; And in this they show
‘ more of Religion than the People that urge me
‘ to destroy them *!* We are this Day doing
what the *Primitive Christians* did, and what all
*Genuine Christians* will.

We have Two *Occasions,* to repair unto our
gracious GOD ; we have Two *Petitions* to carry
unto Him. The one is, That we may have the
Grace to *know,* and to *do,* the *Duties,* which the
*Earthquake* does in its hideous Rumbles most sensible call us to. The other is ; That there may
be no such *Returns* of the *Earthquake* as to lay us
in Desolations, and make our *Plagues wonderful.*
But, the *success* of our Supplications, will very
much turn upon our Attention to the Voice of
our glorious GOD in the *Earthquake* which is
now

now affrighting of us. Don't we remember those Divine *Retaliations*; *As He cried, and they would not hear, so they cried and I would not hear, saith the Lord of Hosts.* And again, *Because I called, and ye refused, I will laugh at your Calamity, and I will mock when your Fear cometh*; *when your Fear cometh as Desolatioa, and your Destruction cometh as a Whirlwind*; *when Distress and Anguish cometh upon you?* Yea, I may say unto you, The *Dispositions* of PIETY, will be so many *Supplications*; and indeed, the best sort of *Supplications*, the most proper and the most potent *Supplications*; There are *pure Hands lifted up* in our *Supplications* when we *Do* what our GOD has oblig'd us to.

Wherefore, as a Præliminary, and as a Foundation to the Discourse, wherewith I propose to treat you, the TEXT which I now pitch upon is That;

## Mic. VI. 9.
*The Voice of the LORD, crieth unto the City.*

CErtainly, you will not expect, that I should spend any time in proving, That there is a VOICE of the glorious GOD, in all that He *does*, in the World. All the *Works* of *Creation*, and all the *Works* of *Providence*, there is a *Voice* of the glorious GOD in them. He *speaks* in all
that

that He *does.* And there is no place, where
their *Voice* may not be *heard.* O *Deaf* we, if we
hear it not ! —— That *Voice,* — O *Love,* O *Admire,* O *Adore, the glorious One, who does all thefe
things.* O *Fear this GOD, and give Glory unto
Him* !

'Tis very fure; In the *Works* wherein the
glorious GOD goes out of the *Ordinary Road,* or,
His *Extraordinary Difpenfations;* In thefe, His
*Voice* becomes very Notable; and moft inexcu-
fable are they who *Regard not the Works of the
Lord, nor the Operation of His Hands*: He *fhall deftroy them, and not build them up.*

EARTHQUAKES are fuch *Works.* We read,
Pfal. XXIX. 8. *The Voice of the Lord fhakes the
Wildernefs.* There is the *Voice of the Lord,* in it,
when He *fhakes* our Territories. There may be
fome *Earthquakes* more *Supernatural* than others:
We reckon that of Mount *Sinai* One; And fo we
reckon that at the *Refurrection* of our Bleffed JE-
SUS; and yet more confpicuoufly that of His
*Crucifixion.* The *fplit Rocks* at this Day obferved
by Travellers who are *Proteftants,* and fomewhat
Nice in their Credulity, are thought by fome
no Injudicious Men, to be the lafting Monu-
ments and Memorials of it. But ufually, our
*Earthquakes* have *Natural Caufes* affigned for
them. What they are, 'tis now and here, neither a Time nor Place for Philofophical Difqui-
fitions. Whether *Colluctations* of *Minerals* producing Vapours that muft have an Explofion,
may

may caufe thofe direful Convulfions in the Bowels of the Earth, which are felt in our *Earthquakes?* —— Or, whether the huge quantities
of *Waters*, running in the Bowels of the Earth,
may not by Degrees wafh away the Bottom of
the upper *Strata* here and there, fo as to caufe
their falling in?— Or, whether the *Subterraneous
Fires*, getting head, may not by their Sulphureous
and Bituminous Exhalations in the Bowels of the
Earth, caufe a Combuftion that may carry all
before it? — Or, whether —— But it muft be
fomething more *Theological*, that you are now to
be treated with. Let the *Natural Caufes* of *Earthquakes* be what the *Wife Men of Enquiry* pleafe,
*They* and their *Caufes* are ftill under the Government of HIM that is the *GOD of Nature*. Shall
we fay, All this is but a *Chance that happens to us*,
or the meer unguided *Motion* of *Matter?* Ah,
profane *Philiftine!* — 'Tis a Language for none
but a *Philiftine*. A *Chriftian* cannot fpeak fo;
No, He is one that will be fenfible of GOD in
thefe things. Verily, In them, *Lo, GOD fends
forth His Voice, and that a mighty Voice* unto us.

You will yet lefs expect, that I fhould be at
any pains, for proving, That this VOICE of the
glorious GOD, is to be hearken'd to. When the
*great GOD who formed all things*, will pleafe to
*utter His Voice*, What? Shall it not by all that
have the Faculties of *Reafon* in them rendring
them capable of hearkening to it, be hearken'd
to? O moft *unreafonable!* GOD our Maker
fays,

12    *Remarks upon the Earthquake.*

fays, *Unto you, O Men, I call, and my Voice is unto the Sons of Men.*  We are *Bruits* rather than *Men,* and *Colts of the wild Aß,* yea, *Children of the wicked One,* rather than the *Sons of Men,* if we do not hearken to the *Voice* of his Eternal *Wifdom.*  He will not own us, for the *People of His Pafture, and the Sheep of His Hand,* if we do not even *To Day hear His Voice.*  An hardy *Pharaoh* may fay, Exod. V 2. *Who is the Lord, that I fhould Obey His Voice!*  Words to come from the Mouth of none but a *Pharaoh,* and a *Devil!*  But, Ah, *Pharaoh,* ah! Monfter, The Almighty GOD, whom thou fo infulteft, and whofe *Voice* thou fo defieft, what will the affronted JEHOVAH do unto thee! *What will He do unto thee!*

Indeed there is this Argument for hearkening to the *Voice* of our GOD, that if we do it not, we provoke Him to *Render His Rebukes in Flames of Fire* unto us ; We provoke Him, to inflict *great Plagues and of long continuance* upon us.  If we do not hearken to His *Voice,* efpecially in His *Caftigatory Dealings* with us, —— He fays, *If ye will not hearken unto me, I will punifh you yet feven times more for your Sins.*

And therefore, Be now at length effectually *Alarmed,* O Inhabitants of BOSTON, yea, and of the whole Countrey whereof this is the *Metropolis.*  What a *Trial,* Yea, what a Gradually defcending *Trial,* is our glorious GOD making of us, whether we will *hearken to His Voice* or no?  A few Months ago, how fearfully did we

we fee the Heavens blazing over us, with Coruſ-
cations that fill'd People with a *fearful Expectation* of the *fiery Indignation* which is anon to *devour
the Adverſaries* of GOD *!* And how frequently
did loud *Thunder-Claps* rouſe us out of our Le-
thargies ! How frequently did hot *Thunderbolts*
fall where many Objects felt the Force of an
*Arm* which, *What can ſtand before?* But, alas,
Did we *hear Attentively*, and Obediently, the
*Noiſe of His Voice*, or, Mind as we ſhould have
done, the *Sound that went out of His Mouth?* After this, The *Stormy Wind which fulfils His Word*,
came ruſhing down upon us. We ſaw an *Horrible Tempeſt.* A *Storm* came, which tore up the
Trees of our Fields by the roots ; tore down
parts of our Houſes ; Yea, Wounded and Killed ſome of our People. The *great and ſtrong
Wind* which *rent the Mountains*, had a *Voice* in it.
Indeed, it was not a *ſtill ſmall Voice* ; but was it
therefore the leſs to be hearken'd to ? And
now, *After the Wind an Earthquake !* ———— Oh *!*
Let it not be ſaid, *The Lord was not in the Earthquake.* Our GOD ſays, *Now ſurely, they will fear
me, and they will receive Inſtruction ;* ———— *that I
may not proceed unto a more dreadful Extremity, and
cut off their Dwellings, and them with and in their
Dwellings !*

What I am now therefore to proceed unto, is
the Conſideration of that CASE.

C                    *What*

14  *Remarks upon the Earthquake.*

*What may be the VOICE of the glorious GOD unto us, in the EARTHQUAKE, wherein we have had the Earth juſt now trembling under us?*

O People *Trembling* before the Lord; *Hear now my SPEECH, and hearken to all my Words.* For indeed, I may declare unto you, The *opening of my Lips will be of Right Things*; and you will not *underſtand Wiſdom*, nor be *of an underſtanding Heart*, if you do not hearken to them.

I. The VOICE of the glorious GOD *crying to the City* in His *Earthquake* is This; O Glorify the *Perfections* of the glorious GOD, which are diſplay'd in the *Earthquake*; And very particularly, the *Power* and *Mercy* which He diſplays when He cauſes the *Earth*, and the Inhabitants thereof, to tremble before Him.

Syrs, Don't you *clearly ſee* the *Eternal Power and Godhead* of Him, who can *ſhake the Earth*, yea, ſhake it all to pieces at His Pleaſure? Oh! ſee it, and *ſhake* before it! As when He *ſets faſt the Mountains*, He ſhows that He is *Girded with Power*; So, when He *ſhakes the Mountains* He ſhows that He has a *Girdle* of matchleſs *Power*. This whole *Globe*, tho' the Ambit of it be more than Twenty four Thouſand and Nine Hundred Miles, and in the ſolid Content muſt be more than Two Hundred and Sixty one Thouſands of Millions, yet it is no more than the *light Duſt of* the

*the Balance,* in the Hand of the glorious GOD ;
who made it, and can Tear it and Rend it as He
pleafes.  In our *Earthquake,* the great GOD,
fays to us, yea, to the greateft of Men, with an
infinitely greater Claim, than a Roman Governour could fpeak fo, to any Man, *Knoweft thou
not that I have power over thee, to put thee to Death,
or fave thee alive?*  We cannot but own His Ab-
folute and Sovereign *Dominion* over us, and our
Lives, and if He go to extinguifh our Lives by
an *Earthquake,* we muft own, *We are in the Houfe
of the Potter, and Lord, Thou mayft break us and lodge
us where thou pleafeft.*  But at the fame time, the
*Earthquake* proclaims the Irrefiftible POWER,
wherewith He can *Crufh a World,* (as He made it)
with a *Word.*  If He touch the Earth, it fhivers
and crumbles before Him·  *The Finger of GOD,*
it can rip open the Earth, and caufe *Caftles,* and
*Cities,* and the largeft of *Territories* to fink into it
in a Moment.  *Lord, who knows the power of thine
Anger !* ―――― O all you that *go on ftill in your
Trefpaffes* and perfift impenitently in Rebellion
againft the glorious GOD ; What are you but
*Fighters againft GOD ?*  What mean you, O Fool-
hardy Wretches?  Dare you *provoke* Him who
is Lord GOD Omnipotent ?  Are you *ftronger than
He ?*  O *Tremble* to continue under the *Wrath of
the Almighty.*  The *Trembling Earth* calls upon
you ; O *Fear Him, that is able to deftroy !* Fear Him,
on whofe order for it, *Earth, open thy Mouth!* you
you prefently go down into the Pit ; you are fwallowed up in a Moment !          C 2          But

16     *Remarks upon the Earthquake.*

But then, O the *Mercy* of our GOD! In the midſt of the *Lamentations* and *Ejulations* cauſed by the *Earthquake*, yet we are to make that Confeſſion, and, Oh! make it with wonderment; *Lord, It is of thy Mercy that we are not conſumed!* If we had our *Deſert*, what would an *Earthquake* preſently do unto us! Our *Hearts* are ſo *Earthly*, that we *deſerve* to be buried in the *Earth.* We Bury our ſelves in it, while we neglect our Souls thro' the purſuits and hurries of it. A jealous GOD may juſtly ſay of us; *Let the Earth ſwallow them up; It has already ſwallow'd them up. They have changed their Center; The Earth is become their Center. Let them go down unto their Center!* We have ſuch a ſhare in the *Sins* of them who dwell on the *Earth,* which have made the *Earth* obnoxious unto *Earthquakes,* that we cannot complain of being unjuſtly dealt withal, if we have our *ſhare* in their *Woes.* By the *Earthquakes* with which the *Earth* has been *viſited by the Lord of Hoſts,* multitudes have *periſhed wonderfully.* That *we* have not, this lays Obligations upon us, for continual Acclamations, *Oh! The patience of a GOD ſlow to Anger and plenteous in Mercy! Oh! the Riches of His Goodneß and Forbearance, and long-ſuffering!* I pray, what are we better than any of them? *Joſephus* writes of a diſmal *Earthquake,* wherein *Judæa* was horribly ſhaken, and near Ten Thouſand People were ſlain by the fall of Houſes upon them. 'Tis likely that in that *Earthquake,* a Towre built over the *Portico's* at the Pool

Pool of *Bethefda* fell, and flew *Eighteen* that were
there waiting for a Cure. Now, have you forgotten what our SAVIOUR faid about *thofe
Eighteen upon whom the Tower of Siloam fell?* This,
This is what He now fays unto us. *Think ye, that
all they who have perifhed in Earthquakes were Sinners above all the Men that are yet walking on the
Earth? I tell you, No; You are all of you fo very
finful, that you deferve to perifh, as much as many of
thofe.*

Oh! Let us be deeply affected, with the *fpar-
ing Mercy* of our GOD unto us. *Behold the Compaffion and Severity of GOD! Severity* to them
who have *perifhed* in *Earthquakes;* But *Compaffion*
towards thee, who haft not fo *perifhed.* —— *Lord,
why am I fpared, and yet ftanding on the Earth before
thee! Why, why does thy Earth yet bear fuch a Sinner againft thee upon it!*

II. The VOICE of the glorious GOD *crying
to the City* in His *Earthquake,* is, This; Let the
*Crimes* that Cry to the Holy GOD for all the
Vengeance of an *Earthquake* upon you, be generally and thoroughly *Reformed* among you.

The Cry is, REFORMATION, O *Degene-
rating Plants,* REFORMATION; *or more Evil
to come upon you!*

'Tis no fond *Superftition* to think, An *Earthquake* ufually carries in it, fome Intimation of the
*Divine Difpleafure;* 'Tis a *Token* which we who
*dwell in the Wildernefs* may be *afraid* of. If God
*over-*

18      *Remarks upon the Earthquake.*

*overturn the Mountains* as He does in *Earthquakes,*
'tis in His *Anger* that He does it.   If the *Earth
Tremble,* as it does in *Earthquakes,* 'tis *at His Wrath,*
that it does so.   When the *Mountains quake,* as
they do in *Earthquakes,* 'tis from His *Indignation.*
It was declared concerning some *Tents of Wicked
Men* ; Num. XV. 30. *If the Earth open its Mouth,
and swallow them up, and they go down alive into the
Pit, you shall understand that these Men have provoked
the Lord.*   Yea, If no Body be kill'd in the *Earthquake,* yet the *Divine Displeasure* against Sin, is to
be apprehended in it.   By such an *Earthquake* did
the Father of our Blessed Jesus testify something
of His Resentment, upon the Wickedness of the
Jews, when, *All their Wickedness was in Golgotha :*
The most nefandous Wickedness that was ever
perpetrated !   Rarely an   *Earthquake* sent any
where, till a People have *sinned grievously.*   If we
search for the *Moral Causes* of an *Earthquake,* a
Prophet of GOD has declared them; Isa. XXIV.
5. *The Earth is defiled under the Inhabitants thereof.*

And shall I now *Cry aloud, and spare not, but
lift up my Voice like a Trumpet,* and *show* unto you,
O our People,   that you   have   *sinned grievously* ?
'Tis true,  Our People are not for the most part
so Abandoned unto *Immoralities,* as they are in
many Ungospellized, or Apostatized and  Antichristian Regions.   But our *Faults* are aggrava-
ted into *Crimes,* because we sin under, and against
the *glorious Gospel of the Blessed* GOD.   We *Rebel
against the light* in what we do amiss ; and a *light*
                                                    which

which teaches us, & quickens us, & gives us many Advantages, to be the *beſt People* in the World. If we are not the *Beſt People* on the Face of the *Earth*, it muſt not be wondered at, if the *Earth* do *Groan*, in the Murmurs of *Earthquakes* under us. It has been thought by ſome, that *Earthquakes* are not mentioned among the *Plagues* in the *Twenty Eighth* Chapter of *Deuteronomy*, becauſe of a Tranſcendency in this beyond all other *Plagues*, [ It is impoſſible to contrive any Defence againſt it ; but it ſays, *Tho' they hide in the top of Carmel, I will find them there!* ] which renders it a more proper Vengeance for Sins under the *Evangelical Diſpenſation.* Our Sins are ſuch. But Oh ! What a *Black Liſt* is there to be formed of them *!*

[ I ſee none *Aſleep* at this Time. 'Tis a Congregation of *Hearers*, that I am this Time ſpeaking to. This very Circumſtance *awakens* a Thought in me; That *ſleeping* in the Aſſemblies of Zion, when it is Indulged, and not a meer Involuntary ſurpriſal upon Infirmity, 'tis *utterly a Fault,* & offers an Affront unto Heaven: But it is a very *Epidemical Miſcarriage* in the Countrey. Now, Syrs, You have an *Earthquake* to give you a puſh like that of the *Goads* given of old, by the *Maſters of the Aſſemblies,* for the *Awaking* of the Drowſy *Sleepers* there. An *Earthquake* is crying in your Ears, *What meaneſt thou, O Sleeper in the Houſe of GOD? Oh! No more ſleeping in this dreadful place! It may ſoon be made ſo.* ] I can go on, and be heard.

How

20          *Remarks upon the Earthquake.*

How do the Sins of *Intemperance* grow upon us ! 'Tis the Defcription of an *Earthquake, The Earth reels to and fro like a Drunken Man.* How does it call for an *Earthquake,* when the *Earth* can fhow fo many ugly pictures of fuch a Thing, in *Drunken Men reeling to and fro upon it !*

How do the Sins of *Unchaftity* under the *Curfe* of Heaven *Increafe and Multiply* among us? The Cities which GOD *overthrew in His Anger,* and funk for the compafs of Eighteen Miles in Breadth and Eighty Miles in Length, and are covered with a Lake that is called, *The Dead Sea:* Was there not an *Earthquake* that help'd in the *overthrowing* of them? If an *Earthquake* do unfpeakable things upon us, let the Impurities of *Sodom* ftand indicted for it.

How do the Sins of *Difhonefty* bring an abominable fcandal on our Profeffion; and the *pernicious ways* thereof, make the *way of Truth* to be *evil fpoken of?* The Habitations, that are not *Habitations of Righteoufnefs,* but built, or fill'd, or fed, by *Difhoneft Gain,* 'tis not wrong, if the *Earth* don't bear them to ftand upon it. GOD fends an *Earthquake* to demolifh the Nefts that have been *Feathered* with fo much *Iniquity.*

To thefe Mifcarriages may we not annumerate the Luft of Exceffes and Vanities in *Apparrel*; the *Coftly Pride* whereof is a Temptation to take Indirect ways, for the fupporting of it? The *Earthquake* fays to us, *Put off fome of your Ornaments!*

And

And shall the Cry of *Defrauded Labourers*, be stifled? I am sure, the *Pulpit* may speak of them; the *Earthquake* does it.

How are we in regard of *Sabbatizing?* The Right and High Strain of it, how is it sadly decay'd with us? An Offended GOD by an *Earthquake* has not suffered us to take the *Rest*, into which we were composing our selves; has fetch'd us out of our Beds, and made us uncapable of enjoying our usual *Rest*. Most Equally punished! We have wretchedly Violated the *Rest* of GOD, by our Profanations of the *Holy Sabbath*, with which He has favoured us.

The *Evening* that follows the *Lord's-Day!* —— I do not plead for holding it properly a part of the *Holy Time* that belongs to the *Christian Sabbath*. Not only the *Scripture*, but also the *Practice* of the whole Church in all Ages and in all Places, have ever made the *Evening* that precedes the *Lord's-Day*, to be a *part* of it; until a certain Writer in *Switzerland* a little while ago, started that Opinion for another *Beginning of the Sabbath*, which now so many run into. But yet, I hope, I may plead, That *this Evening* may not be prostituted unto such *Vile Purposes*, as to spoil and lose all the *Good* of the Day; And that there may no more be such a *Quick Transition* as there often is, from the *Exercises of Godliness*, to all Ungodly Vanities and Lewdnesses. It is complained, That there is more Sin committed on that *Evening* among us, than in any

D                                  *Evening*

22     *Remarks upon the Earthquake.*

*Evening* of all the Week befide. *Young People,*
Where were you, and what was it that you did
laft Night? And in what Airs did the *Earth-*
*quake* find you? Verily, Syrs; The Glorious GOD
has taken the moft *Suitable Evening* that could
have been taken, to fend an *Earthquake* upon
us. A Time, how *Indigitating*! What He *fpeaks*
to us, what He *points* to us, is plainly This.
*Let the Evening that enfues upon my Day, be better*
*fpent than it ufe to be. Spend it more in Employments,*
*that may be agreeable and ferviceable unto the Inten-*
*tions of my Day that is then Expiring with you.* Oh!
That *Houfe-keepers* would reftrain thofe that are
*within their Gates,* from going out of them, and
affign them thofe Things to do, which may be
moft ufeful to them. [The *Societies of Young Men*
meeting to Worſhip GOD and Edify one another, on this *Evening,* how much ought they to
be Encouraged!]

    *Family-Religion*; In what Condition is it?
We are told, they are moft Ominoufly abating
of it, among thofe whom we efteem our *United*
*Brethren* beyond-Sea. But is not there amongft
us alfo, fome Abatement of it? There were
Twelve Sermons on *Family-Religion* lately
preached unto the City, in fo many Lectures of
your *United Paftors.* They were not regarded as
they fhould have been; And GOD now makes
an *Earthquake* fucceed them, which preaches
them over again, in a manner to be *trembled*
at. It is upon Record, That there was a Town
                              in

## Remarks upon the Earthquake.

in *Switzerland*, all deftroy'd by an *Earthquake*: Only One Houfe efcaped, in which the Good Man was at his daily *Family-Sacrifice*. If the *Earthquake* laft Night, had caufed every Houfe to fall, that has not a daily *Family-Sacrifice* to GOD in it, what a rueful Spectacle had we feen this Morning! O *Prayerleſs Houſholders*, How Obdurate, How Obftinate are you, How Inexpreffibly and Prodigioufly given up to a *Reprobate Mind*, if upon this *Earthquake*, which you have outlived, [*But are not fure, that you ſhall Another!*] you do not call your *Domeſticks* together, and let them know, You are exceedingly troubled, that your Family has been fo long expofed unto the *Great Wrath* of GOD, by being a *Family that has not called on His Name*, and that from THIS TIME, fuch *Atheifm* fhall no longer be perfifted in; from THIS TIME you will have them join with you, in *feeking* of GOD that you may *Live*. And BEGIN without any further Delay: Fall down on your Knees before the LORD, with the Expreffions of a Soul Returning to Him; and then Rife up Refolving, *As for me and my Houfe, we will ferve the Lord*.

[I might go on, and ask; Are we not *found faulty* in having our *Hearts divided* as they are, in our foolifh *Factions*? And may not the Glorious GOD caufe the *Earth* to fplit with Chafms and Gafps and frightful *Divifions*; to animadvert upon our finful *Divifions*?

Oh!

24        *Remarks upon the Earthquake.*

Oh ! Let us not be *Impenitent*, and worſe than the *Rocks* which have been moved by this *Earthquake*, — *Impenitent* under ſuch *Reproofs of GOD*, as have been given us. What ? Shall another *Earthquake* be invoked ? —— Or, muſt ſomething like a *Peſtilence* follow upon it ? ]

Syrs, Let every one of us, [ For I call upon you in the Style of the two *Micahs ; Hear this, O all ye People, every one of you !* ] —— I ſay, Let *every one of us*, be awakened, —— Won't a Rugient *Earthquake* awaken us ? —— *To ſearch and try our ways, and turn unto the Lord.* Find out, what Errors in our Lives, our *Conſcience* may Condemn us for. When an *Earthquake* is at work, it will be ſtrange indeed if our *Conſcience* be not alſo at *work*. The *Work of the Law written in our Hearts* will be now exerted. And, O Man, What thy *Conſcience* may now convict thee of, as a Thing to be *Reformed* in thy life ; Bewail it, Abhor it, Repair to thy SAVIOUR, that it may be pardoned, and that He may grant thee, the Aids of His Grace for the avoiding of it. Oh ! That we may now all *ſpeak aright*, in the Ear of the glorious GOD, who *hearkens to hear*, how His *Earthquake* operates upon us ; and that theſe *Two Words* may from every Quarter, be our *Echo* to the *Earthquake !* The one, *What have I done ?* The other, *I will not offend any more !*

But more eſpecially, *Hear the Word of the Lord, Ye Rulers of* BOSTON. —— Has there not been
of

*Remarks upon the Earthquake.*   25

of late, a blameable Intermiſſion of the Laudable and Excellent *Zeal*, with which the *Sword* in
your Hands, is to be and ſometimes has been, a
*Terror to Evil-doers?*   The great GOD by His
*Earthquake* to Night has been *ſhaking* and *jogging*
and *pulling* of you, to make you ſhake off the *ſlum-
ber*, that may be upon you.   Syrs, will you be
prevailed withal, to *meet* and conſult and contrive, what you may do, for the *Suppreſſion of Diſ-
orders*; for the Correction of all *Puniſhable Wickedneſs*; and particularly, for the ſtopping of that
*Language of Fiends*, heard ſo often in our Streets,
from the *Tongues that are ſet on Fire of Hell*; and
for the diſcountenancing of *Idleneſs*; and for the
breaking up of the Execrable *Seminaries for Wickedneſs*, which there are in ſome *Wicked Houſes*! —
You may be the   *Phineas's*, that ſhall *turn away
the wrath of GOD* from the Congregation, and
ſave it from a deſolating *Earthquake*, by the *Zeal*
of GOD *boiling* in you, which is now more loudly than ever called for.

III. The VOICE of the glorious GOD, *crying
to the City* in His *Earthquake*, is This; IMME-
DIATELY get into ſuch a STATE of SAFE-
TY, that no *Earthquake* may cauſe an *Heartquake*
in you; but that you may be Ready for all the
*Events* and *Changes*, which may be intended for
you, and impending over you.   IMMEDIATE-
LY, I ſay.  Stay not for *Another ſhock*.  — The
Rumbles of the *Earthquake*, —— Oh! How do
they

they ring that peal in our Ears ; Matth. XXIV.
44. *Be ye Ready!*  Can any of you tell, when
there may be *Another ſhock.*  And, what horrendous *Effects* it may have ? — I ſay again, What
you do, muſt be done IMMEDIATELY.  You
muſt not put off a *Moment*, what you have to do,
that you may be brought into, *A ſtate of Safety
for Eternity.*

Our LORD mentioning the *Signs* of His
coming to Burn THIS World, and *Create New
Heavens and a New Earth wherein ſhall dwell Righteouſneſs*, He ſays, Luk. XXI. 11. *There ſhall be
great Earthquakes in diverſe places.*

Our SAVIOUR having foretold, That His
*Coming* will be with all poſſible *Surprize* upon the
World ; like that of a *Thief in the Night*, wholly
unlook'd for ; no more look'd for than the Fate
of the *old World*, and of *Sodom*, in the Day that
it overtook them ; and, *The Day ſhall come as a
Snare, on all them who dwell on the Face of the Earth:*
How is this conſiſtent, with ſuch *Signal*, ſuch
Obſervable, ſuch Aſtoniſhing, *Forerunners* of His
*Coming ?*—— It ſeems to me, the *Signs* which
He foretells, were to be Things which were not
ſo much *Immediately to precede* His Coming, and
Rowſe a *ſleeping World*, as to *Prefigure*, and therewith to *Demonſtrate* unto Mankind, *How Things
will be at His coming.*  And it is intimated, as if
they would be given *Immediately after the Tribu-
lation of thoſe Days*, which diſperſed the Jewiſh
Nation.  I ſuppoſe, the Stupendous *Earthquakes*,
which

which in *Thofe Days* more than ever fhook the World, *in Diverfe Places,* and efpecially that un-parallel'd one at *Antioch,* the fecond City of the World, when People were come together to wait upon the Emperour, and celebrate their Sports, from all parts of the World, might fuf-ficiently fulfil what our SAVIOUR foretold, of *Great Earthquakes in diverfe places.* I verily Beleeve, That all the *Signs,* which our LORD promis'd of His coming, have been *given*; and are *paffed,* and *over*; and the Heedlefs Children of Men, under the Intervening Reign of *Anti-chrift,* have taken little Notice of them. For my part, I *can ask for no more!* Neverthelefs, in eve-ry *Earthquake,* there is a *Renewing* and an *En-forcing* of the promifed *Signs:* GOD puts us in mind, of what He is *going to do,* upon a World, that has His *Curfe* lying upon it: And it be-comes us to look upon every *Earthquake,* as a Præmonition of the Day, wherein, as we are certified; Ifa. XXIV. 18, 19. *The Foundations of the Earth fhall fhake; The Earth fhall be utterly bro-ken down; the Earth fhall be clean diffolved; the Earth fhall be moved exceedingly.* We are certifi-ed; Rev. XVI. 18. *There will be a great Earth-quake, fuch as has not been fince Men were on the Earth, fo mighty an Earthquake, and fo great an one.* Every *Earthquake* has that Voice in it, *Make Ready, make Ready, for the Diffolution, which the Glorious LORD is coming,* [*who can fay,* How Quickly!] *to bring upon a finful World.*

But,

28     *Remarks upon the Earthquake.*

—But, what a CONFLAGRATION, will be joined with it!———

When I confider, That the *Coming of the Son of Man in the Clouds of Heaven,* [which muſt mean His Literal, Perſonal, Viſible *Coming* ; We take *the Name of the Lord in Vain,* if we Expound it otherwiſe,] Tis to be at and for the *Deſtruction* of the *Roman* Monarchy, in the *Papal* and *Final* Form of it ; And when I confider, the *Flames,* declared by *Daniel,* and by *Paul,* and by *Peter,* to accompliſh it ; I confeſs, I cannot but admire, how any Men of Thought can content themſelves, with the commonly Received Opinions, about the *Coming* of our SAVIOUR in His *Kingdom,* which are indeed calculated, as if on purpoſe, to lay and keep the *World* in that profound SLEEP, wherein the *Day of GOD* is to find it : *Opinions,* which the *Petrine* CONFLA-GRATION, makes a miſerable *Hay* and *Stubble* of !——— But, if I ſhould own, That I know of *Nothing* that remains to be done, before the Lord *ſhall deſtroy the Man of Sin by the Brightneſs of His coming ;* If I ſhould own, That this Word, is *like a Fire in my Bones, and I am not eaſy in forbearing ;* If I ſhould make the Cry, FIRE, FIRE ! *The Fire of GOD will ſooner than is generally thought for, fall upon a wretched World, which dreams little of it !*——— I ſhould be as much *mocked,* and as little *minded,* as *Lot* was in the *Morning* of the Day when he went out of *Sodom.* The *Sleepy* People of GOD, will not bear to be Awakened : Our
SAVI-

SAVIOUR has foretold, *That it muſt be ſo!*————
Wherefore, I will wave it. I will ſay no more
of *That.* I will ſay, only what no body doubts
of *!* And I will the rather ſuperſede the former
Contemplation, becauſe the very ſame Actions
of Religion, which will prepare for what we are
ſure *cannot be far from us,* [Oh! Let us not make
it an *evil* Day, by *putting it far from us!*] will alſo
prepare us for the *Day of GOD,* which many are
not for, *Haſtening* of; tho' they are *Looking* for
it; but chuſe to put it further off. 'Tis This;
That within a little while, a very *little little
while,* we ſhall every one of us, be *ſwallowed up
in the Earth.* Altho' the Cry of the many more
than *Ten Righteous* ones prevent any further
Earthquake; yet the Opened Mouth of the *Earth,*
will ſhortly *ſwallow every one of us up!* It will do
ſo, in the common way of *Mortality:* At our *In-
terment* it will do ſo. Indeed, there will be This
Difference. In that way we die, and go *one after
another,* and not *All together.* And in that way,
we are not *Buried* at once on the ſpot where &
when we expire; but are carried from the *Houſe
where we die,* to the *Houſe appointed for all the Living.* But ſtill, We may *die* as very *ſuddenly,* as if
we were ſuffocated by an *Earthquake:* and we
may *go down into the lower parts of the Earth,* before another Week be over with us. For this,
*Of the Day and the Hour knoweth no Man.* There
is no Man in this very Numerous Collection of
People, does *know,* whether *This may not before*

E　　　　　　　　　　　　　*this*

*this Day Se'nnight be his Portion.*

Wherefore, in taking the Methods of PIETY which are to be taken, for our *Safety*, the *Voice* of our *Earthquake* is, *Do with thy might what thy hand finds to do.* More particularly, An *Earthquake* awakened a poor Man to cry out, *What shall I do to be saved?* Oh ! That upon our *Earthquake*, this Enquiry were more made among us. I am upon answering that Important Enquiry.

First. A *Process of Repentance*, I say, A PROCESS OF REPENTANCE : You must go thro' *That* IMMEDIATELY. You can have no *safety* in an *Earthquake*, till *That* be done. For a Man to have *This to Do*, when the sudden Convulsions of an *Earthquake* are upon him, —— I say unto you, I would not be in the Circumstances of that Man, for *ten thousand Worlds* !

The perils of an *Earthquake* bring us all into that woful plight ; *Thy Life shall hang in doubt before thee, and thou shalt fear Day and Night, and thou shalt have no Assurance of thy Life.* Yea, there is not one Unregenerate among us, but what may say, *I have no Assurance, that I shall not be in Hell before to Morrow Morning.* How can any Man dare to live so ? Now, an Immediate *Process of Repentance* is the only security.

There was an *Earthquake* at the giving of the *Law.* An *Earthquake* should bring us to a Reflection on our breaking of the *Law.* Retire, O sinful Man, Retire ; and first Confessing the *Sovereign Grace* which must shine forth in enabling

of

of thee, if thou art enabled ever to turn unto
GOD, then *Confider thy ways.* Take the *Ten
Commandments,* with the Expofition of the *Cate-
chifm* upon them ; and Refle&ing upon thy Tref-
paffing againft what is *Forbidden* and what is *Required,* in the *Commandments,* loath and judge thy
felf before the Lord, for thy many and heinous
*Trefpaffes.* Go back to thy *Original Sin,* which
has been the fource of all thy *Actual Sins,* and of
*Innumerable* Evils : Thy fhare in the *Guilt* of the
firft Apoftafy : Thy deriving from thence an
Heart that is *Defperately wicked,* and a *Mother of
Abominations.* Full of *Self-abhorrence,* prefent before the glorious GOD, the *Blood* of His own
SON, which *Cleanfes from all Sin* ; Admiring the
Merit and Virtue of that *Blood,* Beg and Hope
on the account thereof to be *cleanfed from all thy
Sin.* Do this, and weep to a *GOD Ready to par-
don* ; until His good SPIRIT has raifed a *Comfor-
table Perfwafion* in thee, *that He has pardon'd thee.*
At the fame, take up a *full purpofe of Heart,* that
thou wilt *cleave* to Him, and *walk* with Him, in
perpetual Endeavours to *keep a Confcience void of
Offence* before Him, to the period of thy Days.
*This is the way,* Oh ! *walk* in it ; and thou fhalt
find *Reft for thy Soul* ; A *Reft* wherein tho' an
*Earthquake* may tofs about the *Earth* under thy
feet, thou fhalt yet fing ; *The Lord is my Defence,
I fhall not be moved !*

Secondly ; A fpeedy Flight unto the only
REDEEMER : This is the ONE THING
NEED-

NEEDFUL. 'Twill procure our *safety* in an
Earthquake. *As they fled from before the Earthquake
in the Days of Uzziah King of Judah,* so let us now
*Flee* unto the LORD whom we fee on *a Throne
high and lifted up* ; the *High-prieſt* upon the *Throne*;
the SAVIOUR who calls upon us, *Come unto me!*
We read much about being *fafe* and *lodg'd* and
*hid* in the *Tabernacle of GOD.* But, O! what? O!
where? —— is the *True Tabernacle?* Truly, our
Bleſſed JESUS is *Tabernacle of GOD* ; Our Bible
calls Him fo. In Him there *perſonally dwells the
Fulneß of the Godhead*; Here the *Shechinah.* My
Friend, Get into a CHRIST, and thou art in all
the *fafety,* in which the *Tabernacle* of GOD can
cover thee: A *Tabernacle* that no Earthquake ever
can reach unto.

    But, How is this to be done? Briefly, A glori-
ous CHRIST has in a *Covenant of Redemption* engaged unto His FATHER for His People ; That
He would furniſh them with a *Sacrifice* and a
*Righteouſneß,* in Relying whereon they ſhould be
*Forgiven* and *Accepted* with Him ; And, That He
would then fill them with the *Love* of GOD and
their Neighbour, and Heal all that is Amiſs in
them, and fit them for and bring them to *all the
ſpiritual Bleſſings in the Heavenly places.* Now confent unto it, O Gofpellized Soul, That thou mayſt
be comprehended in this *Covenant* of thy SAVI-
OUR. beg it of Him ; *O my SAVIOUR, Do for me
all that thou haſt engaged unto thy FATHER to do for
all thy chofen !* This Confent brings thee into the

Cove-

*Covenant of Grace.* Thy SAVIOUR takes thee under the *shadow of His Wings*; And what can any Earthquake do unto thee there? My Neighbours come about me, and Cry, Oh! *What shall I do, if I see the Earth opening under me, and feel my self going down into the Pit?* I cannot for my life think on a better Answer than This; *Get and keep a fast hold of a CHRIST, and you are in eternal safety.* I have just now told you, how to do it. Soul, Thy SAVIOUR calls to thee, *With me thou shalt be in safety.* Oh! Repair to Him, and say, *Lord, I am Thine; save me!* If an *Earthquake* should now sink thee down, thou hast a SAVIOUR that will fetch thee up again.

—— And now, O EARTHQUAKE, *Do thy worst. Thou canst not make me miserable. My SAVIOUR is my Friend, I will not fear; what can an Earthquake do unto me!*

Thirdly; A Life of Serious, Watchful, Prayerful, and Fruitful PIETY; *This* will do. *All its Ways are Ways of Tranquillity, and all its Paths are Safety.* He that *walks with* GOD, what has he to fear, tho' he should have the Earth *trembling* under his Feet? The *Life of GOD*, come into *That*, and thou hast what can't be *kill'd*; No, Not by an Earthquake. Beleever, Get a Soul as full of a CHRIST as ever thou canst; especially, in *Precious Thoughts* of Him. Let thy *Life* be fill'd with *Devotions* towards GOD, and with *Benignities* towards Men. Make the *serving* and *pleasing* of GOD in them, the main *Scope* of thy Actions;

Make

## 34 *Remarks upon the Earthquake.*

Make the *seeing* and *serving* of GOD by them, the main *Sweet* of thy Enjoyments. Be daily *devising of Good*, and have a peerless Delight in doing of it, and, *Be not weary of well-doing.* If an *Earthquake* find thee *so doing,*—— how *Safe*, how *Safe*, art thou ? *What can harm thee*, if thou be such a *Follower of the Good One?*

Alas, When I see the Epidemical Decay of *Real* and *Vital* PIETY, and how *Lukewarm* we are in all that is Good, with how few *Agonies* the affairs of Salvation are carried on, methinks, I see sufficient cause for *Earthquakes*, to throw us into *Agonies. Laodicea* had this charged upon her, *Thou art Lukewarm.* Tis *Our* unhappy and prevailing Temper. But what is become of *Laodicea ?* Tis intirely lost, in amazing *Earthquakes.* No Travellers can find where *Laodicea* stood /—— It is entirely absorb'd and vanished, in horrible *Earthquakes.*

Lastly. What a Contempt is due to an *Earth*, whereof we see all the Possessions lying under such a dismal *Uncertainty !*

We find People *casting away their Idols*, when they see the LORD *arising to shake terribly the Earth.* The *Earthquake* wherein we just now saw the Glorious GOD *arising to shake terribly the Earth*, has in it this *Voice* unto us ; *Don't Idolize this Earth ! Set not your Hearts upon an Earth, which may easily and suddenly prove a Grave unto you, and unto all that you have upon it !* If we could look into the *uncertain Ground* which we stand upon,
and

and build upon, and could fee the deep, the wide, and hideous *Vaults* below, and how liable the thin *Arched Roof* over the hollow Receffes of the *Subterraneous World* may be to fail and break & fink upon the Expanfion of the Vapours there, certainly it were enough to make us almoft fwoon with Fear, and in a fhuddering Horror, and our Hearts even die away within us.    The dreadful *Abyfs*, over which there is bent and laid the fhallow *Bridge*, that fuftains us, and all that the *Men of this World* have to fubfift upon, or find comfort in !  Syrs, we have no *earthly* Poffeffions, but what may be call'd, *Moveables* ;  Our very *Houfes* are fo !  O you that *mind Earthly Things*! What of this *Idolized Earth* is there, that you can be fure of ?  How does all appear, when an *Earthquake* fhews you *truly* what it is ?  How Undone !  How Undone !  How Damned are you, if you are put off with a *Portion* here ?  The Text, of which the *Earthquake* is a Cogent and a Pungent *Sermon*, is that ; Col. III. 2. *Set your Affections on the Things that are Above, not on Things that are on the Earth.*  My  Fellow-Travellers ; Let us live like *Strangers on the Earth*, and even as *Dead* unto it ; and maintain a wife *Indifferency* to all the Enjoyments and Endearments of it. *As Dying, and behold we Live!*

I have done. — But now, *Return and difcern between the Righteous and the Wicked ; between him that ferveth GOD, and him that ferveth Him not.*

And here, firft, fee the forlorn and frighted Afpect

pect of the *Wicked*; How their *Countenance is changed*, and their *Thoughts trouble them*, and their *knees
do smite one against another* ! Their *Flesh* it self evidently quivering, and their *Hearts failing for fear,
and for looking after the Things that are coming on the
Earth* ! —— And NOW, they wish, Oh ! *That I
were in good Terms with Heaven* ! They think; Well,
If they may escape *this once*, how they will *Exercise themselves unto Godliness* ; how Regularly they
will *order their Conversation* ; how conscienciously
they will *work out their own Salvation* ! —— Sayst
thou so, *Friend* ? — But, Oh ! *Let not Pharaoh deal
deceitfully any more* ! We shall see, how they remember the *Vows* of GOD upon them ; how
they behave themselves.

But then, the *Righteous* ! *Mark the perfect Man,
and behold the Upright* ; See the *Peace of GOD* that
fortifies him, even, when he has a prospect of his
*End* just come upon him. There is indeed a *Reve-
rence and godly Fear* with which he regards what
the great GOD is doing in an *Earthquake*. Even
a *Moses* himself is an Example of it. He is neither
a *Stoick*, nor a *Mocker*. But yet — not *Afraid with
any Amazement* ¡ — you may see an Amiable *Se-
renity* in him, when all the World about him is in
an uproar. How free from the *Commotions*, and
Convulsions and Confusions, with which the rest
of the World is agitated. Even an Heathen Poet,
celebrates it among the priviledges and preroga-
tives of a Virtuous Man, *Let an Earthquake break
and sink the World*, [Impavidum ferient Ruinæ]
*he*

*Remarks upon the Earthquake.* 37

*he is not frighted at the Ruins!* But O the Triumphs of the Man that indeed *Lives unto G O D,* and feels a CHRIST, *living in him !* He is affured, *If the Earthquake put a ftop to my Breath, my Soul will be in the Paradife of G O D before the morning.* Like *Paul* & *Silas,* he can *Sing* in the midft of an *Earthquake* ; he can *Sing for the Majefty of the Lord* ; he can fay, *O Death, where is thy fting ! O Earthquake, where is thy Victory !*

Thus do we turn to *fee the Voice !* ·-- We read, Rev. XI. 19. *The Temple of G O D was opened, and there were Voices, and Thundrings, and a great Earthquake.* We are this Day come into the *Temple,* that we may hear the *Voices* of our *Great Earthquake.*

A *Great Earthquake* is called in the Bible, *A Trembling of G O D.* But, O ! If we may *Tremble* more than the *Earth,* and be thofe whom GO D *fhall fee Trembling at His Word* ; This, This would be a *Trembling of G O D* indeed: Such as, Bleffed are they that come into it.

In fome Expectation, that *GOD giving forth His Thundring Voice,* in and by the *melting* of the *Trembling Earth,* His *Voice* will be hearkned unto, and that our *Earthquake* will prove the *moft ufeful Difpenfation* that ever we have feen, in all the Days of our Pilgrimage, We fhall now conclude ; and prefently Sing part of the *Forty fixth Pfalm,* with the *laft Verfe* of the *Fourth Pfalm* annexed unto it.

F

AN

# AN
# *APPENDIX.*

[ Written *Saturday*, Nov. 4. ]

BEFORE Six Days from the Firſt Shock of our EARTHQUAKE are Expired, we are able to Relate, That it has reached, as far as 'tis poſſible for us in this Time to learn, upon all points of the Compaſs. We already know of it's reaching from *North* to *South*, near one hundred & forty Miles. It ſeems, to have been at the *Northward*, rather more formidable than in our parts. The *Roar* of it *longer* and *louder*, and the Noiſe of the *Explosion* ſomewhere or other, after more than an Hours *murmur*, more audible, and more terrible; equal to that of many diſcharged Cannon. It affects Travellers to ſee, not only vaſt Quantities of *Stone-Wall* thrown down by it, but alſo mighty *Rocks* either overſet, or ſunk ſome way into the Earth. 'Tis not known, how many *Houſes*, or *Chimneys* are damnified. But then, That no *more* ! --- That no *Worſe* ! --- That no *Lives* that we yet know of, Sacrificed ! ⸺

Scarce a Night has paſs'd all this Week, without a ſenſible Repetition of the *Shocks*, with the concomitant Rumbles in many Places. But the

[ 2 ]

the fmell of *Sulphur*, which is affirmed by ma-
ny to have been plain unto them, — adds to a
*Fearful Expectation* of a *Fiery Indignation*, -- in
GOD's Time and way to be proceeded in.

Indeed, the Glorious GOD has heretofore
fpoke to *New-England*, by leffer *Earthquakes* ;
and our Predeceffors made fuch an Holy Improvement of them, that they proved *profitable
Difpenfations.*

About, *Jun.* 2. 1638. there was an *Earthquake* that fhook the Houfes, and fhook down
the Things that ftood upon Shelves in them ;
and People that were abroad, could not ftand,
but laid hold upon what was next them, to preferve them from falling down. A fecond *Shock*
fucceeded, but not equal to the former. The
*Sea alfo was troubled* ; and the Veffels there
felt the Shock, with furprize and confternation.

GOD was at the fame time, *fhaking* the
Churches in the Country, with a Shock that
would have torn them to pieces : if *G O D in
the midft* of them, had not prevented their being *moved* : Their GOD and SAVIOUR *helped*
them, in that *Morning* of the Colony.

On *Octob.* 29 1653. there was an *Earthquake* ,
on which the Aged Hand of the famous Mr.
*Peter Bulkly*, the never-to be-forgotten Paftor
and Glory of *Concord*, could not forbear taking
a Pen, and Writing this Epigram. [ Taken
from, His *Life*, in the *Magnalia C H R I S T I
Americana.* B. III. p. 98. ]

F 2                                    *Ecce,*

[ 3 ]

*Ecce, D E I Nutu Tellus Pavefacta tremiscit,*
   *Terra tremens mota est sedibus ipsa suis.*
*Nutant Fulcra Orbis, Mundi compago soluta est ;*
   *Ex Vultu irati Contremit ille D E I.*
*Contremuit Tellus, imis Concussa Cavernis,*
   *Ponderibus quamquam sit gravis illa suis.*
*Evomit ore putres magno cum murmure Ventos,*
   *Quos in visceribus clauserat ante suis.*
*Ipsa tremit Tellus Scelerum gravitate Virorum,*
   *Sub Sceleris nostri pondere Terra tremit.*
*O Nos quam duri! sunt Ferrea pectora nobis !*
   *Non etenim gemimus cum gemit omne solum.*
*Quis Te non metuit, metuit quem Fabrica Mundi,*
   *Quemq; timent Cæli, Terraq; tota timet !*
*Motibus a Tantis nunc tandem Terra quiescat ;*
   *Sed cessent potius Crimina nostra, Precor.*


Another Aged Hand assumes the Honour of so
   Tranflating it :
Lo, Our Great GOD by His Almighty Beck,
Makes the affrighted *Earth* to move & break.
The Pillars of the World all shake ; The Frame
Of Nature fails, when once His Wrath shall flame.
The *Earth* all trembles, and it's Inwards move ;
Their weight can't bear the ponderous Load above.
It belches noifome *Winds*, with hideous Roar,
Which in it's Bowels lay shut up before.
It shakes, press'd with the heavy Guilt of Men ;
The Earth can't bear the Burden of our Sin.
   O! moft Obdurate WE ! O Hearts of Steel ;
That *Sigh* not, when the *Earth's* loud Sighs we feel !
                My

[ 4 ]

My GOD, who will not Fear a GOD whom *All*,
*All* Creatures fear,and ſhock'd before Him fall!
*Lord*, Put an End unto the *Shocks* betimes :
But, Oh! *Firſt* put an End unto our *Crimes.*

In the Year, 1658. *New-England* felt another
conſiderable *Earthquake.* Nothing memorable
is left upon Record concerning it. It had Con-
comitants that were *too Memorable.*

In the Month of *January*, between 1662 and
1663, there was an *Earthquake*, whereof we
find this Account given by that worthy Man,
Mr. *Samuel Danforth* of *Roxbury* ;

‘ *Jan.*26. & 28. The Foundations of the Earth
‘ trembled, and ſome our Houſes rocqu'd like a
‘ Cradle. Six or ſeven times did the *Earth ſhake*
‘ under us, in the ſpace of Two or Three Days.
‘ It was then tho't & ſaid, That theſe *Earth-*
‘ *quakes* might portend the ſhaking the Founda-
‘ tions of our Churches, and of our Civil State.

In the Year 1705. there was a ſmall *Earth-*
*quake* felt by the *Maſſachuſet*-Province on *Jun.*
16. And in *Connecticut*-Colony, *Jun.* 22. On
which occaſion Dr. *Increaſe Mather*, preached
and printed, *A Diſcourſe concerning Earthquakes.*
In that Sermon, there are theſe among other
Paſſages :

‘ The Lord ſeldom Viſits any Town or Coun-
‘ try with deſolating Judgments, but He firſt
‘ gives them Warning of it, by one means or
‘ another ; and many times by *Earthquakes.*

‘ A

325
## [ 5 ]

' A Roman Hiftorian obferves, that the City of
' *Rome* never felt any *Earthquake*, but fome ter-
' rible Judgment foon followed.  In the Scrip-
' ture, it is faid, *There fhall be Earthquakes in*
' *diverfe Places*;  The Next Words are ;  *And*
' *F A M I N E S & P E S T I L E N C E S. Earth-*
' *quakes* are fometimes *prodromous* of thofe other
' Judgments. ———— But, ---We have at this
' Day Reafon to expect that a Notable COMING
' of the LORD is near at hand   Yea, we may
' fay, *The Great-D A Y of T H E  L O R D, is*
' *Near, it is Near, and it Hafteth greatly.*

There have been more than One or Two leffer *Earthquakes*, befides thefe, at feveral Times
in the Country.  But never any that on all Accounts has equalled T H A T which is now
Alarming of us.

We will at prefent conclude, with a few
Lines extracted from a little Treatife entituled,
*Geologia Norvegica* : written  by a Danifh Minifter, whofe Name was *Michael Peterfon Ef-*
*cholt*, on the Occafion of ( what he calls ) *That*
*very great & fpacious Earthquake, almoft quite*
*thro' the South Parts* of *Norway, Apr.* 24. 1657.

He fays, ' It carryed fuch a Noife & Sound
' with it, that the People at firft knew not but
' it was the Noife of Thunder, until they per-
' ceived the Houfes fhook, and all their Move-
' ables totter. —— Yet it hath not done any Re-
' markable Harm ;  for which we ought to be
' very Thankful unto GOD.—— Neverthelefs,
' in

[ 6 ]

‘ in regard  that this *Earthquake* was of fuch a
‘ Length  and  Breadth,  namely  an  hundred
‘ and fixty  Miles,  we need  not doubt but that
‘ it may fignify fome Remarkable Change and
‘ Alteration.    The ancient Hiftoriographer *He-*
‘ *rodotus*, has recorded it ;  That when any Re-
‘ markable Change or Calamity approaches, it
‘ is  commonly  fignified  by  fuch  preceding
‘ Tokens ! ——

—— ‘ When GOD  Almighty,  now in thefe
‘ laft Times of the World, fhall permit fuch
‘ *Great & Spacious Earthquakes*, for fo many
‘ many Miles in length to happen, Men ought
‘ not carelefly to flight them, and think no more
‘ of them : No, But regard & receive them,  as
‘ partly fignifying  fome unufual Accident Im-
‘ pending  or Approaching ;  and partly  as in-
‘ fallible *Forerunners* of the D A Y,  which the
‘ *earneft Expeftation of the Creature waiteth for*,
‘ *yea, Groaneth and even Travaileth in Pain.*’

# F I N I S.

# Dr. *Mather*'s

# E S S A Y,

## On the *Good Impreſſions*

### produced by the

# 𝕰𝖆𝖗𝖙𝖍𝖖𝖚𝖆𝖐𝖊𝖘.

Boanerges.

# A Short ESSAY
to preferve and ftrengthen the
# Good IMPRESSIONS
Produced by
# 𝕰𝖆𝖗𝖙𝖍𝖖𝖚𝖆𝖐𝖊𝖘
On the Minds of People that have been
## AWAKENED with them.

With fome Views of what is to be *Further* and
*Quickly* look'd for.

Addrefs'd unto the *Whole People* of NEW-
ENGLAND, who have been *Terrified*
with the Late EARTHQUAKES ;

And more Efpecially the *Towns* that have had
a more fingular Share in the *Terrors* of them.

1 Chron. XXIX. 18.
*O Lord GOD, Keep this for ever in the Imagination of the
Thoughts of the Heart of thy People, and confirm their Heart
unto thee.*

*BOSTON*:
Printed for *S. Kneeland*, and Sold at his
Shop in *King-Street*. 1727.

( 3 )

# Good Impreſſions cultiva-
ted.

---

### Pſal. LXXVIII. 34, 36, 37.

*When He ſlew them, then they ſought Him,
and they returned and enquired early after
GOD.*

*Nevertheleſs, they did flatter Him with their
Mouth, and they lied unto Him with their
Tongues.*

*For their Heart was not Right with Him, nei-
ther were they ſtedfaſt in His Covenant.*

AND this was the Wretched Iſſue of all
the GOOD IMPRESSIONS which
the Terrors of GOD had made upon
them. 'Tis the ſtory of what has been
done millions of times; of what is daily done by
millions of Men! O! may we, on whom *the End
of the World is come,* and who have had *theſe things
written for our Admonition,* take warning from it!

The Pſalm which relates the matter, contains
a compendious *Church-Hiſtory,* of Divine *Favours*
conferred, and of Divine *Judgments* inflicted, on
the

4      *Good Impreſſions cultivated.*

the Nation of *Iſrael*, from their Bondage in *Egypt*
even to the Reign of *David*. The Rebellions of
that People, againſt the glorious JEHOVAH,
who made them His People, and His wondrous
Patience, and Mercy, and Juſtice, towards them,
under theſe Rebellions, are the main ſubjeƈt of
this Hiſtory.

In the particular Article we have now before
us;

Behold, firſt, a poor People under *Good Impreſſions* in a time of *Danger*; and from an Apprehenſion of the Glorious GOD coming to *ſlay* them.
He *ſlew* ſome of them; Yea, an Horrendous
EARTHQUAKE, was the way wherein He *ſlew*
a Number of them. The Survivers were a while
under *Good Impreſſions* from ſuch occurrences.
When they were afraid, that GOD was going to
*ſlay* them, yea, to *Damn* them, for their Sins, *Then*
they Bethought themſelves; *Then* they thought
they would become the *Diligent Seekers* of GOD;
*Then* they thought they would no more Deſpiſe
their SAVIOUR. But then,

Behold, next, what becomes of all theſe *Good
Impreſſions*, when the *Danger* ſeems to be a little
over with them. They are not *Effeƈtual* ones;
They are not *Abiding* ones; They all go off, with
miſerable Demonſtrations, that their *Hearts* were
the ſame they were before. They are not *Sincere*,
and ſo they are not *ſtedfaſt* in the Declarations
they made, when the *Good Impreſſions* were upon
them. It becomes apparent, that all their ſhort-
lived *Piety* was but *Flattery*. The *Good Impreſſions*,
what are they *but a Vapour, which appeareth for a little while, and ſoon vaniſhes away?* They ſoon *Eva-
porate*

*porate.* The Sinners in a very *little while* are juſt
ſuch Murmurers and Infidels, as they were before.

My Friends; There is a melancholly obſervation that I have made; *A grievous Viſion is declared
unto me!* What I have obſerved, muſt be the
DOCTRINE which I am now to infiſt upon;
But which, Oh! Allow me to ſay, *I beſeech you,
Brethren,* to do all you can for the practical Confutation of. 'Tis This;

*The ſentiments of PIETY, and the GOOD IM-
PRESSIONS, which People have in the Time
of DANGER,* [Say, The Time of EARTH-
QUAKE] *are too eaſily, too uſually Forgotten,
when they think the DANGER is over with
them.*

There was a Notorious Exemple of this DOC-
'TRINE, in the Infamous *Pharaoh,* whom a Sovereign GOD *raiſed up, that He might ſhow forth His
power* upon Him. GOD was Revenging on the
*Egyptians,* the Injuries that had been done by them
unto His *Iſraelites.* No leſs than Ten Remarkable *Plagues* did the wrath of the Almighty ſend
upon them: and probably all of them within the
ſpace of *one Month. A Month devoured them!* So
memorable were theſe *Plagues,* upon the *Egyptians,*
that the *Philiſtines* Four Hundred years after ſpoke
of them, with ſome Conſternation; Yea, ſo memorable, that we find in Pagan Antiquity, the
*Egyptians* did for many Hundreds of years with
Mourning, and Howling, and lighted Candles,
keep up an *Anniverſary Commemoration* of them.
They were ſuch terrifying *Plagues,* that tho' *Setho-
ſis,* the Succeſſor of the King who was now upon
the

6          *Good Impreſſions cultivated.*

the Throne, did celebrated Exploits in the Eaſt, in the firſt Nine years of the *Iſraelites* being in the Wilderneſs, yet he durſt not meddle with a little Handful of *Iſraelites,* in whoſe cauſe the GOD of Heaven had ſo appeared.   One of thoſe plagues, was accompanied, with terrible *Thunders,* that filled the Land with *Flaming Fire,* and ſcattered *Hot Thunderbolts* upon it.   *Pharaoh* too, the King, whom the old Chronologies diſtinguiſh by the Name of *Amoſis,* was *Thunderſtruck,* into ſome *Sentiments* of PIETY, and ſhow'd ſome *Good Impreſſions* upon them.   *Pharaoh* changes his Note : *Moſes,* The Man of GOD, whom *Pharaoh* hated above all the Men in the World, even *him* does *Pharaoh* under his *Good Impreſſions* apply unto, and ask his *Prayers* for him.   The Servant of GOD, foreſaw and foretold what the *Good Impreſſions* would come to.   Said he, Exod. IX. 29, 30. *The Thunder ſhall ceaſe.*—— *But I know that you will not yet fear the LORD GOD.*   Methinks, I ſee *Pharaoh* Trembling while he hears the Almighty *Thundring,* and ſees the Corruſcations in the Heavens, with which the Lord GOD Omnipotent, can ſtrike the moſt haughty Monarch *Dead in a Moment* ; [And before now, *He has done ſo*] He *Trembles* ;—— And who would not ?  He cries out, *I am ſorry that I have abuſed the People of GOD! I am ſorry that I have deſpiſed the Servants of GOD! I am ſorry that I have detained any thing that GOD has called me to part withal. I will do any thing that the Great GOD would have me to do:*  Well ; The *Thunders* go over :  *Pharaoh* outlives the *Thunders.* And now, How is it ?  Alas, He is *Pharaoh* ſtill !

Thus

Thus it is, even among *Iſraelites* as well as *Egyptians.* People who apprehend themſelves in *Dangers* of a deadly Aſpect upon them, do commonly Think and Speak many *Good Things.* But they do almoſt as commonly *Forget* thoſe *Good Things,* when their Apprehenſions are over. The Thoughts and the Frames, which are frequent with People, when they are *frighted* by *Earthquakes* and by other Dangers, are ſoon *Forgotten!* Soon *Forgotten!* The *Frights* are no ſooner over, but People *Forget* the Thoughts, and the Frames, and the *Vows,* to which the Terrors of GOD awakened them. The Hebrew Name for, MAN, ſignifies, *Forgetful Man.* I mind this Elegance and Emphaſis, in the words of the Pſalmiſt, Pſal. VIII. 4. *What is Forgetful Man, that thou Remembreſt him!* O *Forgetful Man,* Thou ſheweſt what thou art, by nothing more than thy ſoon *Forgetting* of the *Good Impreſſions,* which *Dangers* make upon thee.

9. We will begin with a more *General Aſſertion.* DANGERS of all ſorts, eſpecially all deadly *Dangers,* often are moſt *Hypocritically* plaid withal. O the *Hypocriſy* in the *Heart* of Man, which is *Deceitful above all things, and deſperately wicked!* All ſorts of *Dangers,* do frequently drive People into ſome *Sentiments* and *Purpoſes* of PIETY: But when the *Dangers* are over, the *Sentiments* are worn away, the *Purpoſes* are laid aſide ; the PIETY is no further proſecuted ; and the *Religion* which was but a *flaſh,* is all forgotten.

Firſt. We ſee, *Dangers* make People *Devout* and Serious. People uſe to be devoutly diſpoſed, when deadly *Dangers* are impending over them. *Affliction*

B                    and

and *Affrightment* is how often, the *Mother of Devotion*! I wish, it may not be said, a *Spurious Devotion*. Imminent and sensible *Dangers* of Death, make Men grow *Thoughtful*; and it will be strange, if the Advance of the *Leviathan* do not cause them to *purify themselves*. They whom a sense of *Death* approaching does not compel to some *Sober Thoughts*, what are they ? Harden'd and Frantic —— one can't say, *What*! —— Not *Rational Men*! They do not act as Creatures exercising *Reason*, who cast off all Thoughts of *Religion*, when they have *Death* staring on them, scaring of them. It was once expostulated with a Malefactor in the Jaws of *Death*: Luk. XXIII. 40. *Dost not thou Fear GOD, seeing thou art under Condemnation ?* But that was a Monster of a Man. Shall it be said of a Man, *He does not Fear GOD, when he is in a Danger that looks like a sentence of Death upon him ?* Verily, 'Twill be a very monstrous Character.

We will Enquire, first, after the *Ground*, then, after the *Proof*, of this unhappy matter.

First ; The *Ground* of it, is, A *Conscience* excited by *Dangers* unto its Operations. In deadly *Dangers*, the *Conscience* comes to operate. By *Dangers*, the Minds of Men are chased from those things which drown'd the Murmurs of their *Conscience*. Yea, in *Dangers*, People are compelled not only to hear the *Murmurs* of *Conscience*, but also the *Whispers* are turned into *Thunders*. There is a *Preacher* in the Bosom of every Man ; and upon *Dangers*, this *Preacher* becomes a *Thunderer*.

There are Three Things, which the *Thundering Voice* of CONSCIENCE will speak to People, when *deadly Dangers* are upon them.

One

## Good Impreßions cultivated. 9

One Admonition of *Conscience*, is This; O Man, There is the *Providence* of GOD in the *Dangers* that have now overtaken thee. *Dangers* don't come, nor so much as a *little Bird* fall into them, without the *Providence* of GOD. There is the Hand of GOD, in all the *Dangers* that are brought upon thee. GOD has taken thee into his Hand, when he thus brings *Dangers* upon thee. *Conscience* now subscribes to That; Amos III. 6. *Shall there be Evil in a City, and the Lord hath not done it!* O Thou exposed one, GOD is the *Doer*, in all the *Evil* that is hanging over thee.

A Second Admonition of *Conscience*, is This: 'Tis a GOD *offended* by thy *Sin*, who sends thy *Dangers* upon thee. Thou art a *Sinner*. Thy *Sin* has been an *Offence* unto GOD; Thy *Sin* makes thee obnoxious unto the *Anger* of GOD; lays thee open unto the *Vengeance* of GOD. It is a Thing of the greateſt Importance, that the *Displeaſure* of GOD. ſhould not remain burning againſt thee; A diſpleaſed GOD is an Adverſary, which — *how can thy Hands be ſtrong, or how can thy Heart endure,* to encounter with Him *!* *Conscience* now subſcribes to That; Prov. XIII. 21. *Evil purſueth Sinners.*

A Third Admonition of *Conscience*, is This: REPENTANCE, REPENTANCE *! That* is the moſt likely way to eſcape thy *Dangers.* O *wicked* one, *Forſake thy ways*; O *unjuſt* one, *Forſake thy Thoughts*; *Return to the Lord, and He will have mercy!* If thou *Repenteſt not*, thou mayſt Fear, that the *Arrows prepared* on the *bent Bowe* of GOD, will be let fly upon thee. The Language of *Conſcience* now is That; Jon. III. 8, 9. *Turn every one from his evil way,* ——— *who can tell, but GOD*

*may*

10     *Good Impreſſions cultivated.*

*may turn away from His fierce Anger, that we periſh
not.*

When the *Conſcience* begins to *Thunder* at this
rate, and make a Noiſe like the hideous Rumblings
of an *Earthquake*, it muſt needs throw the Threatened People into ſome *Religious* Diſpoſitions.

As a *Supplement* unto this Meditation, let this
be added. The Glorious GOD throws Men into
*Dangers* on this very *Deſign*; To make them hearken unto what He ſpeaks by the Mouth of His
Deputy, their *Conſcience*, to them. Truly, Syrs,
this is the very *Errand* that your *Dangers* are ſent
upon. The *Conſcience* in Man, may complain, as
in Jer. XXII. 21. *I ſpake unto thee in thy proſperity;
But thou ſaidſt, I will not hear.* Men are Deaf to
*Conſcience*; It Groans, it Cries, it Thunders, and
they do not regard it. GOD now does caſt Men
into *Dangers* on this Intent; *Man, Hear now, what
thy Conſcience has to ſay unto thee: It has a Meſſage
from GOD to thee!* From this it is, that Men ſo
ſeem to be *Religious*, when *Dangers* are upon them.

Secondly; The *Proof* of it; For this we will
repair unto *Experience*. And, *Hear this, O all ye
People, every one of you:* May we not ſay, 'Tis *your
own Experience.* The *Scripture* tells us, of ſome;
Iſa. XXVI. 16. *Lord, In Trouble have they viſited
thee; they poured out a Prayer, when thy Chaſtening
was upon them.* Yea, but our *Experience* will every
day tell us, Lord, How many are they, who when
they are *afraid of Trouble*, do ſay, *They will viſit
GOD every day as long as they live!* How many
are they who *pour out a Prayer*, when *Danger* is upon them! O that the Sermon of this Day, might
be a *Sermon to bring unto Remembrance!* How many,

ny, O our dear People, How many of you, may *Remember* the *Dangers,* wherein you were at that paſs; Jer. II. 20. *Thou ſaidſt, I will not Tranſgreſſ!* *Remember* you not, what you ſaid, when you lay *Sick,* and like to *Die* of your Sickneſs, and pale *Death* look'd you in the Face, and you look'd on yourſelves as *deprived of the Reſidue of your years,* and Summoned before the Tribunal of GOD? *Then* you ſaid, *Oh! If GOD will ſpare my life, I will do nothing but ſerve the GOD of my life : I will hate and loathe and ſhun all the Sin that once I loved ; and lead a life of all Godlineſſ and Honeſty!* *Remember* you not, what you ſaid, when a *Storm* at Sea had almoſt ſwallowed you up, and you were caſt into Horror, by the *Horrible Tempeſt* ; Your *Soul* was *melted becauſe of Trouble;* You ſaw yourſelves going down into the *deep Waters* ; You fear'd you were going down into the *Eternal Burnings?* *Then* you ſaid ; *Oh! If GOD will pleaſe, that I may out-live this Death, I will never Sin againſt Him any more as heretofore! I will do nothing that may render my Death uneaſy and unwelcome to me!*

The *Memorandums* are not over yet. My Friend, *Remember* you not, what you ſaid, when you were in the *Land* and the *Hand* of your *Enemies* ; you *ſat in Darkneſſ,* and in the *ſhadow of Death* ; and you had little Hope of ever being again in the Arms of thoſe, who were now *put far from* you? *Then* you Cried unto the Lord ; and you ſaid ; *Oh! If the Lord will Reſtore me to my Liberty, with what an Enlarged Heart ſhall I run the way of His Commandments.*

And will the Daughters of *Eve* give me leave to be a *Remembrancer* unto Them? When the
Time

Time of your *Travail* and your *Trouble*, and the *perils of Child bearing* drew near, and you conceived yourſelves entring the *Valley of the ſhadow of Death*, You *Then* ſaid, *Behold, The Handmaid of the Lord*! *If the Lord carry me to and thro' my Time, I will forever behave my ſelf as becomes an Handmaid of the Lord.*

In fine, Do you Remember nothing of what you thought when you felt the Earth trembling and rumbling in a tremendous *Earthquake* under you? Did not your *Hearts* then *ſmite* you for your keeping at a diſtance from your SAVIOUR ; and for the various Miſcarriages of an ungodly and unrighteous Life? And was it not the purpoſe of your Hearts, *I will not offend any more* ?

If you don't *Remember* what you ſaid, GOD *Remembers* it ; it is all down in the *Book of His Remembrance.* Perhaps, New *Dangers* and Sorrows are coming upon you, to bring it unto your own *Remembrance* ; *In the latter Days ye ſhall conſider it* !

I muſt now paſs on to a Second Remark. But, one that *is a Lamentation, and ſhall be for a Lamentation.*

Secondly; Men uſe quickly to *Forget* how *Devout* they were, when their *Dangers* were upon them. T'was all but a *Religious Pang.* Ah, Deceitful *Pang* ! like the *Morning Cloud*, and the *Early Dew* ; *It paſſes away.* We read of ſome, Pſal. CVI. 13. *They ſoon forgot His Works.* Even ſo, Men ſoon *Forget* what *workings* they had in their own Hearts, when they ſaw the *Hand of GOD lifted up to ſmite them.*

Of

OF this thing, we are every where entertained with a mournful Evidence. The *Bad lives* of Men, make it moſt notorioufly Evident. The moſt of Men lead *Bad lives:* They do not *Live unto GOD.* With what pungency may they feel it faid unto them ; *Can you ſay,* That you lead ſuch a *Life* as you *faid,* you ſhould and would, when *Deſtruction from GOD* was a *Terror* to you? When our SAVIOUR was in the *Temple,* the Hearers that were *Convicted in their own Conſcience* by what He faid, *Went out,* and, *Lo, He was left alone.* Oh, How far, *how far!* —— would it go towards breaking up the Congregation, if all ſhould *go out,* who may be *convicted in their own Conſcience,* that they do not live, as under the *Terrors* of GOD, they faid, They would. A great Man once putting that Cafe to a good Man, *How ſhall I order my life, that I may glorify GOD?* He only gave him this Anfwer; *Live as when you lately apprehended your ſelf a dying, you thought you would live, if GOD would let you live.* There are many who do not *glorify GOD.* And we may conclude, They don't *live,* as in their *Dangers,* they faid, *They would.* Where one is *Reformed,* a Thoufand are *as they were!*

But, *whence does this come to paſs?* 'Tis, From the *Spirit of the Old Covenant* in Mens Inclinations and Refolutions. When the People of old were appall'd at the *Lightnings* and *Thunders* and *Earthquakes* of the Burning Mountain, they faid, *All that the Lord ſhall ſpeak we will do.* But it was with the *Spirit of the Old Covenant* that they faid it. GOD therefore faid upon it ; Deut. V. 28. 29. *I have heard the Voice of the Words of this People, which*
*they*

*they have ſpoken ; They have well ſaid, all that they have ſpoken: Oh! That there were ſuch an Heart in them!* ――― Even ſo, People remaining yet in the old *Covenant of Works,* will ſay, *This* and *That,* and *they will ſay very well in all that they ſpeak.* Oh! But there is no more than a *Voice of Words,* in all that they have *ſpoken:* There wants a *New Heart* in them ; There is no *Heart* in them to *do* what they *ſay.* Frighted People *ſay,* that they are *Fallen out with Sin.* But it is only from ſome *External Compulſion* upon them. The SPIRIT of GOD has not yet *Internally Changed* the *Biaß* of their Minds: The *Love* of *Sin* yet reigning in their Hearts is not extinguiſhed. They *ſay,* They will ſet themſelves to do the *Things that pleaſe GOD.* But they ſet themſelves about it in *their own ſtrength.* And thus, *All* preſently comes to *Nothing!*

No *Dangers* are enough to Convert a Sinner. I have ſeen Men brought from the *Gallows,* who yet have not been brought from the *Wicked Courſes* which had brought them to the *Gallows.* In going to their expected Execution, they have declared unto me, *That they had rather Dy that Afternoon, than return to the ways of wickedneß which they formerly lived in.* They have had a *Reprieve,* and a *Pardon.* But how after *That!* Alas, I have ſeen the *Dogs return to their vomit* ; and go on ſtill in their old *ways of wickedneß.* Ah, ſinful Men! If One *went unto them from the Dead,* yet they *will not Repent.* The Devils and the Damned, with the hideous Chains and Flames of the *Horrible Pit,* appearing to them, would not cauſe them to *Repent.* Should *Hell* be ſet open before their Eyes, and ſhould they be held over the *Smoke of the Tor-*

*ment*

## *Good Impreſſions cultivated.* x5

ment *which Aſcends forever and ever*, t'wil do no-thing to take out the *Helliſh Tang* of *Sin* which is in their Souls. Till *that* be taken out by the *Spirit of Grace*, there will be no *Frighting* Men out of their *Sin*. He that is *Filthy* will be *Filthy ſtill*. When the *Dangers* are over, you'l find it ſo!

We read of mighty *Legions*, who after they have been Damned for ſeven Thouſand years, and have been actually, in the direful Torments of the Damned for one thouſand of them, yet being let looſe again, they play the *Devil* again juſt as they did a Thouſand years before ; and again attempt with a Satanic Aſſault of *Temptations* to diſturb the *Camp of the Saints,* and with Diabolical Deluſions and Stratagems, draw in thoſe in the *Hidden places of the Earth,* who *go up* from under the *Breadth of the Earth,* to join with them in their War againſt the *Holy ones. Hell* it ſelf won't fetch out the *ſinful Tendencies,* in the Souls of the wicked. Not only *if One went from the Dead* unto the wicked that are not yet *gone to the Dead,* they will yet re-fuſe to *Repent,* but alſo if they that are there were permitted themſelves to *go from the Dead,* yet even Theſe would *not Repent* : Except with *New Lives* they ſhould alſo have *New Hearts* given them from Above. They that *go down to Hell,* with the *Luſts* in them which were the *Weapons of their War,* and have their *Iniquities* in their very *Bones,* if they that have been *ſhut up in the Priſon,* ſhould *after many Days be Viſited,* and Releaſed ; they would again be as wicked as they were before.

Be ſure, *Earthquakes* alone, will not cure the *Love of Sin* in Men, and cauſe them to Turn and Live unto GOD. If People ſhould feel what may

C            force

force them to *flee for their Lives,* with the utmoft confufion, from an all-devouring *Earthquake,* —— *As they fled from before the Earthquake, in the Days of Uzziah King of Judah,* —— This will not caufe them to *flee from their Sins.* If People fhould fee what is not now a *New Thing,* the *Earth open its Mouth, and fwallow up* their Neighbours by Hundreds at a Morfel, and a multitude *going down a-live into the Pit,* and the *Earth clofing upon them,* yet in flying from the *Tents* of wicked Men at their lamentable Cry, *Left the Earth fwallow up them alfo,* —— it would be no *New Thing,* if they do not fly from the *Ways* of Wicked Men. Are there not Nefandous Inftances of People continuing in the *Actual Commiffion* of Diforderly Things, even in the very Time of an *Earthquake?* Yea, People making themfelves *Drunk,* and Reeling to and fro with *ftrong Drink,* while the *Earth* has juft been *Reeling to and fro like a Drunkard* under them, and roaring againft them? And *Robberies* committed, even while the *Earthquake* has afforded an *Opportunity* for the Theeves to exert their curfed Faculty? Hardened Sinners! There is no Reclaiming of them!

It is a Remark very near akin to This. How do amazing *Thunders* ufually operate? People are *Afraid* even *with much amazement* under the *Thunderclaps;* Afraid of Irrefiftible and Far-terebrating *Thunderbolts.* When the *Lightning is directed unto the Ends of the Earth, and after it a Voice roreth; and God Thunders with the Voice of His Excellency; God Thunders marvelloufly with His Voice;* Lo, At this our *Hearts* tremble, and are even *removed out of their place.* But how quickly, how fadly, do the *Thun-*

*ders*

*ders* loſe their Efficacy! The *Thunders do ceaſe,* and yet Men do not *Fear the Lord God,* as when it *Thundred,* they ſay, *They would.*

O the *Inconſtancy* of our *Carnal minds!* *Conſtant* only in their *Enmity* to GOD! People ſeem to be very Good while they have the loud peals of the *Thunders* diſcharging over them; and they fear leſt the Next Flaſh of the *Lightenings* render them a *Pillar of Salt.* But they are not the ſame after the *Thunders* are over, that they were in the Time of the *Thunders.* —— How often have I thought! —— O! If my dear Neighbours were diſpoſed *after* the *Thunders* as they are *under* them! — How *Happy* would they be! How *Holy* would they be! What a Religious Neighbourhood; and how full of PIETY!

From this Remark on *Thunders,* I return to *Earthquakes,* which are of the ſame Family with them: And, my Remark upon them is, That it is very plain, the *Earthquakes* which have lately ſhook the *Earth* under us for many Hundreds of Miles, and which in many places have been continued for diverſe Weeks together, have produced very *Good Impreſſions* on many Thouſands of Minds. If there be a few *Stocks* and *Stones* and Prodigies of *Impiety,* which have had no *Good Impreſſions* made upon them from the *mighty Voice* of GOD *ſent forth* in theſe *Earthquakes,* verily, they are not only moſt unaccountably *Sottiſh* Wretches, but even worſe than *Bruitiſh* ones: I ſay, worſe than *Bruitiſh* ones; For it might have affected even thoſe profane *Indolents* themſelves, to have ſeen the *Horrors* which theſe *Earthquakes* raiſed in the *Brutal World,* at the Moments of the Tremors: How the greater and

the

the ſmaller *Cattel,* and the very *Dogs* themſelves, expreſs'd themſelves moved, and horribly terrified, when they felt the *Earth* moving under them. They that now had no Awe upon them, and no Senſe of a Glorious GOD and their Duty to Him, and felt no *Good Impreſſions* on their Minds, what ſhall be thought of them ! —— I ſuppoſe, there were very few ſuch *Monſters* to be ſeen, in our Land. No ; There have been *Good Impreſſions* made upon the Minds of People every where in Town and Countrey. The like was never ſeen in our Land! The many that fly into the *Covenant* of GOD, as unto the *Horns of the Altar,* that they may be ſheltered from the Miſchiefs of *Earthquakes* there, moſt certainly run thither with *Good Impreſſions* on their Minds. Yea, there are multitudes with whom it is a Time of ſuch *Good Impreſſions* as they never felt in their Lives before. But now, O ! The Extreme *Hazard* which there may be, left theſe *Good Impreſſions* do *quickly* dy away, *quickly* wear off, *quickly* come to nothing : Extreme *Hazard,* left People anon be juſt what they were before, and *will not yet Fear the Lord GOD,* whoſe Voice has thus loudly called upon us. For my part, my Heart more *trembles* at this, than at an *Earthquake.* ——

¶ Wherefore from *Aſſerting,* we will proceed now to *Exhorting.* And, Oh ! *Suffer the Word of* EXHORTATION, which is now in a *Few Words* to call upon you.

We are very ſollicitous, that when our *Earthquakes* are over, the *Good Impreſſions* which they have cauſed may not be *over* too. But what was

it

it I ſaid? —— when our *Earthquakes* are *over!*
Who can ſay when *That* will be! I will mention
a Thing which is not generally known among us.
The Celebrated *Earthquake*, which terrified *New-
England* in the latter end of *January*, between the
years 1662. and 1663. not only reached unto
*Canada* to the Northward of us, and, as the French
Hiſtorian ſays, *Occaſion'd incredible Deſolations on
the ſurface of the Earth for above four hundred Leagues
throughout that Countrey:* But alſo continued Five
or Six Months together. Who can ſay, what
may be our Portion? I am ſure, there can be
nothing more ſeaſonable, than the *Exhortation* I
am coming to.

We read concerning Two Miniſters, upon
whom our Lord put the Name of BOANERGES.
The Name will ſignify, *Sons of Earthquake,* as well
as what we commonly take it, *Of Thunder.* Our
Lord in impoſing that Name on theſe two Miniſters, might have Reſpect unto that Prophecy,
*I will ſhake all Nations, and the deſire of all Nations
ſhall come.* Theſe Miniſters might have a Notable
Delivery, as *Nazianzen* intimates, by the Advantage whereof what they delivered might come like
*Thunder* on the Hearers. But this is not all; There
were to be mighty *Commotions* even like thoſe of
an *Earthquake,* in ſubſerviency to the Intereſts of
the Goſpel; and our Lord would make a ſingular
uſe of theſe Miniſters in thoſe *Commotions*; who
were to carry the Goſpel with a Force like that
of *Thunder* alſo, thro' the Jewiſh Nation.

Oh! That one of the *Boanerges* were here to have
the management of this EXHORTATION; and
that he who is a *Son of Earthquake,* in Eſſays to
ſerve

20 *Good Impreſſions cultivated.*

ſerve the Intentions of the preſent *Commotions,* might be a *Son of Thunder,* in bringing with it the *Right Words* that ſhall be *Forcible!*

The EXHORTATION that now *ſpeaks* unto you, and muſt not be *Forgotten,* is This. Let thoſe that have had *Good Impreſſions* on their Minds from the *Earthquakes* which have newly *ſhaken* us, Beware leſt they loſe the *Good Impreſſions*; Exceedingly Beware, Infinitely Beware, leſt when they imagine the *Earthquakes* are *ceaſed,* it appear that that their *Heart was not Right* in, and not *Reach'd* by, the *Good Impreſſions,* nor were they *ſtedfaſt*; But they Forget what they Thought and Said and Vow'd, when the *Earthquakes* were upon them.

At the Time of the Battel between thoſe two Grand Robbers, which were diſputing the Empire of the World, there was a *Great Earthquake*: But the *Buſineſs* of the Battel ſo engaged the combatants, that they took not the leaſt Notice of it. Few People have been ſo *Buſy,* or ſo Drowſy, or ſo Stupid, as to take no Notice of the Repeted *Shocks* and *Roars,* wherein GOD has from a *Trembling* Earth ſent forth His Thundring *mighty Voice* unto us. I wiſh, we may not be ſo *Buſy* about our Worldly Affairs and Pleaſures, as to take too little Notice of what that *Thundring Voice* has declared unto us. But we read of ſuch a Thing as That, Hoſ. VII. 16. *They are like a Deceitful Bowe.* The Thing whereof there is a moſt grievous Hazard, is, That the Wicked *Bent* of many Minds for the ways of Sin, having by the *Earthquakes* had ſome *ſtrain* upon it, upon the *ceaſing* of the *Earthquakes,* the *Deceitful Bowe* will return where it was; the *ſtrain* being taken off, they will return to their old

*Good Impreſſions cultivated.* 21

old *Bent*, and they will *go on ſtill in their Treſpaſſes.*

O our dear People, and all you that have had the *Right Thoughts of the Righteous* by the *Earthquakes* at all awakened in you, Our *Hearts Deſire and Prayer to* GOD for you, is, That the *Good Impreſſions* upon you may not end, in any thing ſhort of a Thorough TURN to GOD and CHRIST and PIETY: And that ſuch a *View of Things* as you had in the Minutes of the *Earthquakes*, may in an *Effectual Work* of Grace, abide with you ; and the Fruit thereof be, that you will *Fear* GOD *all the Days that you live upon Earth ; and paſs the Time of your ſojourning here in the Fear*, not of *Earthquakes*, but of the glorious GOD, who has *the deep places of the Earth* in His Almighty *Hand.*

In order to THIS, let theſe *Admonitions of the Lord* find a due Entertainment with you.

I. A NEW HEART, a NEW HEART, is the *Firſt Thing* to be made ſure of. Be ſure, that you do not reſt in a *Superficial, Defective, Deluſive Work*, or ſtop ſhort in any thing leſs than a *Thorough* CONVERSION, from the *Error of your way*, with a *Work* of *Real* and *Vital* PIETY upon you. A lamentable thing, is that *work of the Wicked*, which is a *Deceitful Work.* If the *Heart* be not *Right*, O *Iſraelite*, thou wilt not be *ſtedfaſt*, in adhering to thy *Good Impreſſions.* A *Thorough* CHANGE of STATE, and therefore and therewith a *Thorough* CHANGE of HEART, is requiſite, that ſo the *Good Impreſſions* made upon you, may *continue* with you ; *In theſe is continuance, and ſo you ſhall be ſaved!* Without a *principle* of PIETY, reſtoring to the Glorious GOD His *Throne* in your Souls, your *Good Impreſſions* from the *Earthquakes*, will be a ſort of

of *Muſhrooms* riſing from the *Earth*, and preſently
Wither, and Moulder, and Crumble, and come to
nothing.   Unleſs the *Love of GOD*, which is the
*Root of the Righteous* be implanted for a living
*Principle* of PIETY in your Souls, your *Good Im-
preſſions* will be like the *Alcherva* of *Jonah*, and
Wither in a Night or two.

When the *Earth* was in *its* Convulſions, and
threw you into *yours*, This was the *Firſt Thing*,
which threw you into Agonies ; *Alaß, I am a
miſerable Unregenerate* ; *I am ſtill in my ſins* ; *I am
not Reconciled unto GOD* ; *I am falling into thoſe Hands
which it is a fearful Thing to fall into* !   And This is
the *Firſt Thing* that you have to look to.   Oh !
Look to *This* ; That you may have a Thorough
CONVERSION to GOD and CHRIST, and a
Life of that *Acquaintance* with Him, whereby *Good
will come unto* you.

But, How ſhall *This* be come at ?   Very ſurpri-
ſing is that Command ; Ezek. XVI. 31. *Make
your ſelves a New Heart*.   What ?   When, O Sinner,
Thou art *Feeble and ſore Broken*, and mayſt ly *Roaring by reaſon* of the *Deſperate Wickedneß* in thy *Heart*,
from which, none but an  Almighty GOD, *Oh !
wretched one that thou art !* —— None but an Almighty GOD can *deliver* thee !   It is none but an
Almighty GOD even one who can transform *Stone*
into *Fleſh*, that can give thee *Another Heart* ; None
but one who can *Create* a whole World, can *Create
a Clean Heart*, and can make a *New Heart* in a
Sinner that is *Accuſtomed to do Evil*.   Wherefore
when our GOD bids thee, *Make thy ſelf a New
Heart* ;  His meaning is, *Look unto me, to make it
for thee* !   The *Good Work* begins, in an Hearty
*Weeping*

*Weeping and Making Supplication* to GOD for a *New Heart.* Seeing and Feeling and Owning thy own *Death,* and *lying among the ſlain,* Oh! Make thy Moans and thy *Groans,* even *the Groans of a deadly wounded Man,* unto a GOD, whoſe *Name* is, *The Lord GOD, Merciful and Gracious and abundant in Goodneſs.* Groan at this rate unto Him ; *Turn thou me, O Lord, and I ſhall be Turned!* O *Great GOD, Make me a New Creature, and beſtow a New Heart upon me!* It looks *Hopefully,* —— as if the *Fear of GOD* were actually *beginning* in thee, and as if the *Beginning of Wiſdom* were dawning on thee, when thou art come into a *deſire to Fear His Name.* The *Good Work* has its *Beginning* in the *deſire* of it. GOD will be *attentive* to the *Prayer* of ſuch as *deſire to Fear His Name. Life* is beginning to ſhew it ſelf in *Breathing* after it.

In ſhort, The Method of CONVERSION is This. The *Foundation* of the work muſt be laid in a *deep Humiliation* of Soul, confeſſing, That thou art *Unable* to *Turn* unto GOD, and *Unworthy* that He ſhould enable thee, and yet *moſt Worthy* to periſh if thou do it not. Being thus *Humbled unto the Duſt,* now *Cry* from thence to the glorious GOD. *Quicken me, O GOD of Sovereign Grace; Quicken me, to Turn unto thee, and Fly unto my SA-VIOUR.* And hereupon *Try,* whether He do not Help thee. *Try* particularly, whether thou canſt not give an Hearty Anſwer to the Calls of the Goſpel. The Goſpel calls, *Be ſorry for thy Sin. Try* whether thou canſt not Heartily ſay, *Lord, I am ſorry, I am ſorry, that I have wandred from thee!* The Goſpel calls, *Let the great Salvation which thy JESUS has for thee, be welcome to thee. Try* whe-

D　　　　　　　　ther

ther thou canſt not Heartily ſay ; *Lord, The Bene-fits of a JESUS, are all welcome to me, all welcome to me !* The Goſpel calls, *Reſolve upon a Life of Obe-dience to GOD all thy Days.* *Try* whether thou canſt not Heartily ſay, *Lord, The way of thy Command-ments, with paying of acknowledgments to Thee in all my ways,* I *Reſolve* upon it, I *Reſolve upon it* ! ———— Behold, Thy *Calling and Election made ſure* in thy Arrival unto this.

To ſet the Matter in a yet further light ; The CONVERSION ſo importunately urged for, *is,* A *Tranſlation* from the *Firſt Adam* to the *Second Adam.* Wherefore, O *Convert paſſing from Death to Life* ; Get thy Heart very ſtrongly affected with the *Evil Circumſtances,* into which thy Fall from GOD in the *Firſt Adam* has reduc'd and ruin'd thee.   Let *Horror take hold* on thee when thou doſt behold the Univerſal *Diſorder* and *Corruption* with which the *Poiſon of the old Serpent* ſo imbibed has infected thee ; and behold the Innumerable *Tranſ-greſſions* and *Rebellions* wherein thou haſt wickedly *denied the GOD that is Above.* Go on to behold, the violated *Law* of GOD binding thee over to ſuffer all the *Evil that purſueth ſinners* : Behold the *powers of Darkneſs* enſlaving of thee, and thy Soul diſtempered and languiſhing with *grievous Diſeaſes* ; Behold how obnoxious thou art unto the *Strange Puniſhment reſerved for the workers of Iniquity* in a Future World.   And now, Fly away to the *Second Adam* for thy *Help* under all theſe Diſtreſſes ; *Help* laid on one that is *mighty to ſave.* Behold the Bleſſed JESUS offering to take thee and make thee *His own,* and *ſave thee to the uttermoſt.* Beg of Him, and Hope in Him, That by the *Sacrifice* which

which he made of Himſelf on the *Accurſed Tree,*
and by Influences, derived from Him, all the
Miſeries convey'd unto thee from the *Forbidden
Tree,* may be releeved and removed. Put thy
Truſt in the Bleſſed JESUS, for a *life* that ſhall
be the *Reverſe* of all the *Death,* which the unhappy
parent of thy Fleſh has entailed upon thee. Entreat of Him ; *O my SAVIOUR, let thy Spirit fill
me with the life of GOD.* Entreat of Him ; *O my
SAVIOUR, Fit me for, and fetch me to, all the ſpiritual
Bleſſings of the Heavenly places.* Rely on Him, as
thy Redeemer. And this with a *Comfortable Per-
ſwaſion* of thy *Favourable Reception* with Him.
Thus a CONVERSION is accompliſhed.

But yet, eſteem it not accompliſhed until you
can ſay thoſe Things, which are the Three Grand
MAXIMS of *Real* and *Vital* PIETY.

The Firſt. *The ſerving and pleaſing of the Glorious
GOD, and my being and my doing of what may be a
grateful Spectacle unto Him, who is acquainted with all
my ways, is what I cloſe withal as the chief END,
which all my Motions are to center in.*

The Second. *My Eyes are continually to a Glorious
CHRIST, that I may be made Righteous and be made
Holy by Him ; and I long to have His Image inſtam-
ped on me.*

The Third. *I do not indulge my ſelf in any Ill Frame
towards my Neighbour, but am willing to do as I would
be done unto.* ——

Now, *It is Finiſhed !* Now, thou ſhalt *never be
moved.* Thus *doing the Will of GOD* thou ſhalt
*Abide forever* ; And ſo ſhall the *Good Impreſſions* that
He has made upon thee.

II. Whatever *Miſcarriages* in your *Lives,* you

felt

felt your *Hearts*, when the *Earthquakes* rowſed them, *ſmite* you for, Oh! Forſake them, Oh! Reform them; After the *Earthquakes* are over, Oh! Don't return unto thoſe *Miſcarriages*. When the *Earth* was *Trembling*, were you conſcious to no *Miſcarriages*, which the præſages of a *Judgment to come* ſet you a *Trembling* for? Perhaps, the *Rumbling Earth*, which turned *the Night of your pleaſure*, [ unto many, *Too much ſo*! ] *into Terror*, made that Murmur in your Ears, which, once made the Ears of a *Shimei* to tingle; 1. King. II. 44. *Thou knoweſt all the wickedneſs which thy Heart is privy to.* The Wretch who in the Defiances which by *Swearing* and *Curſing* and the Language of black Fiends, proclaimed a *Tongue ſet on Fire of Hell*; in the Time of the *Earthquakes*, doubtleſs he felt his Heart miſgive him; *The Great GOD whom I have inſulted and affronted, may now ſend me down into that Fire of Hell, where a drop of water to cool the ſcorches of my Blaſphemous Tongue will be in vain wiſhed for!* The Beaſt which threw away ſo many precious Hours at the *Tavern*, and was *Drunk* ſo often with the *Liquors* wherein is *Beſotment*, and was intoxicated ſo often with a *Cup of Exceſs*; in the Time of *Earthquakes*, doubtleſs he felt his Heart miſgive him; *A Juſt GOD now makes me ſtagger by other means than I uſe to do it; and gives me a Cup of Trembling! How ſhall I drink off the Dregs of the Cup which there is in the Hand of the Lord for the wicked of the Earth?* Such as *walked after the Fleſh in the Luſts of Uncleanneſs*, in the Time of the *Earthquakes* doubtleſs felt their miſgiving Hearts griping of them, and ſaying, *Am not I one of the Filthy Inhabitants under which the Earth is defiled? Is there not a Day of Judgment coming wherein fuch wickednefs as mine is to be punifhed?* Shall not I have my part in the perdition of ungodly Men, when the Day comes that fhall burn like an Oven? The *Falfe-dealer,* and fuch as had *Robbed* or *Cheated* their Neighbours, doubtlefs in the Time of the *Earthquakes* felt their mifgiving Hearts reminding them of their *Difhoneft Practices,* and faying; *Haft thou ftole? O fteal no more; But Reftore as foon and as far as thou canft, what has been ftolen.*

The Great and lewd City of *Lima,* fome while ago, felt an *Earthquake* that funk a large part of it, and brought in the Sea hideoufly rolling over it. In their Great Perplexity upon it, the Survivers profefs'd much *Attrition* of Soul, and laid afide the Quarrels that were among them, and cried out, *Our Oppreffion, our Injuftice, and our Extravagances have brought all this upon us.* Thofe poor *Spaniards* may be our *Monitors.*—— But I have not faid all. The *Sabbath-breaker,* doubtlefs in the Time of the *Earthquakes* felt fome Twitches and fome Wifhes of a Mifgiving *Heart; The Holy GOD, who won't let the Earth reft under me, now lets me know, that if I go on to break His Holy Reft, He will fend me where I fhall have no Reft, neither Day nor Night, but the fmoke of the Torment will afcend forever and ever. Lord, Help me to Sabbatize better than I ufe to do.* But, What am I fpeaking of? Of SABBATIZING! The Thing which *pure and undefiled* RELIGION, either *Lives* or *Dies* withal. Our *Sabbath!* —— NEW ENGLAND, Thy *Sabbath,* 'tis thy *Beauty* and thy *Defence.* Oh! let nothing of This World ever take away thy *Crown.* Let thy *Sabbath* be thrown away

way, and ſinn'd away, and an *Ichabod* will ſoon
be written on all thy *Glory*. ——— Sirs, I cannot
go on, without ſpeaking a *Good Word* for the *Beſt
of Days*. ——— Where, where are the True *New-
Engliſh Sabbatizers?* Muſt we repair unto the *Se-
pulchres* of our *Fathers* to look for them? Where
are the *Houſholders* that *Remember the Sabbath*, and
make *all within their Gates* to do ſo? Where are
the *Nehemiahs*, who will do all they can to lay
Reſtraints upon thoſe, who would *bring Wrath upon
us* by *profaning the Sabbath?* Can the *Miniſters* of
the Goſpel do no more, that the Remote Inhabitants of their Pariſhes, where many ſtay at or
near the Meeting houſes all the Time that inter-
venes between the two public Meetings, may be
put into the Beſt Method of ſpending the *Holy
Time* in the Beſt manner; and keep up the zeal
of *Sabbatizing?* If we won't *Reſt* with and in
GOD on His Day, GOD will not ſuffer His *Earth*
to Reſt under us, or permit us to *Reſt* upon it. A
plain Countrey-man once being changed and raiſed into a *Prophet* of GOD, the Date of his Prophecies was, *Two Years before the* [Famous *Uzzian*]
*Earthquake*. Now, having foretold, That in that
*Earthquake*, the Lord would *Rore out of Zion*, he
mentions the *Tranſgreſſions* that would call for ſuch
a thing. One of them is This; [Amos VIII. 5.]
*Ye ſay, when will the Sabbath be over?* They could
not forbear entrenching on the *Sabbath* with ſecu-
lar Affairs, or ſenſual Frolicks. It follows, *And ſhall
not the Earth Tremble for this?* ——— An *Earthquake* enſues upon it.

I will not have this called, *A Digreſſion*. However, I will go no further in *This*; but go on to
ſay,

ſay, We read, 1. Joh. III. 20. *If our Hearts Condemn us, GOD is Greater than our Hearts, and knoweth all Things.* Now, *Bring Things to mind, O Tranſgreſſors.* In the Time of the *Earthquakes,* the Glorious GOD, ſet up his *Tribunal* in your *Hearts,*
and ſet you as before His *Judgment-ſeat.* Every
Thing in your ways, which the *light of GOD* in
your Hearts, then *Condemned* as an Evil Thing,
Oh! Hate it, Oh! Shun it, Oh! Avoid all *occaſions* of it: And if you are *Tempted* at any time
hereafter to Repeat it, Anſwer and Conquer the
*Temptation* ſo: *If I felt the Earth now ſhaking under
me, and gaping for me, ſhould I venture to do ſuch a
wicked Thing?* It *were as bad as to leap into the
direful Chaſms of the Earth opening in an Earthquake,
to do ſuch a wicked Thing!* When the *Egyptians*
would venture into the Deep, at a Time when,
as it is hinted in the LXXVII. Pſalm, *The Earth
trembled and ſhook;* what came of it? We read,
Exod. XV. 12. *Thou ſtretchedeſt thy Hand and the
Earth ſwallowed them.* Hardy ſinner, Wilt thou
venture on, to do as thou didſt uſe to do? To
do ſo is to challenge the *out-ſtretching* of that *Hand,*
that can ſoon cauſe the *Earth* to *ſwallow* thee.

III. *Make Haſte,* and, Oh, *Delay not* Immediately to *keep thoſe Commandments* of GOD, in
which the *Earthquakes* made you think, *Without
any further delay, this Duty ſhall be complied withal.*
Not only *Sins of Commiſſion* but alſo *Sins of Omiſſi-
on* had in the *Earthquakes* the *Reproofs of GOD*
given unto them. Truly, The Beſt Thing that
can be deſired for you, is; That you may *order
your Converſation aright,* juſt as you moſt approved,
at the Time when the *Earthquakes* made you deſire
the

the *Salvation of GOD.* Some in the Time of the *Earthquakes* are for getting as near to thoſe whom they take to be *Good Men* as they can, profeſſing their *Choice to dy with ſuch.* But, *Children,* whom do you *chuſe to live withal?* There are Points of a *Good Converſation in CHRIST,* which perhaps you were not fully come up to. But in the Time of the *Earthquakes* you thought, *I will now do what I know to be my Duty.* Now, with the *Earthquakes* there was that *Roaring out of Zion* unto you; Heb. III. 7. *To Day, Oh! Hear the Voice of GOD.* There can be no greater Part or Proof of Prudence than This; For a Man to think, *What have I left undone, that if I were now a dying I ſhould wiſh to have done?* And go do accordingly. And now, My Friends, Think with your ſelves. If you felt the *Earthquakes* cauſing your *Houſes* to fall upon you, and cruſh you to *Death* in the Ruines of them; Or, if you felt the *Earthquakes* cauſe thoſe formidable Apertures in the Ground, which would be the *Gates of Death* hideouſly opening for you; Think, *What is the Duty which I have lift undone, the Neglect whereof would now make me feel the Bitterneß of Death upon me?* The *Religion of the Cloſet,* and, *Family Religion,* and, *The Holy Table Religiouſly approach'd unto;* Such as theſe are Points of PIETY, which *Earthquakes* compel the Minds of Men, to confeſs their Obligations to, and Chaſtiſe them for the neglecting of. If you ſaw your ſelves going down into the horrible *Caverns,* which *Earthquakes* may ſink you down into, would it not exceedingly terrify you, to think, *I have not this Day been on my Knees in ſecret before the Glorious GOD?* If *Earthquakes* made it

not

*Good Impreffions cultivated.*

not fafe that you fhould ftay in your *Habitations*, and yet made you at a lofs where to be fafe by running out of them, would it not exceedingly terrify you to think, that you had never, or feldom, or poorly called upon GOD in your *Habitations*? There is the Duty of Commemorating the *Death* of our SAVIOUR at His *Holy Table*, whereof the precept is as plain as any words can make it; *THIS DO!* For the Epidemical Negle&t of this Duty, the ufual *Apology* is a very wicked one. Tis, *I have not prepared for it!* Man, The very *Apology* is it felf an *Impiety*. 'Tis thy *Crime*, that thou art not *prepared*. It is pleaded; *It is not in me, I can't prepare my felf.* But, Haft thou done all that is *in Thee*, and as much as *Thou canft*, that thou mayft be *prepared?* The Negle&t of this Duty is always a *Grief of Mind* on a *Death-bed*, unto fuch as are not *Hardened in their Sins*. It muft needs be a *Grief of Mind* in an *Earthquake*. T'wil then be a Difconfolate Refle&tion: *There is one Thing, wherein I have difobey'd, and have difhonoured my SAVIOUR all my Days.* Not *prepar'd*, you fay! But fuppofe it could be told you, *Before this Month is out, a formidable Earthquake fhall put a ftop to your Breathing on the Face of the Earth any more!* What would you do to *prepare* for it? With *Madnefs in your Hearts* you are *going down to the Dead*, if you do not now Immediately, all that were Neceffary to be done that you may *prepare* for This. Now *prepare to meet with your own Death*, as you are given up to a *Reprobate Mind* if you do it not, and you will *prepare to fhew forth* your Lord's *Death* at His *Holy Table* as you ought to do. The jogs of the *Earthquakes*, have been as *Goads* upon you, for ftimulating of you to

E         *your*

your Duty. Methinks, you may hear your SAVI-
OUR from the *Earth* calling to you, as once from
*Heaven* to another ; *Soul, Soul, Why doſt thou keep at
a diſtance from me ?  It is hard for thee, and it cannot be
ſafe, to Kick againſt the Goads.*

When *Rabab* joined her ſelf to the Church of *Iſrael,* ſhe had a *Scarlet-Cord* given her, and ſomething
to ſhow for her preſervation, when an *Earthquake*
threw down the Walls of *Jericho.*  Truly, To come
with the *preparation of the Sanctuary,* and join your
ſelves to an Inſtituted Church of the GOD of *Iſrael,*
and ſo to *dwell in His Tabernacle,* 'tis to *ſeek a Refuge
under the covert of His Wings.*

IV. The *purpoſes* of PIETY which you take up
from the *Terrors of the ſhadow of Death* in the *Earthquakes,* let the *Covenant of Grace* give *life* unto them :
And with the Spirit of that *New Covenant* proceed
unto the *performing* of what you have *purpoſed.*  The
*Good Impreſſions* made by the *Earthquakes* do ſhoot
forth Firſt, in *Good purpoſes to walk according to that
Rule,* which brings *Peace* to the *Iſrael of* GOD.  The
*Good Impreſſions* are loſt, when thoſe *Good purpoſes*
fail of being Executed.  And they will fail if you
keep up the Spirit of the *Old Covenant,* when you
ſet about the Execution of them.  The Firſt Thing
you muſt ſee to, is, That your *Good purpoſes* be not
made in your *own ſtrength :*  Or with an Imagination of your being Able to *will and to do at your own
pleaſure ;*  If they be ſo, there will be no *ſtrength* in
them.  The *Adverſaries of the Lord,* and of *Good purpoſes* to walk with Him, O Man, By thy *own
ſtrength,* never, never ſhalt thou *prevail* againſt
them.  Under the Horrors of the *Earthquakes,* you
*purpoſe* to expreſs a *Reſpect unto* theſe and thoſe, and
even

even *All the Commandments of* GOD. You Truſt
you ſhall *do* as you *ſay*; never *do* as you have *done*.
You have no *Fear* of it. But, *I have*! —— In whom
do you *Truſt*? In thy *own Heart*, O Vain Man!
Then thou art a *Fool*. All will ſoon come to Nothing. There is a Clauſe of more than ordinary
Significancy, which muſt be an Ingredient of all
*Good Purpoſes*; Even That; Phil. IV. 13. *THRO'
CHRIST WHO STRENGTHENS ME.* The *Cove-
nant of Works*, the Frame and Strain of *That*, will
choak all *Good Purpoſes*, and kill them in the Bud.
The *Covenant of Grace*, is that which alone will
Preſerve them, Secure them, Nouriſh them. And
you are thus to conceive of it. There is an Eternal COVENANT between GOD the FATHER,
and GOD our SAVIOUR. In that *Covenant of
Redemption*, your SAVIOUR promiſed, not only
that He will pay the *Price of Redemption* for you,
[*which has been done*!] but alſo, that He will
*Quicken* and *Incline* and *Strengthen* the People,
whom He brings under the *Shadow of His Wings*,
to Glorify GOD, and Live unto Him. Your
*Good Purpoſes* are beſt expreſſed in the Form of
giving the *Conſent* of your Souls, that the Bleſſed
JESUS, who is your *Saviour* and *Surety*, ſhould
*Aſſiſt* you unto the Doing of all the Good, which
you *Purpoſe* to do. I freely own to you, that I
am not entirely ſatisfied in a *Form of Covenanting
with* GOD, wherein we act our ſelves as *Princi-
pals*, and a Glorious CHRIST is brought in only
as an *Acceſſary*. Tho' *an exceeding great Multitude
which no Man can Number*, have been brought
home to GOD in that *Form*, yet, I judge, the
more *Evangelical* the *Form* is, and the more that

CHRIST

CHRIST is *All* in it, it is the Better, and the *Surer,* and the *Faſter.* The Style of your *Good Purpoſes* is to be ſuch as This; ' O Great GOD, ' Be Thou *my* GOD.   I am not able to pay unto ' Thee the Homage of PIETY, in the Duties of ' it, which I owe unto Thee.   But, I Deſire, I ' Deſire to do it; I deſire to do theſe *Duties.* My ' Bleſſed JESUS has engaged that His People ' ſhall, thro' Him acting as a *Principle of Life* in ' them, do theſe *Duties*;  And it is my Deſire to ' be comprehended in this Engagement, and be ' *Found in Him.*   I Conſent, I Conſent, That ' He ſhould cauſe me to do them; and *work in* ' *me all that is well-pleaſing in the ſight of* GOD.   I ' put my ſelf under His Conduct, that He may ' do ſo.   And even in my giving this *Conſent,* it ' is His Help that has brought me to it.——— Now, O *Evangelized* Soul, *Go on, and proſper.*

But, Oh! Remember at the ſame time, to lay aſide all Thoughts of going to *Eſtabliſh your own Righteouſneſs,* or of making to your ſelves a *Righteouſneſs* of your own *Obedience,* to the Commandments of GOD; No, Tho' it ſhould be in the *Evangelical Way* carried on.   You muſt propoſe to ſtand *Juſtified* before the *Thrice-Holy* GOD, only in the *Righteouſneſs* of that *Obedience,* which the Bleſſed JESUS yielded unto His *Law* for you. And you muſt not ſo much as Propoſe to be *Recommended,* unto the Liberty and Priviledge of pleading that ſpotleſs *Righteouſneſs,* by your own *Obedience,* or by your *Good Purpoſes* of it : But come to it with no *Recommendation,* but the Character of the *Poor* that muſt make This their *only Refuge.*   If you take up *Good Purpoſes,* with the

*Indirect*

*Good Impreffions cultivated.* 35

*IndirectViews* of a *Self-Jufticiary*, they will all foon *die* away, and be laid under that Epitaph, *My Purpofes are broken off, even the Thoughts of my Heart.*

It will be well for you, if you fall into the hands of *Skilful Divines*, and *Paftors* that will wifely *lead* you *in the Paths of Righteoufnefs.*

V. Allow me to Conclude with one brief Direction, which I tender as an *Appendix* to the reft. There is a *Stratagem* of your *Adverfary the Devil*, which you are to be warned of.

In the *Concern of Mind*, which the *Earthquakes* raife in you, be not fo concerned about *leffer*, and perhaps *doubtful Matters*, as to overlook the more *Weighty matters of the Gofpel*. The *Good Impreffions* from the *Earthquakes*, may be much damnified, by being diverted from the MAIN THINGS that are called for; Or, by Exclamations againft the *leffer Faults* in *others*, putting by and fhifting off, the Charge of much *Greater* in *our felves*. There may be the fine-fpun *Devices of Satan*, in a Prepofterous and an Irregular, and a Self-Opinionated *Zeal*; And we fhould not be *Ignorant of His Devices.*

As for *Garments*, by all means, let all *Exorbitances* and *Extravagances* be rebuked, and retrenched; All Trefpaffes againft the *Modeft*, and *Shamefac'd*, and *Sober Apparrel*, which the *Word of GOD* requires, be Redreffed. GOD, as well as Good and Wife Chriftians, is difpleafed at them. Yea, 'tis now a proper feafon to make Humble *Abatements*, even of fome lawful *Ornaments*. For the reft, let us keep to the *Word of GOD*, and moderately ufe, *every Creature*, which He has there granted us a

*Charter*

*Charter* for. And not fall into the *Arrogant Pride,*
of making Things to be *Sins,* which the *Word of*
GOD has never made ſo : [But may be as lawful as
for a Man to wear an *Hat of Beevers Fur,* or a *Cap*
of *Sheeps wool* upon his Head.] Nor let us lay the
*Main ſtreß* of our Demands, on Things, which the
*worſt* People in the World, can as eaſily come to,
as the *Beſt.* But while we are *zealouſly affected,* as it
is a *Good Thing* to be, againſt the *Vanity* and *Luxury*
of a few *Fooliſh People* in their *Garb,* and the like,
let us be *Proportionably zealous* againſt thoſe *groſſer*
efforts of *Ungodlineß* and *Unrighteouſneß,* which
have the *Wrath of GOD reveled from Heaven* againſt
them. And let our *Main care* be for, a SOUL ſo
full of *ſubmiſſion* to GOD, a SOUL ſo full of *Con-*
*formity* to CHRIST, a SOUL ſo full of *Benignity*
to *Men,* as the Goſpel calls for. This is what all
Wiſe Men are *agreed in.* While there may be thoſe,
who may ſee *Falſe cauſes of Puniſhment,* and may
*enquire not wiſely* upon them.

If we will be Nice at *ſtraining of Gnats,* I beſeech
you, let it be *Enquir'd,* [Not as if *That* were one !]
What is to be thought about the *Cry of DEFRAU-*
*DED LABOURERS going up to the Lord of Sabaoth.*

Yea, if Things not yet by all Good Men *Agreed*
*on,* may be ſpoken of, let it be Enquired, Whether
Chriſtians do generally pay to a glorious CHRIST,
the *Dues* which they that would count themſelves,
the True Sons of *Abraham,* ſhould be induced eaſily to Confeſs, belonging to our *Melchizedek* ?
And whether they Devote unto PIOUS USES,
that *portion* of their *Income,* which the *pattern* of our
Father *Jacob,* and the *precept* of the Goſpel, has
plainly declared for ? And whether the SON of
GOD,

*Good Impreſſions cultivated.*

GOD, be not *Robb'd*, as in a *Sacriledge*, when this *portion* is witheld from Him? And whether if this *portion* were *honeſtly paid* unto the LORD, a very *ſmall Moiety* of it applied where it ſhould be, would not put a ſtop to the Cry of many DEFRAU-DED LABOURERS? But it ſeems, this is, Not *Agreed* on. And I know very well, what I ſay of this matter will be little regarded ; But ſee, whether a perpetual *Series* and *Succeſſion* of *Impoveriſh-ments,* and *Remarkable ways deviſed* by the Juſtice of Heaven for it, be not what our Land will be doom'd unto. —— I have done. Behold the Me-thod for preventing of an *Abortion* on our *Good Im-preſſions,* and this unhappy Account of them, *We have been in pain, we have brought forth wind, we have not wrought any Deliverance for the Soul that has been going with us.*

I come to the *Concluſion of the Matter.* It may be hoped, The *Good Impreſſions* from our *Earth-quakes,* will be ſuch, that the *Trembling* of the *Earth* under us, will prove the moſt *uſeful Diſpenſation* of Heaven, that ever we have met withal: Many *Children* of GOD, will Bleſs Him to Eternal Ages, for the *Excitations* which the *Earthquakes* have given unto the PIETY which was too languid in them. And many *Elect* of GOD who were not yet His *Children,* are made ſuch, by the *Earthquakes* driving of them, into thoſe Motions of PIETY, which carry them to their SAVIOUR. The *Lord of Hoſts* coming to *ſhake the Earth,* hereupon the *Deſire of all Nations has come,* and *fill'd* their Hearts with *His Glory.* As we read, *The Voice of the Eternal* GOD *makes the Hinds to bring forth ;* By the ſtart-ling Roars of the *Thunders* over them, when
they

they are *Travailing*, they are thrown into *Frights*
that force their Off-ſpring from them :   So the
*Voice* of the Eternal GOD, in the ghaſtly Roars
of the *Earthquakes* under us, will cauſe many a
Soul to be *New Born*; and many Slow, Dull,
Dilatory *Intentions* of Doing the Will of GOD,
will be *brought forth* into *Endeavours* that never
will be repented of.   The Churches in the Capital City of the Province, and many other Churches throughout the Countrey, have ſet apart
Whole DAYS of *Supplications* to Obtain the Bleſſings of a *Succeſsful Goſpel.* We have ſtood waiting for ſome while, and wondring what was become of our *Prayers.*   The *Succeſs* was not preſently what we look'd for.   We did not preſently ſee the *Anſwers* of our *Prayers.*   But, Lo, as we
read of the Primitive Beleevers, *When they had
prayed, the place was ſhaken, and they were all filled
with the Holy Spirit.*   Even thus, the Glorious
GOD *ſhakes* the *place* where theſe *Prayers* are
made, and grants thoſe Effuſions of the *Holy Spirit* for which we made our *Prayers.*   Yea, *By Terrible Things in Righteouſneſs* He *anſwers* us, as the
*GOD of our Salvation,* and grants us the *Petitions
we have deſired of Him.*   O Wonderful ! O Wonderful ! Our GOD inſtead of ſending *Earthquakes*
to deſtroy as He juſtly might, He ſends them to
fetch us home unto Himſelf, and to do us the
greateſt Good in the World ! If theſe *Good Impreſſions* grow, and hold, and laſt, and come to a due
Maturity, it looks as if ſome *Salvation* may be
nigh to us, and *Glory* may *dwell in our Land.*

What a Deplorable Thing is it, That ſome of
our *Congregations* have ſuch Contentions and Con-
fuſions

*Good Impreſſions cultivated.* 39

fuſions in them, as greatly to defeat ſuch an En-
joyment and ſuch an Improvement of *Good Impreſſions* as others are exceedingly Rejoicing in!
O *Lord JESUS, pity them*!

On the other hand; A *Relapſe* is always dangerous. If the *Good Impreſſions* on the Minds of People
from the *Earthquakes,* quickly vaniſh, and People
become generally as *Worldly,* and as *Prayerleſs,* and
as *Vitious,* as before the *Earthquakes,* and if the *Goodneſs* whereof there is a ſhow made on the *Earthquakes,* do *go away* with them, we may *Tremble,* we
may *Tremble,* at, *what is a coming*! They who *dwell
in the Wilderneſs* have cauſe to be *afraid of the Tokens.*

As for the Miſerables themſelves, it looks awfully, as if it muſt be ſaid, *All is in vain; They are a
Reprobate Metal; the Lord has Rejected them.* It looks
awfully, as if this were the *Doom* from GOD upon
them, *Never, Never ſhall any Fruit be found upon them*;
and as if the *Oath* of GOD were gone out againſt
them, *That they ſhall never enter into His Reſt.* There
ſeems to be that ſentence from the Mouth of GOD
upon theſe Obdurate Sinners; Ezek. XXIV. 13.
*Becauſe I have purged thee, and thou waſt not purged,
thou ſhalt not be purged any more, till I have cauſed my
Fury to reſt upon thee.* That there ſhould be *Earthquakes* extending for more than Five Hundred
Miles; and in ſeveral places the *Roars* continue
every Day for ſome Weeks together, and the *ſhocks*
be given many *ſevens* of times in theſe Weeks; and
not *one life* be loſt in all! —— O *the Goodneſs and
Forbearance, and Long-ſuffering* of our GOD! But if
this be trifled with, what a *Wrath,* O Hardened
ones, what a *Wrath,* are you *treaſuring up againſt the
Day of Wrath*! It will be well, if ſomething of

E

*Peſtilen-*

40     *Good Impreffions cultivated.*

*Peſtilential Aſpeƈt* be not quickly ſhot among us, wherein the *ſlain of the Lord may be many.* — I ſay, ſomething of a *Peſtilential Aſpeƈt.* Our LORD having ſpoken of, *Earthquakes in diverſe places,* preſently proceeds to ſpeak of, *Peſtilences.* Upon the amazing *Earthquakes,* wherein the mighty City of *Antioch,* with many other places was demoliſhed, before our Apoſtle *John* could be well cold in his Grave, which, I ſuppoſe, our Lord in His Prædiction had His Eye-firſt upon, there came on ſuch a *Peſtilence* that it look'd as if the World was going to be diſ-peopled ; and the Reliques of it remained even to the Time of the Martyr *Cyprian.* When there had been an *Earthquake* in the Wilderneſs, where the People aſſoon as they Recovered out of the Cries into which it had thrown them, diſcovered an *Incurable Obſtinacy* in their Vile Tempers, and their Baſe Doings, the *Next News* is, A *Peſtilence,* which deſtroy'd many Thouſands of them. After the never-to-be-forgotten *Earthquake* in one of our well-known Iſlands, that ſome now among us were preſent at, Half the People ſaved from the perdition at *Port-royal,* died of a *Peſtilence* at *Kingſton* ; where five hundred Graves were dug within a Month, and ſometimes Two or Three buried in one Hole together ; And the reſt of the Iſland had a deep Draught in that *Cup of Aſtoniſhment* which GOD gave them after He had cauſed the *Earth* to *Tremble* under them. Indeed, the Exemples of Mineral and Malignant Steams, from *Earthquakes* terminating in a raging *Peſtilence,* have been very Uſual and very Diſmal. Yea, *American* Exemples of ſuch a thing. Tho' the proper *Plague* was never known in *America* ; it is well known,

that

that after some *Earthquakes,* which overturned almost the whole Capital City of *Chili,* in the
*South-America,* not very many Years ago, almost
all the surviving Inhabitants died of a *Pestilence,*
more Mortal than a proper *Plague* use to be. We
are not certain, that our *Earthquakes* will have a-
ny such Effects. The Methods of *Repentance* may
prevent them. Our Flight unto our SAVIOUR
with the Faith of the XCI. Psalm; This may
save us from them. Yet, In Conformity to what
our SAVIOUR spoke of some Tragical Accidents which had happened a little before, whereof one seems to have been an *Earthquake,*——— *Except ye Repent,*——— I will venture to say, I verily
Fear, That the Glorious GOD, having within a
little while singled out several Towns, that were
*None of the Worst,* [Not *Sinners above all Men!*] but
full of Godly People, and ordered the *Destroying
Angel* to make a *Doleful Havock* among them, He
has therein shot off *Direful Warning-pieces* to all
the Land: I say, *Direful Warning-pieces!*— And
His Voice to the whole Countrey, is, O! *Let there
be a General Turn to GOD, in a Life of Serious PI-
ETY, lest a more General Stroke do make fearful Devastations upon you!*

I do not speak these things, as a *Melancholy Vi-
sionary,* or because of any *Delight* I can take in
keeping my Neighbours under a *Fear* which has
*Torment* in it. And indeed I am sorry to see,
that ever now and then, upon some Idle Rumours
and Whimseys, the *Heart of this People is moved, as
the Trees of the Wood are moved with the Wind;*
More *moved,* alas, than they are by the *plain Word*
of GOD brought unto them: Sorry, sorry, to
fee,

fee, That *foolifh Notions* ever now and then ftarted
by the Devil, to torture us, and to triumph over
our Guilty Souls, will work more upon us, than
all the plain Comminations of that Word, wherein we have the Glorious GOD *marvellouſly Thundering* over us! No, But *knowing the Terror of the
Lord,* we would *perſwade* you, unto that PIETY,
which may divert the Iudgments of GOD, that
may be hanging over us. And we would have
you *fing in the ways* of that PIETY; fain have
you *Live Comfortably,* and be bravely above the
*Fear of Evil.* You know the Courſe that *Ninive*
took, and how it ſucceeded. What? Shall a *New-
England* be worfe than a *Ninive?* GOD forbid *!*
Syrs, They whom *Earthquakes* do chafe into a
Life of PIETY, do the beft Thing that can be
done, to procure a *Mark* of GOD upon them,
for their Prefervation, if He ſhould ſend an *Over-
flowing Scourge,* and pour out the *Vials* of His
Wrath on the *Children of Difobedience,* and of *Un-
perſwadeableneſs.* O Beleevers, Thus taken under
the Protection of your SAVIOUR, Hear Him
now faying unto you, *Fear not, for I am with thee :
Be not difmayed, for I am thy GOD.*

But, *Lifting up a Voice like a Trumpet,* I declare
unto you that are *Impenitent* under and after ſuch
*Earthquakes* as have come to rowfe us from the
*Dead ſleep* upon us, *Earthquakes* are not all the *Arrows,* in the *Quiver* of GOD, *ordained* for thofe, by
whom He is *provoked every day.* But if *Earthquakes*
will not move you, it feems come to a, *Conclama-
tum eſt.*—— Alaſs.—— It looks as if the laſt Means
were uſed ; and all that remains were only this ;
*He that being often Reproved, hardens his Neck, ſhall
be deſtroyed ſuddenly, and without any Remedy.* Yea,

## Good *Impreſſions* cultivated.

Yea, A General Impenitence under and after ſuch *Earthquakes*, what will it betoken, but that theſe *Earthquakes*, are no other than the *Beginning of Sorrows!* There have been tremendous *Earthquakes* in former and later Ages; The *Hiſtory* of them were enough to caſt a wicked World into all the Trepidations which a *Mene Tekel* threw a *Belſhazzar* into. The Motto on the *Title-Page* of ſuch an *Hiſtory*, might be That, *Come and ſee the Works of* GOD ; *He is Terrible in His Doing towards the Children of Men*. But I am certain, a Greater *Earthquake* than all of thoſe, is what we have cauſe to live in *Expeĉtation* of : Even that *Earthquake*, whereof we are warned, Rev. XVI. 18. *A Great Earthquake, ſuch as has not been ſince Men were on the Earth, ſo Mighty an Earthquake, and ſo Great an one.* I again, and again, declare it unto you ; *The Coming of the Son of Man in the Clouds of Heaven,* 'tis what we know of Nothing to Retard it or Protraĉt it. We are told, It muſt be at and for the Deſtruĉtion of that *Roman Monarchy*, for which the laſt Period of *Twelve Hundred and Sixty Years* are moſt certainly upon their Expiration. An Excellent Pen, which *New-England* will have Singular cauſe to know, has in an Incomparable Treatiſe on the *Sacred Prophecies*, with much Erudition ſhown, and with much Demonſtration prov'd, That there is abundance of cauſe to think, the Expiration of that *Black Period* may have been above Ten Years ago. What *Pauſe* our Glorious LORD may now make, before the *Next Thing* which we have to look for, and what He may pleaſe to Do in this *Pauſe*, and whether in this Pauſe a more General, and a more Terrible *Slaughter*

44     *Good Impreſſions cultivated.*

*ter of the Witneſſes,* may not be carried on, we cannot ſay ; For my part, *I have not the Knowledge of
the Holy ones.* But for the *Coming of the Son of Man
in the Clouds of Heaven,* which, O *Vain Men,* will
not be found a *Metaphor,* It may, *for any thing I
know,* be the *Next Thing* that is to be look'd for.
All that the *Oracles* of GOD have mentioned, as
Things to be done before it, are Accompliſhed : I
ſay, *All Accompliſhed !* Certainly, The *Kingdom of
GOD is at hand :* And in the Introducing of it,
*The Foundations of the Earth ſhall ſhake ; The Earth
ſhall be utterly broken down ; The Earth ſhall be clean
diſſolved ; The Earth ſhall be moved exceedingly.* O
*Kiſs* the Feet of the SON of GOD, whoſe *hot wrath
will quickly flame ;* and then, *Bleſſed are they who
truſt in* Him. Our Lord is coming to *ſend a Fire on
the Earth ;* [But it ſhall be *Viſited* of the *Lord of Hoſts*
with *Earthquake* as well as *Fire :* ] and, what *if it
be* in the ſubterraneous Receptacles, *already kindled?*
From this Conſideration, I beſeech you, let not the
*Good Impreſſions* of the *Earthquakes* be laid aſide : I
ſay, This Conſideration, That more *Earthquakes*
are to be look'd for ; from which you can have
no *Refuge* but This : O *my SAVIOUR, Under the
Shadow of thy Wings will I make my Refuge.*

History gives us the Names of ſome Philoſophers among
the ancient *Pagans,* who upon ſome Circumſtances obſerved
in the bottom of *Wells,* and ſome other ſuch Occurrences,
foretold *Earthquakes ;* which came to paſs accordingly. We
*Chriſtians* have a *more ſure Word of Prophecy,* according to which
we may foretel, That our *Earthquakes are not all over yet ;* It
muſt not be thought, That *Earthquakes* have done all they
have to do, upon a World ſinking under an Enormous Load
of *Wickedneſs,* which with an Accumulation of *Guilt* from
*Former Ages* lies upon it. I am not ſo much of a *Natural Phi-
loſopher,* as to form any Judgment on the Conſtitution of
                                                      our

## Good Impressions cultivated.    45

our *Soyl*, which is well known to be vastly replenished with stores both of *Iron* and of *Sulphur*; Tho' I am aware, what a surprizing Imitation of *Earthquakes*, the Dust of these Mixed and Warmed, will afford unto us: And some it may be, would from hence raise a Suspicion, That our *Earthquakes* may by'nd by issue in some *Fiery Eruptions*; and may proceed anon to a *Fire*, that *shall burn to the Foundations of the Mountains*. But I am so much of a *Christian Philosopher*, as to suspect, that when the *Grand Period*, which cannot but be now very near unto us, is coming on, stupendous *Earthquakes*, will be some of the Things, which an *Earth*, from whence a *Cry* to Heaven still waxing Louder for the *Days of Vengeance* to come upon it, must be torn withal. O thou *Land*, where GOD has been so *Forgotten*, and which hast so impiously *Denied the GOD that is Above*, Thou shalt be *torn to pieces, and there shall be none to deliver thee*! Yea, There is more cause to suspect than it is now and here proper to Declare, That the *Holy* and *Mighty* ANGELS of JEHOVAH-JESUS, who are His *Ministers*, to *do His Pleasure*, and very much concerned in the Management of *Earthquakes*, when it pleases Him to Order them, are coming down with *Commissions* to do those Things whereupon it shall be said, *Come, Behold the Works of the Lord, what Desolations He has made in the Earth*. Doubtless, In GOD's Time for them, There are *more Earthquakes to come*; And it is of the Last Consequence unto us, that in the ways of PIETY, we be brought into a *State of Safety for Eternity* before they come; and that when they come, the *Good Impressions* made by *Former Earthquakes* be found Abiding on us, and Abounding in us.

---

BOSTON-Lecture. Dec. 14. 1727.

---

# ( 46 )

# An APPENDIX.

### Written Dec. 25. 1727.

---

## A Collection

Of some

## Obſervable Occurrences,

Which the preſent *Earthquakes* of
NEW-ENGLAND,
[The *Shocks* and *Roars* whereof, we had no lon-
ger ago than the Laſt Night awakening of us,]
Lead us to take Notice of.

---

### I. The Firſt OBSERVABLE.

THE Occurring of EARTHQUAKES in
DIVERS PLACES, is what our SAVI-
OUR has adviſed us to conſider of. Truly, In
*this Year* of NEW-ENGLAND's *Trembling*, there
are occurring EARTHQUAKES in DIVERS
PLACES. If the jogs given to *France* and *Britain,*
do little to rowſe the *Europæan* World from the
Lethargy of the *laſt Time*, yet it may be hoped ſome
in *America* may *hear Attentively the Noiſe of the Voice
of GOD* in them, and the *Sound that goes out of His
Mouth.*

In our coming to relate the *Earthquakes* of *this
Year*, it may not be amiſs, but be a decent Introduction, to relate, that ſo lately, as a little above a Year
ago,

*Appendix.*

ago, in the Night between the firſt and ſecond of *September*, between the Hours of Ten and Eleven, the City of *Palermo*, in *Sicily*, felt ſome ſhocks, of an *Earthquake*, which were not at firſt very Violent. But they ſoon increaſed with great Fury for above Twenty Minutes; whereby about a quarter part of that great City, was overturn'd & overwhelm'd, and made an Heap of amazing Rubbiſh: From whence *Three Thouſand of the Dead*, were drawn out, five days after, fearfully cruſh'd and maſh'd, and miſerably broken to pieces. In one Ward of the City, a whole *Street* gaped at once with an hideous and horrid Noiſe; and from the Chaſm, there iſſued out *Flames*, which were mixed with calcined Stones, and a Torrent of *Burning Brimſtone*, whereby in leſs than half an Hour, the whole Ward was conſumed. It was computed, that about *Fifteen Thouſand* People periſhed in this Deſolation. But *This Year* is what we are now confin'd unto. We are informed that in the Month of *May* laſt, they had ſeveral Shocks of an *Earthquake*, at *Arles*, in *France*; and one ſo Violent, that all the Inhabitants ran out of the City, for fear of being overwhelmed under the Ruines of their Houſes, and continued encamped in the open Countrey, till they hoped the Danger was over. Some of the Shocks were more Violent about *Languedoc*, than at *Arles*.

Our Accounts from *Great Britain*, inform us, That on the Nineteenth of *July* laſt, there were *Earthquakes* felt at *Swanzy*, before which there was heard a mighty Noiſe, like that of *Thunder* at a Diſtance. The Houſes trembled; The Walls of Gardens rocqued; The tops of Chimneys fell,

G  Many

48 *Appendix.*

Many left their Habitations.—— At the fame time they felt the like at *Highworth*, & the Neighbouring places, where the People were thrown into the greateft Confternation, from the Apprehenfion of their Houfes falling upon them. An Alteration in the Face of the Sky, and the Colour and Quivering of the Luminaries there, before it, was very much obferved. At the fame time the City of *Briftol* had a fhare of the Confternation.

About *Exeter*, they had the *Earthquake* which gave dreadful Concuffions; People could not ftand when they felt it; It rang the Bells in the Steeples; And fome Damage was done by it. From feveral other parts in the *Weft*, there have come in the like Accounts.

The Relation from *Wales*, is yet more Expreffive. ‘ On *Wednefday* the *Nineteenth* of *July*, a little after Four in the Morning, we had a moft
‘ terrible *Earthquake*. They that were in the Field,
‘ and heard it coming (as they fay, from the *Eaft*,)
‘ could not tell what to liken it to, but to Great
‘ Guns, firing under Ground, or fome terrible
‘ Thunder. The *Hedges* and Trees feemed to
‘ walk, or move from their Places; The Birds
‘ flew out from thence, as if they were frighted;
‘ The Walls of the Park and Gardens [at *Margam*]
‘ were fhook down; The Doors of the Church,
‘ and of feveral Houfes flew open, tho’ Lock’d
‘ and Bolted. The Bells tolled of themfelves; fe-
‘ veral Stacks of Chimneys were thrown down;
‘ Houfes untiled; Windows and Shutters broken.
‘ The Milk-People in the Fields, declare, That
‘ the Earth trembled fo, that the Milk dafh’d o-
‘ ver

' ver the Edges of the Pails. The Rivers fwelled
' feveral times higher than was ufual, and the
' Water changed unto the Colour of Whey. The
' Houfes and Beds rocqued like Cradles.

Befides thefe Things; on Aug. 25. In the Vale
of *Good-Cheap*, adjoining to the Parifhes of *Wye*
and *Hinxhil*, feveral Brooks were on Fire for many Days together; which People were, as well
they might be, very much furprized at.

The Second OBSERVABLE.

We foon knew, that our EARTHQUAKE extended more than *Five Hundred Miles*. But fhall
we reckon it a part of *ours*, if we find an EARTH-
QUAKE within a Day or Two before *ours* affect-
ing the *Caribbee-Iflands*? Reader, Confider what
we are going to Relate, and think, with a juft
Reflection, How deep the *Fires* may ly, which
may give fo near *Simultaneous Agitations*, to the
Tottering Arch which is our only *Foundation*; [if
we have no fhare in the *City* that has better *Foundations*!] and what a mighty Force they may a-
non exert upon it!

We have Advice, that the *Earthquake* we had
here; (if it may be faid fo) Oct. 29. between Ten
and Eleven in the Evening, was felt at *Barbados*
the Day before, about *Noon*; which is near *two
Thoufand Miles* diftant from us; And much after
the manner we had it here. The *Houfes* were in
a very frightful Convulfion; The *Streets* rofe and
fell, even like the *Waves* of the Sea; The People
in utmoft Confternation from an Apprehenfion
that the Earth might fink under them, ran to the
Wharfe, that they might get into Veffels for their
fafety.

G 2                                        We

We have Advice alfo, that *Martineco*, A Day or two before the Time of our *Earthquake*, underwent a more terrible one, than that of *Barbados*, or, that of *New-England*. Their *Temple* and their *Prifon* were thrown down; and many of their *Sugar-works* ruined; and their Negros kill'd. The *Noife* as well as the *Shock*, was beyond Expreffion hideous; They that have arrived from thence unto us, difcover an *Abiding Horror*, at what they heard and felt and faw, in what they are efcaped from.

It may be added, That fome of our Veffels, which were at a confiderable Diftance from us, in the midft of the *Huge* and *Wide Atlantic*, at the Time of our *Earthquake* were *vifited* with fuch *Thunder*, as they had fcarce ever known to be parallel'd.

### III. The Third OBSERVABLE.

There was *This Year*, a very ftrange occurrence in *Ireland*; which drew as in *Miniature* a moft *lively Emblem*, of what it is that EARTH-QUAKES come for; and of the Condition and Confufion which falls upon *Forfaken Sinners*, when held in the *Cords* of their *Sins*, and fiez'd by the Irrefiftible Vengeance of Heaven. The Story is worth telling; and by the ordering of GOD it is come to pafs, that it is told among the Nations; Yea, and in *America* too this *lively Picture* is now exhibited. Here it is; look upon it.

On the Fourteenth of the laft *Auguft*, (1727.) as one *John Byrn*, a Wretch of a very Diffolute and Abandoned Life, ftood at the Gallows in *Kilkenny*, with a Rope about his Neck, in order to be executed for the Murder of one Mr. *Taylor*,

and

and was relating the Murder with an amazing
Indolence and Insolence, a Noise like *Thunder*
was heard under the Gallows, and the *Earth fell
a Trembling*, with the terrible Shocks of an *Earthquake*, for many Yards round about the Place, but
not extending any further. It was look'd on as an
amazing Expreſſion of the Divine Diſpleaſure,
and the *Wrath of GOD reveal'd from Heaven*, a-
gainſt the Crimes of ſo horrible and obdurate a
Criminal. The aſtoniſhed Sheriff, and his Guards,
and the Spectators, which were very numerous,
all ran away with the utmoſt Conſternation and
Expedition ; and with ſuch Diſtraction, that the
Malefactor being left alone, had a ſtrange Opportunity, to have made his Eſcape, if he had attempted it. But he was himſelf ſo terrified and
confounded, as to be found preſently *Stupified*
when the Sheriff returned, and finiſhed the Execution.

### The Fourth OBSERVABLE.

Our EARTHQUAKES unavoidably lead us
to the Conſideration, of what is to be expected
from the *Subterraneous Fires*, in the *Day of the Lord
that ſhall burn like an Oven* ; when they ſhall con-
ſpire with the *Fires*, which at the *Glorious Appearing of our great GOD and SAVIOUR*, ſhall fill and
cleanſe the *Heavens*, and thoſe *High places* which
are now occupied by *Wicked Spirits*. When *the
Lord our GOD ſhall come*, and *a Fire ſhall devour before Him, and it ſhall be very Tempeſtuous round about
Him*, Then the *Fire and Brimſtone* which will in an
*Horrible Tempeſt* be *Rained like Snares*, upon the
*wicked*, even upon all but thoſe Holy and Humble
*Walkers with GOD*, that ſhall have His *Mark* upon
them,

them, and with a furprizing *Change* upon them
fhall be *caught up to meet the Lord*: This *Fire* will
meet with, and give an Attractive and Amazing
*Energy* to, the *Subterraneous Fires*, in which the
*Trembling Earth* is to fall a *Sacrifice*.

Now, if the *Eighteen* on whom the *Towre of Siloam fell*, were to be conftrued as a *Figure* and *Fore-
tafte*, of what was to befal incredible Multitudes,
by the *Fall of Towres* upon them, in the approaching Deftruction of *Jerufalem*; Why may not the
*Hundred and Eighteen* that perifhed the other Night
in the Barn at *Barwel*, be fhown unto the World,
as a *Type*, of what fhall be done to many Millions,
in the CONFLAGRATION, which is to come
*as a fnare upon all them who dwell on the Face of the
whole Earth?* If one would fee a Tragical *Pour-
traiture*, of the *Bufinefs* which the World is very
much taken up withal; Yea, and very much of the
*Religion* which is in the World pretended to; and
of the *fudden Deftruction* by *Fire*, which the miferable People of the *Earth* will find themfelves, beyond all poffibility of efcaping, referved for; Let
them look into the Barn at *Barwel*. 'Tis a difmal
and a fhocking Story; The Relation is thus convey'd unto us,

About Eight o' Clock, in the Evening that followed the Ninth of *September*, 1727. at a place
called *Barwel*, in *Cambridge-fhire*, (about Three
Miles from *New-Market*) there was a *Poppet-Show*
acting in a Barn, which was built with *Barwel-
Stone*, and thatch'd with *Straw*. The Man going
to give his Attendents the fight of the Show, not
only *Lock'd* but alfo *Nail'd*, the Door. There was
a Place adjoining to the Barn, which had in it a
Quantity

*Appendix.*

Quantity of *Hay* and *Straw*; and a Boy who set a Wooden Lanthorn with a short Candle down, while he peep'd in to see the Spectacle. A Man, who had threatened, that if he were not let in to see it for nothing, he would set the Barn on *Fire* over their Heads, beat the Lanthorn about, so as to set the *Hay* and *Straw* on *Fire*, and ran away. The Flaming *Hay* and *Straw* presently set the *Barn* on a *Flame*; which had a Floor above the People; and the *Fire* getting into the *False Roof*, ran like Wild-fire; and the falling of the Floor hastened the Death, of the smothered Miserables. The People could not get out; but about Five or Six escaped the *Flames*; The rest, which were about *One Hundred and Twenty*, among whom there were several *Young Gentlewomen* of considerable Estates, miserably perished. Some had their *Legs* burnt off, some their *Hands*, and some their *Heads*; and some were intirely incinerated. The *Merry-Andrew* that belonged unto the Show, got out, but so horribly burnt, that he lived no more than a Day and a Night. It was for some little while the melancholy Employment of the Neighbouring-place, to see whether they could not pick out the Roasted and Mangled Carcasses of their *Particular Friends*; but most of them were carried in Carts, and put into an Hole in the Church-yard. And about Seven or Eight Houses of the Neighbourhood, were consumed in the same Disaster.

*Whoso is wise, will observe these things.*

# F I N I S.

## DATE DUE